BETWEEN FORM AND FREEDOM

A practical guide for the teenage years

BETTY STALEY

HAWTHORN PRESS

Published by Hawthorn Press, Hawthorn House, 1 Lansdown Lane, Stroud, Gloucestershire, GL5 1BJ, UK

Tel: 01453 757040 Fax: 01453 751138 email: info@hawthornpress.com
www.hawthornpress.com

Cover photography by Fred Chance
Cover design by Bookcraft Ltd, Stroud, Gloucestershire
Design and typesetting by Bookcraft Ltd, Stroud, Gloucestershire
Printed in the UK by Athenaeum Press Ltd, Gateshead, Tyne and Wear

First edition published 1988
Second edition published 2009
Reprinted 2011, 2013 by Berforts Information Press, Oxford

Every effort has been made to trace the ownership of all copyrighted material. If any omission has been made, please bring this to the publisher's attention so that proper acknowledgement may be given in future editions.

The views expressed in this book are not necessarily those of the publisher.

The excerpt from *Another Brick in the Wall* © 1979 Pink Floyd Music Publishers Ltd is reproduced with permission.

The Logical Song by Rick Davies and Roger Hodgson from Supertramp *Breakfast in America* © 1979 Almo Music Corp – Delicate Music, is reproduced with permission from Rondor Music (London) Ltd.

The excerpt from *Mending Wall* from *The Poetry of Robert Frost* edited by Edward Connery Lathem © Estate of Robert Frost, is reproduced with permission from Henry Holt and Co Inc NY and Jonathan Cape Ltd, London.

British Library Cataloguing in Publication Data
Staley, Betty
Between Form and Freedom: a practical guide for the teenage years.
(Lifeways)
1. Adolescents. Development.
I. Title. II. Series
305.2'35

ISBN 978 1 903458 89 1

Contents

Dedication

This book is dedicated to my three children – Andrea, George and Sonya – and to my high school students. They all have again and again taught me the great lessons of life.

This book is also dedicated to my father, Israel Jehuda Kletsky, otherwise known as Izzy. He was one of the many idealistic Russian immigrants who came to the United States to find freedom and to contribute their fire and energy to the betterment of this land.

His dreams for a better society inspired him to teach me about those people who cherished liberty and to hold out a hope that one day we would all live in peace.

Through his concern for his fellow workers, he organized a union local, participated in demonstrations and pickets, and taught me the importance of sacrifice.

His dedication to those who were fighting for racial equality made me an enthusiastic fan of Jackie Robinson and the Brooklyn Dodgers, as well as giving me an understanding of social justice.

His love gave me the confidence that I could be whatever I willed to be.

Foreword

Joseph Chilton Pearce

An editorial entitled *What's Wrong with These Kids?* was reproduced in newspapers and magazines across the country. The author asked with self-righteous indignation: "… after all we've done for them, why do today's kids act the way they do?" There followed a long, glowing account of the materialistic benefits, the erotic freedoms, information accesses and technological wizardry, which we, the generation of the Great Depression and World War II, have given our young people. The article pointed out that, though deprived of all these freedoms and wonders, we, the elders, had come through pretty well and built a marvelous world. Ignored was the glaring fact that today's youth, "given everything" materially, are starved on emotional-spiritual levels. These may have been scanty in our childhood too, but we had the nurturing of marvelous imaginations, dreams, and hopes. Erotic materialism, "giving everything", is bought at a price.

Most public, and private, educational systems treat today's child and adolescent as prospective consumer-producers vital to the gross national product. Most parents demand of education only that it equip their child to get a "good job" and make lots of money. The criteria and model presented for the child's imprinting from birth is that of being no more than a dollar commodity value in our economic schemes. A major magazine devoted a serious article to "today's materialistic kids", pointing out that through use of the right psychological inputs, we could, by age six, "determine the child's buying patterns for life." With such attitudes reflected by parents, teachers, and all media, the young person has no access to any other self-evaluation or self-image. With such a violence to the natural development of intelligence occurring from the beginning of life, small wonder that violence among our teenagers becomes endemic.

Until we again recognize the spiritual side of life as primary, particularly in childhood and adolescence, our mounting social catastrophe can only continue. For only through the recognition and nurturing of the spirit can a true intelligence unfold. In this excellent book, Betty Staley has given us a compassionate, intelligent, and intuitive look into the mind of children and adolescents. Even the most casual reader of this book will never again respond to children and adolescents in the old mechanical ways.

Young people unconsciously look continually for some signal from their world that the true inner needs of their life might be met. The strength and power of Steiner or Waldorf education lies in just this recognition, and in providing young people with proper guidance, stimuli, and help at the proper times. The fact that most Waldorf educated children are happy, intelligent, adaptive, cooperative, and, above all, love their school and love learning, indicates that our young people, given such a message, will themselves respond positively and overcome many of the culturally induced negativities and dysfunctions facing them outside the school.

My own spiritual journey has been different from, though in some ways roughly parallel to, that of Rudolf Steiner, founder of Waldorf education, and the major model for Betty Staley's work. In no way do my personal qualifications of the Steiner system "disqualify" it. My points of disagreement with Betty are minor and no more than statistical, incidental when faced with the overwhelming need our young people have for genuine developmental models and guidance, which Waldorf certainly approaches. Steiner education is easily one of the most beneficial systems currently available (rivaled, perhaps, only by Sister Grace Pilon's *Workshop Way*), just as Steiner's philosophy is an extraordinary and profound insight.[1] Any shortcoming that I find therein are dismissable within the overall picture of optimistic hope Waldorf offers all educational systems.

This book is about the development of intelligence in the whole person, which subject I would make compulsory in all education, at all levels. What happens, or is supposed to happen, in the early years, the middle years, and the adolescent period? At present we enter into these periods in "dark ignorance" – totally unprepared. Our parents, teachers, and leaders are equally ignorant of what is at stake and what the needs are. We pass this ignorance on, unknowingly, generation after generation. What kind of world would we have were we not entering into each stage of life in such ignorance and darkness? The Steiner schools, and works like Betty Staley's, are a significant step in the movement toward breaking this cycle and achieving a true knowledge – knowing our needs and how to meet them.

This book is not, however, just for Steiner teachers, parents, or those familiar with Steiner. It offers a wealth of information and insight for every teacher, parent, and individual interested in breaking from the suicidal trends of our day, and opening toward the life of the spirit within us. Some of Steiner's language may seem archaic, some of his terms may seem from a past era. I ask, however, what have our clever, sophisticated, mechanistic "naked ape" terms given us? What kind of world and society has the erotic materialism of the behaviorists, currently shaping academic and public belief, actually given us? I claim only a slide toward global suicide and despair.

An ancient Egyptian hieroglyphic stated that there were two sources of knowledge: intuition, coming from a general intelligence; and analytical logic, coming from individual intellect. The same information can be obtained by either system; the difference lies in that information from the intuitive mode always leads to wholeness and life; information through the analytical mode always leads to fragmentation and death. The evidence for this is overwhelming us today. Analytical intellect, divorced from the intuitions of intelligence, has led to the scientific-technological nightmare of our day. To look within this fragmenting process for our solutions is madness. The same process, however, in service of intuition and intelligence, could lead to a remarkable world. Steiner represents a striking synthesis of these polar approaches, and Betty Staley's book mirrors this balance. Naively, one could only wish this work were a best-seller. Practically, I can only hope it will be read by a significant number of significant people – namely, parents, teachers, and, indeed, adolescents themselves.

Introduction

Being an adolescent today

As parents, we often forget our adolescent years. We, too, had to find our way, leave behind the customs of our parents, and venture into a strange and wonderful world. The ideals, values, and goals we live by today were formed during our adolescent years. The memories of activities of those years are with us today as adults. The ideas we thought about, the people we admired, the image we carried of ourselves – all these live within our adult personalities. I have often heard adults comment that they are grateful not to be adolescents in today's world.

"Back when I was a teenager, standards were pretty straightforward. There were good girls and bad girls, and the lines were pretty clear. Of course, we got into trouble. We drank and smoked, but we couldn't damage ourselves as easily as kids today can. We might have fooled around on weekends, but we respected our elders, we did our homework, and we carried out our chores. We worked for pocket money and had very little extra to spend."

The message was clear. You were good or bad. You knew what the risks were and you were careful. Quite a different situation exists for today's teenager. The pace is fast, the costs are high, and the risks are great. Young people today have to make their way through a world that tells them, "Be appealing, be sexy, be cool, be aggressive. Enjoy, experience, and be smooth." What does this mean?

By the time pre-teenagers enter seventh grade, they are aware of marijuana, alcohol, cocaine, sexual perversions, abortions, homosexuality, divorce, promiscuity, suicide, violence, runaways, and child abuse. Their sophistication makes the teenage experiences of their parents seem to be back in the Dark Ages. Such a precocious awareness of difficulties and dangers affects youngsters so that they feel insecure and lack trust in the people around them.

They had expected the world to be secure; they had thought adults knew what they were doing; they had believed that life was worth living. These expectations have been shattered for this generation which lives with divorce as a common experience, with the loneliness and insecurity of parents who turn to their children for companionship, with the threat of climatic change now a greater perceived danger, and with a general lack of belief in divine guidance or protection.

Is life worth living? Is there any meaning? Is there a future? These are the questions that hide in the shadows of the young teenagers' minds. Messages in the environment call upon youngsters to get stoned, make lots of money, have a fancy car, attain power, feel good, and "make it" in the world. There are fewer voices in the environment telling them how to build relationships, live meaningfully in their communities, how to care about other people, how to take responsibility, how to heal the earth, and how to find God.

It is a tribute to the strong nature and good will of youngsters that they remain interested in positive contributions to society despite the destructive words that drum into their psyches, despite adult cynicism about politics and social change, and despite the social ills they see around them. The Divine persists in each young person, celebrating the higher meaning in life.

Young people want to serve, they want to make a difference, and they want to find effective models in the adult world. They look for adults who commit themselves to action, to principles, to ideals. They respect adults who care enough to set limits, who have expectations of them, who talk with them, and most of all, who believe in them.

Many, many adults give endless hours helping teenagers find their way through this confusing period of life. We parents cannot live an isolated existence. We cannot bury our heads in the sand, pretending that our children don't see or hear what is going on. We cannot, despite our most sincere efforts, protect our children from harmful influences without completely isolating ourselves from modern life. We can, however, raise our children to be sensitive, caring, responsible people. We can guide them through these dangerous years.

To do this, we have to help each other. We have to seek help from agencies when necessary. We have to look for appropriate schools and summer programs. We have to be willing to make major changes in family life, to provide strong guidance, to ask hard questions, and to evaluate our priorities. Today we cannot afford to be casual parents. Parenthood in the 21st century is a difficult and conscious task – the most challenging and worthwhile work there is.

The view of the human being put forth in this book is based on the work of Rudolf Steiner, an Austrian philosopher, scientist, and seer who was born in 1861 and died in 1925. Steiner's world-view is called anthroposophy, or spiritual science, and is based on a spiritual perception of the universe. Students of anthroposophy have developed Steiner's insights into practical spheres including education, architecture, medicine, social organization and agriculture. Over four hundred Waldorf schools located in many countries across the world offer a vital creative approach to learning, based on Rudolf Steiner's view of the child. Parents who have become interested in these ideas have asked me to develop them further in the context of child raising and family life. Other parents who have neither contact with Waldorf education nor with Rudolf Steiner's views have responded to what I have been able to share through my own struggles and insights during lectures and parent workshops. They have asked me to elaborate these thoughts and share them. In response to these requests, I offer this book.

PART I

The Nature of Adolescence

Chapter One

How do you get to be an adolescent?

Phases in child development

> Our birth is but a sleep and a forgetting;
> The Soul that rises with us, our life's Star,
> Hath elsewhere its setting,
> And cometh from afar;
> Not in entire forgetfulness,
> And not in utter nakedness,
> But trailing clouds of glory do we come
> From God, who is our home.
> William Wordsworth

The child enters life

William Wordsworth, in the words above, shares a living imagination of human incarnation. Our birth is a sleep and a forgetting – yet so often we think of our birth as a waking and the world we have left behind as enclosed in a dark sleep. Ancient cultures spoke of a golden world left behind when the soul descended to earth. The earth, the new home, was then experienced as a land of shadows.

When we are born, we forget the world that has previously been our home. Gradually, we come to know our new home – the planet Earth.

Although we do not remember our pre-birth state, dim memories live within the soul and emerge from time to time as the child grows and comes to accept the imperfections of the everyday Earthworld.

Life unfolds in seven-year rhythms. Each of these life-phases has a special quality. During each, some capacities are lost and others gained, and during the middle of each, the child is especially sensitive to memories of pre-birth experiences.

The child's thinking is very different in each phase, which means that learning is radically different, depending on the child's age. In the first stage, between birth and age seven, the child thinks through doing and learns through imitation. Between seven and fourteen, the child thinks in pictures and learns through the feelings. Between fourteen and twenty-one, the young person thinks conceptually and learns through the intellect.

The first phase: birth to seven

During the first seven years, children's energies are directed to growing, walking, speaking, and thinking, as they establish themselves in the family. The love and care surrounding the young child lead it securely into the world, minimizing the dangers and welcoming it into the human community.

Young children explore the world by imitating the actions of others. They crawl, walk, run, dig, and throw. They are busy all the time becoming familiar with the earth, their new home. Young children are connected to the world through their will-activity and through their senses. They take in all that meets them through their senses and imitate what is in their environment.

Because they think through doing, they learn through imitating.

As soon as someone in the environment is doing something – chopping wood, hammering nails, beating eggs – young children are there to do it also. They throw themselves into these tasks with gusto.

By the seventh year, this phase comes to a conclusion. The child's physical body is basically complete. The child has mastered the human abilities on which the rest of life will depend – the ability to walk, to speak, and to think.

The second phase: seven to fourteen

The second phase is the heart of childhood. It begins and ends with a new state of consciousness expressed through physical changes. The marked physical growth of the first phase of childhood comes to a final expression in the change of teeth – from the uniformly shaped milk-teeth, already under the baby's gums at birth, to the individually shaped second teeth. The second phase ends with the maturation of the sexual organs, changes in the larynx, a growth spurt in the arms and legs, and increased activity in the thyroid gland.

During the second phase — from seven to fourteen — the soul develops. Children leave the security of the family and venture into the larger world of neighborhood and school. They come to feel at home in the wider circle of their community. They relate to this new world with their feelings, which are expressed in extremes. One hour they are happy; the next hour they are sad. They love you; they hate you. They say no; they say yes. They feel powerful; they feel powerless. The parent is overcome by the rush of intense feelings which the youngster expresses. Just as the parent tries to deal with the feelings expressed, the youngster's mood changes, and the adult is left nursing confused and hurt feelings, unsure what the youngster was actually trying to express.

The feeling life is developed in private, in a world of dreams, hopes, and fantasies. As their inner worlds develop depth, children begin to have secrets. The two worlds — the inner private and the outer public — interact, causing tension as children slowly learn to feel comfortable in both worlds.

Because the child approaches the world in this way, the most natural way of learning is through the feelings.

As children experience their new feelings, they show an increased interest in adventure stories. They relish the swing of emotions that they experience while listening to or reading a story filled with terror and suspense.

Their imaginations are filled with picture images, and their state of consciousness is a dream state where one image follows another without logical sequence. Indeed, the kind of thinking children do during the main part of the second phase of childhood is *picture thinking*. Out of this kind of thinking, they develop a *sense* for things rather than an *understanding* of things.

Toward the end of this phase, puberty occurs, heralding adolescence. The children have developed their habits, attitudes, temperaments, self-images, and social skills. Now, everything is thrown into chaos as the youngster passes into the next stage of life.

The third phase: fourteen to twenty-one

The third phase — fourteen to twenty-one — is the 'official' period of adolescence. *During this phase, children learn through the intellect.* They move from picture thinking to *abstract thinking*. Then, youth experiences the range of human emotions, ideals, goals, and expressions of personality as it prepares for the spiritual birth of the individual self, the ego, somewhere around the twenty-first year.

At this time the young person is able to act with self-direction and objective judgment. Childhood is completed.

Chapter Two

Stages of adolescence

Please understand me.
I am happy.
I want to be free
To fly in the wind.
My hair is a wing
My hand will propel.
My heart will love
Forever.
Me

Ninth grade girl

For the child, adolescence is new territory, uncharted and unexplored. Even parents often feel as if they are trying to navigate this unknown territory without a map. Imagine how the adolescent feels!

Adolescent development occurs in two recognizable phases which can be referred to as *negation* and *affirmation*. In the first phase, negation, adolescents want to oppose everything, they want to refute and criticize the world. In the second stage, affirmation, adolescents try to find their way into the life of the outer world. The polarity which expresses itself during adolescence is similar to an earlier polarity expressed when three-year-olds said 'No' to everything, followed by four-five year-olds who embraced the world with a mighty 'Yes'.

Negation

In the beginning of adolescence, young people are searching for their spiritual home, which expresses itself unconsciously as an undefined inner longing. Boys and girls look for the wonderful or the perfect, and when it cannot be found, they feel let down and disillusioned. Then the outer world seems strange and disappointing. They see ugliness where they had expected beauty. They see human weakness where they had expected perfection. This is frustrating and depressing. They become defiant, test everything and everyone – particularly anyone representing authority. They oppose everything that is out in the world and side with the underdog, especially against adults.

"Adults are nothing special" is the unspoken motto of many rebellious teenagers. Such teenagers may go so far as to torment an adult. However, if that same adult should do anything to cause the young teenager discomfort, a pained, withdrawn, and hostile response is evoked: "No one understands me".

It is not unusual for cyncism to develop out of unfulfilled expectations. Some adolescents never recover from their initial disappointment in the world. As adults, they feel justified in abusing other people to compensate for the previous hurts and disappointments they have suffered.

Disappointment causes the loneliness of adolescents to intensify, and this makes life very difficult for the adults, who, in this situation, can do nothing right. There are even moments when thought is absent and adolescents are capable of violent action, untempered by thinking. Out of curiosity, they may be outrageously rude, set a house on fire, or even pull a trigger. Some adolescents feel so removed from other people that they wonder if anyone anywhere thinks or feels as they do. They question whether there is a friend out there for them, and the search for a friend becomes an overwhelming priority in their lives.

The role of the 'crush'

Adolescence is the time when something akin to the Romantic Era of history is experienced in the individual life. The young person wishes to feel part of Nature as in Shelley's "Ode to the West Wind".

> Make me thy lyre, even as the forest is:
> What if my leaves are falling like its own!
> The tumult of thy mighty harmonies

Will take from both a deep, autumnal tone.
Sweet though in sadness. Be thou, Spirit fierce,
My spirit! Be thou me, impetuous one!

Because the young person's soul has become free and the feelings are more active, a deep longing for the spiritual world is felt. The soul's unconscious search for its lost spiritual home is characteristic of adolescence. Although many young people have deeply religious experiences, they usually keep them private or share them with only a trusted few.

The young adolescent longs to meet a kindred spirit who comes out of the spiritual world. How many songs describe the soul-mate as an angel or one who comes out of a dream? The soul realizes that it does not yet fit into the physical world, and it yearns for a creature to help it feel whole again.

The search for the spirit expresses itself in the soul life as a 'crush'. In this state, the person being adored does not have to be near. In fact, to adore from a distance is more satisfying because the adored one is not subjected to scrutiny but is held up to be worshiped. Godlike qualities are often projected onto the person who may be of the same sex or of the opposite sex. Teenagers model themselves after relatives, family friends, and teachers. In addition, girls tend to choose movie stars, camp counselors, rock stars, or upper classmen, while boys tend to choose slightly older boys, sports stars, historical figures, movie stars, television heroes, or rock stars.

In the crush, the object adored represents perfection. This helps the adolescent deal with the disappointment that the world is not perfect because he or she can concentrate on a figure who does represent perfection. Sometimes, a very close friendship produces the same effect as a crush. The best friend fills a similar role as the adored one, and best friends, their identities often merged, do everything together. They dress alike, enjoy the same music, share the same observations about people, and cling to each other in the storm of life. In the crush, adolescents feel the reflection of the higher world; "heaven" is in their hearts. Between thirteen and fifteen, the crush reaches its greatest intensity, although it may continue on into the late teens.

The crush may be projected onto an activity or an idea as well as onto a person. Teenagers can become fanatically devoted to a game and lose all sense of time. The game may involve a complicated system of rewards and punishments through which the youngsters can test their intellectual skill, or the game may be based on chance, which has its own excitement. They may devote themselves to a sport with similar fanaticism, using every possible moment in the day to shoot baskets, practice pitching, or kick a soccer ball. Sports have helped many teenagers get through the early adolescent period without becoming too obsessed with themselves. If the adults concerned with the sport create an atmosphere of support, cooperation, and camaraderie, the youngsters can receive great benefit. If, on the other hand, adults foster cut-throat competition, creating pressure on the teenager to win at all costs, they are doing nothing to help the youngster move out of self-obsession, but, in fact, are intensifying unhealthy self-preoccupation.

With a crush, something evokes the kinds of feelings that once were experienced in a far simpler way in the childhood experience of God. That something may be a person – either close-by or unattainable – an idea, or even an activity. At some point, however, adolescents can no longer keep the adored object at a distance. They must connect personally. Teenagers fantasize how the connection will be made, how they and the object of their worship will come together. The youngster may imagine becoming a tragic figure who lives and dies for an idea. Perhaps the teenager will be the only person in the crowd noticed by the cherished singer. This fantasy meeting between the adolescent and the object of adoration carries a storm of emotions which is of great importance for the further development of the individual, and it leads the adolescent over to the second stage of adolescence – affirmation.

Thus, the first love – be it baseball, a cultural hero, or an older girl or boy – often is the bridge from the stage of negation to the stage of affirmation at about fifteen or sixteen. No experience will ever have quite the impact on the young person as this event does. Its power lies in the innocence and freshness of the experience. However, the kind of influence this strong experience has on the developing person depends on the way the crush is resolved.

Transition

The fifteenth-sixteenth year is the pivotal time for adolescents. Teenagers are coming into their own, and they are beginning to accept the world as they see it. This usually begins to happen at the end of tenth grade and the beginning of eleventh grade.

At this time, teenagers are coming out of the extreme of being either too withdrawn or too aggressive and are beginning to laugh more, to feel accepted, to be accepting, to be friendly and outgoing, to be communicative, to relate better to teachers and parents, and to understand their siblings.

Boys still hang around with boys but now they look at girls. Girls hang around with girls and survey the boys. There is usually a friendly "in" group in each class or school made up of popular and successful girls who spend endless hours on the telephone, laughing and talking about everybody. Their exuberance and energy, their optimism and expansiveness are infectious, but it is sometimes doubtful whether they are having as good a time as it seems.

The pressure to act in a certain way so as to be part of this group can cause tremendous strain. The price paid for acceptance is the sacrifice of inner growth for outer rewards. Girls who are not included in this group may have a hard time finding where they belong in the social life of the school. Boys also are affected by social pressure although they may not be as conscious of all the ins and outs of the groups as the girls are.

One of the problems of the transitional period is the attempt to do too much. In their eagerness to embrace the world, teenagers often take on too many commitments, which they then have trouble honoring, or they take on such difficult challenges that they have difficulty living up to expectations. They try to think about too many things or plan too many activities, and there is simply not enough time to do everything. This exuberance and confidence also leads them to experiment with danger. Fifteen-year-olds often take risks and test limits, not so much out of insecurity, as a thirteen-year-old would, but because they want to taste life.

Affirmation

After this turning point, the way is prepared for the stage of affirmation, which comes during the sixteenth-seventeenth year. The stage of affirmation is characterized by the transformation of love from early sensuality and self-interest to love for another human being and for the world in general, for affirmation is not limited to love of a person. At this point, adolescents begin to search for ideas or for a picture of the world with which they can be comfortable. The stage of affirmation is the time when the search for truth begins. Adolescents now search for religious answers, for ideal political systems, and for the next step in their education. They become concerned about their future careers.

In the earlier period, young adolescents are not familiar with the world. What they experience is separateness, hostility, and opposition. This evokes distrust and even hatred from youngsters. Slowly, however, teenagers begin to question, analyze, criticize, and doubt, and gradually the distrust and hostility toward the world is transformed into a longing to do great deeds for the world. The young people come to express joy in the world.

This is often stimulated by powerful experiences in nature. The youngster feels, "How good it is to be alive," and a period of stability follows in which he feels less tense and less hypersensitive.

As teenagers feel more confident, more comfortable with themselves, they become more realistic about life. They begin to appreciate their freedom and respect their responsibilities. With this change come a sense of humor and patience. Relationships with parents and siblings become more comfortable (although teeenagers still prefer to be with friends).

Parents are appreciated and cherished, and adolescents begin to feel free to approach them for advice, feeling less threatened and more able to participate in the give-and-take without losing their identities. The adolescents become more self-reliant and more poised. Life becomes relatively peaceful, and fewer arguments occur. Sometimes, older adolescents comment that their parents are becoming smarter or wiser, or at least easier to live with.

With time, crushes fade and in their place come real life relationships. More immature boys or girls may hold on to their crushes for a longer time and often with members of the same sex. At this time, the tables turn and the older adolescents become the object of crushes from younger teenagers. It is amusing to watch eleventh and twelfth graders deal with the admiration of the seventh, eighth or ninth graders. Not quite sure how to handle the situation, the older students often try to be sensitive in the way they respond to their youthful admirers.

Late adolescence: eighteen to twenty-one

As teenagers step across the threshhold of their eighteenth birth-days, they enter young adulthood and are ready for responsibilities. Learning and maturity now become based on life experience. The focus of their development lies in finding a relationship to their times, to the culture in which they are living, and to the people who embody the ideals and values of the cultural age. In the book *Phases*, Bernard Lievegoed writes, "In everyday life among other people he can create his own free world between the laws of the spirit and the laws of nature … The margin of freedom which is the lifesaver for the adolescent may be found between mind and matter. What is important is that despite limitations imposed by physical circumstances and by cultural taboos and the accepted norms of the concrete social situation he *makes* something that is totally and absolutely *personal*."

Whether the young adult is working at a job or at school, there is the need to make a personal mark on life, to see what the limits are, to find one's mentors. It is important during this time to develop social skills, to make strong personal connections with people. These are the years in which the young person finds career direction, is exposed to new interests, travels, experiments with living arrange-ments, and works at a variety of intimate social relationships.

Young adults should not make commitments that tie them down. This should be the time of developing judgment, of flexibility, and of forming the picture of one's life. Youngsters who become tied to adult jobs and to family matters before twenty-one become respon-sible adults, but they often take longer to find their direction. They need time to explore, change, and change again.

(In the many years I have been a teacher, one of the most

pleasurable experiences has been talking to graduates. The changes they go through in the three or four years after graduation are exciting and often unpredictable. Teenagers who were determined to go into one field of study turn one hundred and eighty degrees and go in a different direction. They find so much that is new and challenging, that is calling to them, that is fascinating. Life, the great teacher, is so interesting for them, and it is wonderful to share their insights.)

Those who feel tied down have a harder time exploring new aspects of their personality. They, too, learn from life, but sometimes what they learn is quite discouraging. They often go from job to job and grow quite discouraged when they find that it is not easy to support themselves. After the initial satisfaction of being on their own, there is a let-down. Why? Rather than discovering new aspects of themselves, they feel stifled and confined. They are not finding out who they are in the world. Those who travel, study, work at an apprenticeship, or learn a craft are developing themselves as people. They are expanding their horizons and exploring their skills.

Dangers

If they are not presented with ideals or do not have feelings of comfort about their origin, if they do not find a close friend or object of love, if there is nothing that comes to take them out of self-preoccupation, adolescents can be drawn too strongly into the physical-sexual life as their main source of satisfaction. They are encouraged to do this by movies, television, radio and advertising. The budding young adult can become trapped into sexual preoccupation through overstimulation from outside. With nothing to balance this preoccupation, adolescents become hard and tough. They are thrust into eroticism or the will to power.

Our cities are filled with young people who have nothing to lift them out of their despair or sensuality and whose lives become a series of exploits with few goals other than immediate pleasure or power. When we study biographies, we can see how one special event – a meeting with a person, an experience with music, a kind word, a book given at the right moment, or an experience in nature

– can shake these youngsters loose from this trap and set them going on a wholesome and meaningful path. Those caught in poverty, minority discrimination, or crime often fall into a despair that drags them down unless they have one of the above experiences to free them.

Drama is a special help during this time. By stepping into another character, the young person can experience fear, compassion, terror, joy, and humor. In fear, the person breathes in most strongly. In loving devotion, the person breathes out. The rhythm of breathing out and breathing in of emotional experiences helps the soul establish its independence from the body in a healthful way. Through drama, adolescents are able to try out roles, experiment with anger, confrontation, sensitivity, compassion and sacrifice, and to vicariously experience what happens to people in different life situations.

Another helpful area for teenagers is interest in world events. By becoming familiar with the issues, by learning how different policies and attitudes are formed in response to complex circumstances, they begin to see where change can occur. Rather than becoming cynical, they develop a hopeful attitude, probably because the involvement itself produces the experience of having an effect on events and circumstances.

Interest in the world is also expressed through interest in other cultures. Studying the myths of a culture allows youngsters to understand the ways people think. Studying their values provides the youth with a possibility to reflect on his or her own cultural values. Such an interest often leads to greater understanding of humanity and an enhanced sense of brotherhood.

Adolescents often come up with simple answers to life's complex problems, and adults smile at the naive optimism that trips off the tongues of youths who want to save the world. However, the idealism of youth sets the stage for commitment and involvement during adult life. Interest in the outer world, in ideas, and in social issues also helps adolescents become free of the control which their bodies still have over them. Rather than being self-preoccupied, they become interested and involved in the outer world. Interest in others is one of the first steps of spiritual development, according to Steiner.

Adolescence is not a stable time. It is a period of impermanence, new values, new modes, and new ideas being tried out and discarded. Because adolescents do not fully experience objective reality until around the twenty-first year, firmness, understanding, patience, and love are needed from the adults to help them through the transitional period.

Chapter Three

The search for the self

As I watch the rain run down the window
I think of all the sadness in the world.
… Is there no hope for the future?
Ninth grade boy

Who am I? Where have I come from? Is there a God? Is there meaning in the world? These questions become conscious in adolescence and live with us the rest of our lives. When we feel insecure and separate from the people around us, when we feel spiritually threatened, these questions rise to meet us. As we develop through the cycles of human life, we undergo change in the way we relate to the world. We become different in ourselves; old capacities fade, new capacities awaken. The old answers don't satisfy us any more. As we move from one stage to another, we experience a transitional time when the old approach is no longer adequate, but the new attitude or soul-condition is not yet functioning. Transition periods create discomfort and crisis.

Three major crises occur during the first twenty-one years, and from then on, other crises continue throughout adult life, approximately every seven years. Each crisis is an opportunity for developing increased self-awareness and understanding. The Chinese pictogram for "crisis" has two elements, one meaning "danger" and one meaning "opportunity". The crisis points in the middle of each seven-year period mark the time when the person makes major steps forward or backward – a time rich with opportunity and fraught with danger.

The third/fourth-year change

The first crisis occurs between ages two and four. Until that time, the child has experienced itself as a part of the environment. There has been no strong sense of separation. Everything in the environment is there to serve the child: to feed, clothe, shelter, love and support every need that arises. After the second birthday, the child begins to experience itself as a separate body and finds that the world is not there to provide every need whenever it wants. The anger that is felt is expressed by the name given to that period – 'The Terrible Twos'.

The child senses that it is no longer the center of the universe, but a separate being, an "I". This is manifested in the way that children refer to themselves. Previously, the child may have said, "Johnnie wants that" or "Sarah likes cookies". During this period of transition, however, the mental process itself undergoes change. When the child hears the question, "Do you want another cookie?" a transition is made from "you" to "I", and the child responds, "I want another cookie".

The early experience of the "I" is one of the miracles of human development. It forms the foundation of later psychological and mental growth. It leads to children's new experience as independent physical beings, physically independent of their parents, their houses, the fields, flowers, animals and all else that is around them. Having come through this change, the youngsters gain confidence in themselves and enter the period known as 'The Fearless Fours'.

All children, except those who have severe learning difficulties or have deep psychological disturbances, have a similar "I" experience. They may not remember the process of change, but it is reflected in the change in speech, usually completed by the fourth birthday.

The ninth/tenth-year change

Seven years later, between the ages of eight and ten, the second ego crisis or crisis in self-awareness occurs. The child has earlier experienced the physical separation, and now the separation of soul is experienced. Children come to sense that they are their own selves, that they have their own feelings and thoughts. They are not the same as other people; their thoughts and feelings are different. This leads at first to a feeling of loss and a concern about death.

They no longer feel what their parents are thinking, and, even more, their parents cannot feel what they are thinking and wanting.

They see that they have to explain what is going on inside them, they have to express their needs and wants clearly. This is very frustrating. It was so much easier when they were little and their parents anticipated their needs.

They come to feel soul-loneliness. They yearn for the magic of childhood when small hills were mountains, boulders were forts, animals spoke to them, and the people around them were grand heroes and heroines. Slowly, they are coming to see that the hill is only a hill, the rock is only a rock, and people have flaws. The magic is gone.

As Wordsworth says in his *Ode*, "The things which I have seen, I now can see no more". The commonplace has become the normal way of seeing. After every special occasion, one nine-year-old would say, "Well, that wasn't very interesting". Events which had been exciting to the younger child now had become too ordinary for words.

Adults may experience something of the loss of the magic of childhood when they return to the places of their own early years. Everything is changed. The trees seem so much smaller, the path in the forest is only a scant trail in the bushes. The magic is gone, and the adult, too, is left with a nostalgic longing for what once was.

When children lose the capacity for seeing imaginatively, for seeing the glow around things and people, their focus on the things of the outer world becomes sharper. What once was bathed in beauty and warmth stands cold and unadorned in its objectness. It is as if the child's eyes are opening wide for the first time. Children begin to see what they never saw before. They see unfairness, narrow-mindedness, and inconsistency. Their adored adults topple from pedestals, and this upsets them. If parents are not perfect, whom can children count on? They see imperfection in their teachers as well, and they feel confused. So, they pull back and become aloof because they cannot understand what is happening.

They think about things they are not supposed to do. They feel temptation and guilt. They feel caught between a voice that encourages them to do naughty things and a voice that restrains them. The youngsters look at the world and see that, as Gilbert and Sullivan put it, "things are seldom what they seem". What is supposed to be good isn't always good, and what is supposed to be bad often has an enticing flavor to it.

They see that they can make choices in their lives, so they step out and start expressing what they want. "I want this. I don't want that." They try to exercise some control. They find, however, that they don't always get what they express as their choice. If they make certain choices, they are confronted with responsibility.

Ah! There's the rub! Choice can become a burden. They slowly understand that this new capacity has a price to it – and they aren't sure that it is worth it. They begin to get the message that they cannot have both worlds – they cannot be young children in a little child's world and also exercise more grown-up decisions. The dawning sense that they are accountable for what they do makes some of them want to crawl back into the safe womb of childhood, while others want to dive prematurely into the exciting teen world and prove themselves worthy.

They become critical of everything around them. Often, only their loved cat or dog escapes being a target of this frustrated attention. "I don't like you". "You're dumb". "You never keep promises". "You never let me do anything". "You're not fair". Eight and nine-year-olds going through this change become sullen and moody. When asked, "Is anything bothering you?", typical answers are, "No" and "I don't know".

This new relationship between youngster and parents often is expressed by two questions, "Are you my real parents?" and "What was I like as a baby?" The first question comes from their feeling of separateness and loneliness. Because of this feeling, they often want to escape to the time when they felt safe and connected. They become fascinated with their own childhoods and ask many questions. Some begin speaking baby-talk and resume babyish habits.

The way the ninth/tenth-year change is resolved has much to do with the way youngsters will enter adolescence several years later. *If* they find ways to gain self-confidence, and *if* they have trusted adults to turn to, *then* they tend to resolve the sense of separation and make peace with the world.

So often in life when we suffer a loss, we also experience compensation. This is true with the ninth-year change. Along with the confusion and frustrations that occur, comes an increased ability to do things in the world. This is reflected in the increased skills in physical coordination, intellectual understanding, and interest in the world. The child has reached a balance between an active inner life and outer ability, which makes fourth and fifth grades (and sometimes sixth) glorious to teach. This is the heart of childhood.

As we know, life doesn't always go smoothly. If the youngsters do not gain self-confidence, if they do not have one trusted adult to turn to, if they cannot find a hopeful relationship, they assume an attitude which says, "I don't care," or "I hate everything". The despair of many young dropouts or criminals has its roots during this period. This attitude has been referred to as the dropout syndrome, especially with boys. Obviously, most nine-year-olds do not drop out of school, nor do they run away from home, take drugs, or decide that life isn't worth living. They remain at home and in school, but their gestures say: "Show me", "I don't care", "I can't do it anyway". In a few years, they may easily become twelve-year-olds who do drop out, run away, smoke pot, drink alcohol, or sleep around.

As Joseph Chilton Pearce says in *The Magical Child*:[1]

Forcing the early child to deal prematurely with adult abstract thought can cripple the child's ability to think abstractly later on. The first ten years or so are designed for acquiring a full-dimensional knowledge of the world as it is and learning how to interact with it physically and mentally. This growth of knowledge and ability should lead to the ability to survive physically in the world. With the security of a full knowledge of survival, the young person could then move freely into abstract thought. His/her intelligence could then attend the true maturation of the mind-brain. Not incidentally, the concrete knowledge from which survival grows is also the concrete structure of knowledge out of which abstract thought arises.

A shallow-dimensional world view, based only on the long-range senses of sight and sound, is often the kind of knowledge constructed by the child. Direct physical contact with the world – taste, touch, even smell – are often either discouraged or actually forbidden in the parent's anxiety over the hazards of germs and imagined threats. Without a full-dimensional world view structured in the formative years, no earth matrix can form, no knowledge of physical survival can develop, and no basis for abstraction and creativity can arise. A permanent anxiety and obsessive-compulsive attachment to material objects will result. And anxiety always cripples intelligence; it blocks the development of muscular-mindedness, the ability to interact with the unknown and unpredictable. Anxiety is the source of the fall of the child somewhere around age nine. Its roots are deep, its branches prolific, its fruit abundant, and its effects devastating.

The sixteenth/seventeenth-year change

The next crisis, occurring around sixteen or seventeen, has to do with the feeling of spiritual separation. Even though the emotional chaos is mostly resolved and the rate of physical changes has slowed down, a subtle feeling of discomfort starts to be experienced. Some teenagers come to terms with mortality for the first time. They learn that they have limits, especially limits to their physical abilities. They test their bodies, get too little sleep, ignore nutrition, abuse their health.

Those who tend to be perfectionists suffer particularly during this time. They set very high standards for themselves and feel pressure to measure up to other people's expectations of them. They want to be involved in many activities, carry a heavy schedule, work part-time, and have an active social life. They may also want to participate in competitive sports, practice an instrument, be in musical or dramatic productions, − all within the space of twenty-four hour days. Late nights and anxieties catch up with them, and they sometimes end up sick. The period of convalescence may be valuable because it gives them a chance to rest and think about priorities, but they also may feel added pressure because of missing school. However, the most valuable change that can come out of illness is acceptance that one cannot be perfect and do all things. Choices have to be made, priorities have to be set.

The crisis often confronts the sixteen-year-old with spiritual questions. Is there a God? Is there life after death? Do angels exist? What happens if there's nothing? How can the existence of God be proven? Teenagers thus may box themselves into philosophical corners which leave them few options. They may deny the existence of anything spiritual while yearning for proof that the spiritual world exists. They may convince themselves that the world is completely meaningless. The power of these thoughts may cause deep depression and even hopelessness.

Some are not interested in philosophical questions but prefer their excitement in the physical arena of life. They enjoy thrills of speed and daring, choosing one exciting experience after another. Some confront existential questions when they find themselves in serious situations such as a serious auto accident, a bad decision while drunk or stoned, facing a pregnancy, being suspended from school, or in trouble with the law. Such situations make them think about the meaning of life, whether there is a God, and whether they are alone in the universe. They may decide it is time to outgrow their irre-sponsible behavior and grow up.

Very often, sixteen-year-olds are working out the attitudes devel-oped during the ninth-year change. With a new awareness of them-selves, they are able to make major shifts in their behavior. The potential for change around sixteen is shown by the numbers of adolescents who do a complete turn-around after experiencing a shock. Their higher self (which also may be called their I, or true self, or ego) draws close to their soul and awakens them to the nobler side of their nature.

The spiritual crisis of the third period of childhood – fourteen to twenty-one – leaves adolescents feeling alone on the planet. After an initial period of anger and disappointment, they often decide to involve themselves in the world. They may join a social organization, participate in protest marches, etc. As they sense their mortality, they also experience their own imperfection. As nine-year-olds, they learned to see the imperfections in others. Now they start to see themselves objectively, and they assess their strengths and weaknesses. They begin to stand outside themselves and realize who they are.

In this process, they see the importance of the choices they are making. They think about their goals, their values. They think about whether or not they believe in a spiritual world, and, if they do, whether it is the way adults describe it. They are interested in discussing such topics only as long as they don't feel they are being converted. They realize that they must find their own path to God, and they have serious inner conversations. Youngsters in this phase of life have many painful times. The questioning path is a lonely one to tread, but it is the only one that leads to becoming a free human being.

The seven year stages and points of crisis

Here is a representation of the three crises; each crisis is occasioned by the youngster attaining a new awareness of himself or herself. The first comes with the awareness of the self as a separate human being; the second with the awareness that one has an inner life; the third with the awareness of oneself as partaking in life and death, raising the question of meaning in life.

The crisis usually occurs with the approach of the middle years of the phase. To understand this, it might be helpful to think of hiking in the mountains. Our adjustment comes not at the top of the mountain, but as the flatlands start to rise. Our breathing and pulse quicken as our bodies strives to adjust to the strain placed upon them. Once we have made the adjustment, we find a new pace – a second wind – and we are able to maintain a steady stride to the heights for a breath-taking view. There we feel a sense of accomplishment. Having had these experiences, once again we take to the path, descend the mountain, and gradually adjust our stride. Our lungs and heart also adjust until we return to our flatland home, never to be the same as when we began. Thus the adolescent benefits from the inner crisis around sixteen.

Memories of the experience dim, but they are there to be awakened when a similar experience comes along or when we feel a similar sense of adjustment or of accomplishment. It may be recalled when we are deeply moved or when our own children pass through this period.

The feelings that accompany the crisis live unconsciously in our soul lives. They work behind the scenes as we meet people or situations and may make us feel comfortable or uncomfortable about ourselves or about other people we meet. Each crisis may take several years to resolve, and much of the time we are unaware of anything but a feeling of mild discontent. Many years later, after the crisis period has passed, the mention of it may cause a knot in the stomach or tears to flow. In this way, the adult is alerted to the pain still living and probably unresolved.

The completion of childhood

The childhood of human life is made up of twenty-one years. For the rest of our lives, we look back to those years for clues to our health, our attitudes, our self-confidence or lack of it, our ideals. Often we find that until we penetrate a childhood experience and understand it, we are stuck in it, but once we come to a clear picture of what happened, we are free to go on with our lives. Often coming to a clear picture involves forgiving people for what they have done to us.

Our responsibility as parents becomes greater as we ponder the formative powers we have over our children. Yet we are not the only major determinant. Other people in the environment, heredity, the family's joys and trials, the place and time – all have their influences. However, it is important to recognize that the child's own individuality, the ego coming from before birth and separate from heredity, guides the development of the childhood years and comes to the forefront at around twenty-one.

What role does this ego have? Perhaps an image may help us. Picture a ship. The ship's design has long ago been conceived, the framework has been constructed, the walls filled in, the cabin completed. Then comes the moment when the captain, who has been working in the background, steps forward. The captain has been preparing for this moment for a long time. How well will he/she take hold of the ship? What crew will the captain choose? Where will he/she steer the ship? Will the captain be tyrannical, weak, or wise? Will he/she be respected? Will the captain be responsive to the crew? Will the captain know when to diverge from his/her course to answer a call of distress?

These are the challenges to the captain of the soul, to the human ego, as it takes its place around the twenty-first year. The parents will have completed their major work. Now, as individuals, the young adults have to take responsibility for themselves. The ego is in charge. At twenty-one, young people go forth to seek their fortunes.

Chapter Four

The birth of intellect

Nothing is at last sacred but the integrity of your own mind.
Ralph Waldo Emerson

With puberty is born a new soul force – the force of intellect. The young person begins to form independent opinions based on the experiences of life.

The early teenage years

One twelve-year-old referred to something she had learned when she was eleven. "That was before my brain knew how to think", she said. The birth of the intellect is accompanied by a great interest in facts about the world. At this age, youngsters like a subject even if it's difficult. They begin to read newspapers, listen to the news, and enjoy discussions. Many thirteen-year-olds dig into their homework with a strong sense of satisfaction and accomplishment. During the early teen years, a wide range of interests emerges to meet this new enjoyment of intellectual challenge.

The newly formed intellect, however, lacks discrimination. The youngster uncritically accepts as truth statements made by respected adults and media, and builds a worldview out of the biases and opinions of those around him. This worldview becomes the foundation of his or her judgement. Earlier, the youngster's worldview was based on the feelings in the immediate environment, but now it is ideas and opinions that influence. Consequently, thirteen and fourteen-year-olds often rely on half-truths and undigested facts when they try to make sense of the world. The power of the intellect allows them to receive the information, but lack of experience often results in dogmatic statements that do not hold up under questioning.

Youngsters enjoy being able to express opinions based on a knowledge even though it may be very little knowledge, and it is quite easy for them to think that they know more than they do. They fall in love with their ideas and, like prize fighters waiting to be challenged, they present them to the world. Here we find an interesting contradiction. Having accepted an idea or opinion on the flimsiest of authority, from then on, they will permit no contradiction of it. When challenged, they find it difficult to let go of the idea, even if it is obviously absurd. Discussion easily turns into an argument, hurt feelings, and barbed comments.

At this age, they also sense the power which their opinions have on other people and realize that they can make or destroy reputations at will. In ways that younger children never would dream of, they test their skill by manipulating parents, teachers, and friends. This newly found intellectual power has two sides to it. It can be a reaching out to new understanding of the world, or it can become a cutting-off of oneself from intimacy and love.

The change of thinking in the sixteenth year

Fifteen-year-olds also like to air their own opinions, but they are better at listening to the thoughts of others as well. This is a welcome change, and it is one of the big differences between ninth and tenth graders. Rather than being in love with their own power of thinking, fifteen-year-olds begin to be fascinated by thought itself. They respond favorably to philosophical questions, although they cannot concentrate for long. Their thinking focuses more clearly than before and they express interest in how things came to be and how they have changed. The power to grasp a thought and develop it grows stronger as their power of intellect matures. They are more reflective, and a discussion no longer seems like a prizefight because they are learning to listen.

By sixteen, the brain has attained almost full power. Sixteen-year-olds may lack wisdom but are fully capable of thinking in abstractions and generalizations. They can compare, contrast, analyze and synthesize information. Sixteen-year-olds learn as quickly as teachers and parents do. However, they still are often ready to engage in debate before they have digested the new material. They are not ready to acknowledge their lack of wisdom and experience, and their arrogance can be very irritating to adults. Another endearing aspect of their new-found intellectual power is that they enjoy finding and boasting about flaws in adult reasoning.

Adolescents enjoy sharpening their new tool – reason – and may push it to a ridiculous extent merely to prove a point. However, the force of intellect is the tool for questioning the social structure, the human soul, and the nature of life itself. It also is a tool for probing hypocrisy. By about seventeen or eighteen, adolescents begin to gain perspective. They become interested in comparative ideas and earnestly strive to formulate individual answers to life's questions. The life experiences being accumulated by the seventeen/eighteen-year-old temper the force of intellect and balance it. Now more than a weapon, thinking has become a tool which the young adult can use along with other tools in coming to a conclusion.

New ideas are welcomed. The worldview formed earlier now can be questioned and old prejudices challenged.

The late teen years: from cleverness to the beginning of wisdom

Between eighteen and twenty-one, thinking reaches a new stage. The young adult experiences thought more objectively than ever before. Trying to figure out what is real and what is illusion, trying to separate one's own thinking from that of others, trying to figure out why one person reacts one way instead of another – these are fascinating changes that go on in the mind of the young adult. Through considering such questions, young people begin to distinguish between cleverness and wisdom. They still are vulnerable to indoctrination or dogmatism, but they have more tools at their disposal to use in forming their own judgments.

In college or on jobs, young adults find that they have new strength in their thinking. Problems which they could not have solved during their high school years now seem easier. As one person said, "It is as if something clicked".

The importance of the intellect

Rudolf Steiner pointed out that if intense interest in the riddles of life is not awakened in young people, then the new energies released at adolescence transform themselves into urges of a baser kind – first into delight of power and second into eroticism. Through their intellects, adolescents can be encouraged to engage the world questions. Their new-found energy can be directed outward to develop interest in other people.

Plato described the importance of the intellect in his description of the human soul, which he said was made up of three soul elements. He described the 'sentient soul' and the 'spiritual soul' as two wild horses, pulling in opposite directions. The charioteer holding the rein was the 'intellectual soul'. Through the control of the intellectual soul, Plato felt that human beings could keep in check the pleasures and desires which would pull them into the lower, earthly forces such as eroticism, as well as one-sided spiritual pursuits which would pull them off the earth. In time and with experience, the intellectual soul learns how to control the two opposite needs so that, acknowledged and satisfied, both are able to exist side-by-side in harmony.

The process of balancing the opposites begins in adolescence and goes on during adulthood. It is essential in order to develop maturity and stability.

The nature of the intellect

The intellect in a young person has been developing gradually. In early childhood, it was connected with the will; in the middle childhood period, it was connected with the feelings. Around twelve, it shows the first signs of existing independently of the feelings. The first sign of this is the ability to understand cause and effect. Steiner explained that the capacity to experience phenomena through the intellect alone comes at the same time as children sense the skeletal nature of their own bodies. As they perceive their own bony structure, they also perceive the structure of thought.

Their sense of historic time increases, measurement becomes more important as a way of proving physical occurrences, and abstract concepts begin to be grasped. The mythical, imaginative, dream-like perceptions yield to scientific thinking.

It is particularly difficult for parents who have been attempting to protect their children from premature intellectuality to accept that it is appropriate and in the child's best interests to awaken the intellect, starting at about age twelve. Deadly when fostered too early, systematic thinking now becomes necessary for the soul-life to cross the bridge to its next phase. The child now needs to be connected to the physical world, and the use of reason to develop concepts out of perceptions grounds the child and is appropriate at this time.

However, one has to be careful because one-sided conceptual education hurries the intellectual faculties and encourages premature puberty. Once the intellectual consciousness is awakened, imaginative thinking is stunted. The rich, dream-like world of images recedes, and youngsters learn mainly through the senses and through thinking. They have very little protection from sense bombardment and are too awake to whatever comes from the environment. Childhood is over.

Once adolescents see the physical world as the subject of observation and experiment, they try to manipulate the environment. It is quite easy for them to gain the false impression that they can understand everything through logical thinking. Reality becomes what one can see and measure. Such an attitude fosters a mechanistic view of the human being and of the universe.

Many children's books, especially those on science, foster this attitude and shape the attitudes of many youngsters. For them, the world is only a machine, the heart is only a pump, and the brain is only a computer. Most traditional educational materials take the mechanistic view as their starting point.

Parents interested in a spiritual view of the human being and of the universe should be aware of this bias in most popular scientific material. The material presented is not so much wrong as it is one-sided. A full picture is omitted. As an antidote, adults need to stimulate in young children a sense of wonder and arouse in them awe for the beauty of nature, the mystery of the human body, and the interrelationships of the human being and cosmos. When they are young, that is all they need. Only as they become adolescents is more needed.

As youngsters become more conscious, thinking can lose its liveliness and spontaneity and become dry and abstract. It is a challenge to stimulate feelings which then enliven the thinking. Thinking without feelings can be cold. Feeling should not be confused with sentimentality. For instance, many would consider geometry the epitome of cold, abstract thinking, but it need not be so. If one does geometry with one's sense of awe alert to the wonders of the forms and lawfulness of geometry, one's relationship to the material becomes entirely transformed. The person who does geometry without those feelings has really missed a vital element of mathematics and is engaged in a truly dead activity.

There are many additional ways to awaken livelier thinking. By exploring the deeper truths in mythology, youngsters can develop appreciation for the many levels of meaning in literature. By drawing or painting copies of works of art from different periods, youngsters directly experience the changes in human consciousness. This experience develops appreciation for the great artistic accomplishments of mankind and gives them a feeling for people of diverse cultures. Through listening to or reading biographies, teenagers can identify with the challenges confronted by men and women of high ideals. In studying science, becoming directly involved with the phenomena can enliven the thinking much more than memorizing theories.

The awakening intellect longs to meet the world, to grapple with ideals, and to feel some sense of mastery over the environment. When issues of substance are presented, the intellect is exercised. At the same time, the adolescent comes to feel, "There is more to this than meets the eye". In this way, a sense of appreciation develops as the teenager learns to handle facts, especially if the facts are interrelated.

Dangers

Thinking is the gateway to freedom. Yet, it is possible – even common – for young people to be sidetracked so that they either become so materialistic in their thinking that they lose touch with their artistic and creative capacities, or they so strongly react to the hardness and coldness of modern materialism that they dissipate their ability to think critically in a Nirvana of vague sentimentality.

The first danger occurs when the youngster is rushed too quickly into materialistic thought. Adolescents who have been steeped in a view that nothing is real which cannot be physically measured or detected often feel very uncomfortable when asked to consider the possibility of a spiritual dimension to life. They wish to reduce all life to cause-and-effect thinking. They may even come to feel uncomfortable outside the factual and objective areas of science and technology, such as in fields with an artistic, musical, poetic, or literary content. Charles Darwin went so far in the direction of reducing the world to what he could measure that he experienced pain when he contemplated the world he once had loved. He wrote in his journal:

> But now for many years I cannot endure to read a line of poetry. I have tried lately to read Shakespeare, and found it so intolerably dull that it nauseated me. I have also almost lost my taste for pictures and music. I lament this curious loss of my higher aesthetic tastes … My mind seems to have become a kind of machine for grinding general laws, out of large collections of facts, but why this should have caused the atrophy of that part of the brain alone, on which the higher tastes depend, I cannot conceive.

Some youngsters may be able to accept both the prevailing scientific view and a spiritual view, but only by splitting their consciousness. They place their religious experience into a separate compartment so that it has no connection with their materialistic thoughts about Nature and human development.

Youngsters who are drawn exclusively to cause-and-effect thinking are very comfortable with schoolwork that requires objective fill-in answers. Open-ended essay questions, however, are threatening to them because their minds have been so programed by stimulus-response operation that they cannot handle questions which call for other kinds of thinking. This tendency is heightened by the obsession which such students often have with computers. Life becomes a shallow progression of stimulus-response challenges rather than an intricate web of deep human relationships.

The second danger is that some adolescents will remain too long in a dream world to avoid dealing with the real world. Because they are uncomfortable relating to logic and cause-and-effect thinking, they drift into worlds of images and fantasy. Using the imagination as escape, they resist focusing their thoughts or organizing them. They do not like to be pinned down or asked to be objective.

They resent anyone who tries to make them bring clarity into their rambling descriptions, often labeling such a person as unfeeling and uncreative.

A variation of the dreamy adolescent is the one who is not living in rich imagery but who simply refuses to take the trouble to be clear. Such teenagers wallow in clichés, sprinkling their speech with "Well", "kinda", and "ya know". They share many of the same outer attitudes of the adolescent who is escaping into fantasy, but their resistance to form and rigor comes out of laziness rather than an aversion to the matter-of-fact world.

Balance in thinking is necessary for the teenager. Enthusiasm and feelings are needed as well as objectivity. Either alone diverts the teenager from becoming a free, well-rounded individual.

Development of the ego rests on the balance between form and flexibility in thinking. Such a balance results from the natural maturing of the teenager. In the early adolescent years, the thoughts of teenagers are not their own thoughts. Their thinking is strongly shaped by the images from outside which cascade down on them. Teenagers are at the mercy of those thoughts and lack experience to keep them out. After sixteen, however, thoughts awaken from within the soul. Adolescents then are able to listen and respond to the inner thought process. They become fascinated with thinking itself and especially with patterns in thinking.

When adolescents gain control over their thinking and are no longer at the mercy of thoughts chaotically streaming into their consciousness, they bring will into their thinking. Their thinking becomes disciplined and directed. It has form. It is focused. At this point, teenagers experience freedom – a moment of true excitement.

Chapter Five

Release of feelings

Beauty is truth, truth beauty, – that is all
Ye know on earth, and all ye need to know.
John Keats

When little children are asked how they feel about things, it is not unusual for them to answer, "I don't know". How can children of six or seven or ten or eleven understand their feelings? They certainly experience feelings of pleasure, pain, excitement, and fear. But the child has great difficulty describing – much less, understanding – more subtle feelings such as ecstasy, compassion, sadness, gratitude, or joy. Many feelings of young children are connected with their physical body and with physical needs for food, drink, shelter, warmth, comfort, security and protection. Children assume that everything in their world is the way it is supposed to be. The child feels the way it breathes – naturally and without judgment. For children, the world is good. Even in the most adverse situations, children accept what is.

During the period from seven to fourteen, children live strongly in the life of feeling. All actions, experiences, and thoughts are colored by feelings, most of which are in polarity – sympathy and antipathy, love and hatred, like and dislike. When children embrace the world, their gesture is open, and they meet the world with positive feelings. When they close themselves off from the world, however, their feelings are negative, and they isolate themselves from the environment. We all have seen youngsters who put themselves on the sidelines instead of joining in the fun with their friends. They may even cross their arms and assume a grumpy attitude toward the other children and toward the world at large. Whether they realize it or not, they clearly put out a message: Keep your distance!

The child moves between the inner soul-life and the outer sense world in a Yes-No movement. Feelings accompany everything children do, yet these feelings are never fixed or stagnant. They are always moving, changing, and influencing us. The world of childhood is the world of flowing color, tone and sensation – all of which are rooted in the feelings.

The highest feelings in the child's soul are experienced as beauty. Beauty is a kind person, a warm, sunny day, a happy moment, a cuddly puppy, holding father's hand, kissing mother goodnight. Beauty is the 'Yes' of the world, while ugliness is its 'No'. The child experiences the love of parents and God as the ultimate beauty.

Feelings in adolescence

When children reach puberty, they have a new experience of their feelings. This new experience is unlike any experience the young person has ever had before. The change is gradual, but strange and unfamiliar. Feelings rush in and out. The youngster experiences floods of emotions, moods, and desires. Exaggerated feelings well up, and the teenager is overwhelmed by the strange new sensations.

As with the birth of anything new, it takes time to gain experience and balance. Feelings swing back and forth, changing from moment to moment. Giggles, hysterical laughing, crying, and depression overwhelm the youngster, and control is lost.

Can you remember uproarious times when something happened which struck you as funny, and you couldn't stop laughing? No amount of stern reproach could stop the giggles. Finally, you had to get up and go for a drink "to take hold of yourself". Can you remember crying when you weren't sure what was bothering you? Such experiences begin as the youngster enters the preteen years. The feelings are surging, and the ego is not yet able to direct them. In the midst of uncontrollable feelings, young people find themselves confused.

Extremes in feelings

During this time, youngsters oscillate between extremes. Within a brief period, they may be alternately withdrawn and aggressive, lethargic and overactive. They are moody and oversensitive. Tears burst forth, small incidents set off big reactions, unpleasant comments are exchanged, blow-ups occur, and a period of general unhappiness results.

As adolescents become aware of their feelings, they are confused by them, fascinated by them, and frustrated by them. The see-sawing of their feelings makes them feel and act unpredictably. They are as much a mystery to themselves as to the adults around them.

It is a mystery that the gradual development of control over the feelings coincides with the strengthening of thinking. Both capacities mature markedly around the sixteenth year. As youngsters develop control over their thinking, they see beauty on another level. Beauty in the world of thought is truth. And the teenager seeks truth.

The adolescent gradually develops self-confidence, control, and some perspective. Moodiness continues to come and go, along with periods of happiness and unhappiness, but there is a greater ability to handle feelings until the youngsters experience a new level of emotional stability. This period that emerges, while not without its traumatic incidents, now includes enthusiasm, renewed energy, and a new enjoyment of people. The teenager embraces life, accepts its contradictions and inconsistencies, and says 'Yes' to it.

Young people stand on the threshold of two existences – the childhood from which they have come, the adult world they are about to enter. Should they step out or should they rush back in? Because they feel confused, they usually do both. They want to become adults, but at the same time, to remain children. One young woman demanded to be treated as an adult. When she then was called to task for manipulative behavior, she petulantly countered, "Well, you know I'm just a child. I shouldn't be expected to handle that."

Steiner compared the freeing of the feelings, the development of an independent soul-life, to a continued experience of gentle pain. Teenagers are preoccupied with this sense of inner discomfort and find it difficult to direct their interest to the outside world. Their self-concern makes it easy for them to be self-indulgent and unconcerned about other people's needs. Steiner points out that healthy emotional growth occurs when teenagers become interested in the world outside themselves.

Physical and emotional changes

Physical puberty precedes psychological puberty. Because the maturation of the sexual organs brings on physical maturity, the mistaken impression arises that youth are mature because they can reproduce their kind. However, their emotional level may be years away from maturity. We adults often set ourselves up by expecting more than the teenager is able to deliver. We grow angry and disappointed with the young person, when the real problem is our own unrealistic expectations.

Emotional maturity develops slowly. Major turning points occur at about the third, ninth, and twelfth years. With the onset of adolescence, emotional development becomes a major focus of the teenager's life. Emotional maturity has to do with the child's appropriate reactions to the demands of life at a particular stage. A too-sophisticated nine-year-old may seem to be emotionally mature at first meeting, but, behind that facade of sophistication, one finds a youngster with the needs and insecurities of a nine-year-old child. The maturity is not genuine. On the other hand, the emotionally immature child is living in a past phase. Such children try to meet their needs in ways that were appropriate when they were younger. When you have a twelve-year-old who still runs to his mother every time someone frustrates him, or a high school student who responds with name-calling and bluster, you are dealing with youngsters who are stuck in patterns they should have outgrown.

One of the great steps toward emotional maturity has to do with separation. Children separate from the secure world of childhood – often unwillingly. The separation makes them lonely, forcing them to explore their inner world. Preoccupation with themselves and their loneliness leads them to care about other people. "If I feel this pain, maybe you do too." They slowly step out to meet the world. Sometimes, they step out too far and too quickly and face a world that is unfriendly, even terrifying.

The loss of childhood joy sometimes drives children back inside themselves for protection. Others become absorbed in the teen culture to find solace and reassurance. Most are tossed between feeling confused and understood by nobody.

It is to be expected that young teenagers, confused by new and unpredictable feelings and by a changing relationship with the world, will be moody and irresponsible. They seek new relationships with adults – the old relationships which served them well in earlier years do not satisfy them anymore, and they don't know how to indicate this in a tactful manner. The teen scene is exciting and alluring. It calls to them. The trick for the parent is to permit them to experience enough of it to feel that they are part of their times, without their being swallowed by it.

How does emotional maturity develop?

The foundation of emotional maturity begins already at birth. The parents' attitude to the child in the early days prepares a bond which surrounds the child with security and warmth. The emotions surrounding the child as it learns to lift its head, smile, kick and crawl influence its emotional development. The attitude to the child when it is eating has a special effect. Is the child welcomed into the family? Is it bonded? Or is it an unwanted stranger? Is it ignored? The child's connections with family, with self-image, with attitudes, are developed by the family before the child begins school. Sometimes, these attitudes may be harmful to the child. In such cases, these attitudes can be transformed, but scars remain in the emotional well-being of the child. In each new phase of development, new capacities are released which can be used to transform the past. However, until twenty-one, with the birth of the ego, children are unable to transform themselves; they are dependent on the adults around them.

The first big step toward emotional maturity takes place around age three. If the child experiences the birth of self-consciousness but still feels that the world is good, the child makes the emotional adjustment in a healthy way. When children trust their family environment, they feel secure. Increasingly, however, today's children are encouraged at this early age to make judgments about the world. Having to decide for themselves what they will wear, what they will eat, etc., leaves these youngsters insecure. When the family ceases being an authority in their lives, they seek authority elsewhere – in television commercials, the opinions of other children. Instead of feeling secure, they feel empty.

The next critical effect on the child's emotional maturity begins around the tenth year with the separation from the secure world of childhood. Children explore their inner lives. They try to understand themselves.

They imagine themselves to be great actors, athletes, tragic heroes and heroines. They withdraw into fantasy and spend long periods alone, daydreaming. They compare themselves with others. They want to be alike; they want to be accepted.

A healthy sense of self is slowly built up so that the child can adjust to his or her new relationship to the world. Children need to find out how they are different and how they are similar. They find out what they like, what they don't. They find out how their beliefs are different from other people's beliefs. This is a slow, steady process which allows youngsters to integrate each discovery into their images of themselves. If they continue to feel accepted while these changes are going on, they are affirmed and feel positive about themselves.

Problems arise when children are hurried, when they feel too much stress, when they lose trust in their relationships. If children lose the basic trust that the world is a good and safe place and that people care about them, this impairs their emotional development.

When adults pass their stresses on to their children, when they lean on their children because they themselves are emotionally immature, when they demand premature responsibility from their children, they are rushing them into adulthood before they have had a chance to stabilize their self-images.

When that happens, the protection of early childhood years is over, and the child faces a world which can be unfriendly and sometimes terrifying. The world no longer glows with joy and goodness. The child moves from the sunlight into the shadows of anxiety, fear, anger, self-punishment, and conformity.

Chapter Six

Understanding our sons and daughters

"Are there psychological differences between boys and girls?"
"No, all the differences are caused by society."
"I don't think so. I think we're really different."
"Will we ever be able to resolve this question?"
From a discussion with teenage boys and girls

Male and female differences

In its early years, the women's liberation movement attempted to obliterate the differences between men and women, to say that, except for physical differences, men and women were the same. In recent years, however, research has shown that, in addition to basic differences in psychological make-up, there are also differences in the thinking between male and female.

Respect for each person as an individual should be central in all relationships. Artificial standards and limitations placed on people because of sex have been suffocating and need to be set right. At the same time, our desire to correct past wrongs should not blind us to genuine and significant gender differences.

The emotional life of teenaged girls

In girls, the emotional life is far stronger than in boys. Rudolf Steiner says that the ego of the girl is drawn down into the emotional life early in adolescence, so that she identifies with her emotions. Because the girl's emotional life is strongly penetrated with the ego, which contains the spiritual kernel of her individuality, it is closer to the spiritual qualities of life.

The interrelationship of ego and emotions makes the girl very concerned about her identity – who she is and how she is affecting people. The girl feels tossed and blown by powerful emotions which carry her from one situation to another. She finds it difficult to separate who she is from how she feels. She is overly sensitive and gets easily hurt. She interprets the way statements are made and looks for hidden meaning even when it is not there. She is very concerned about justice and fairness, always ready to defend the underdog or to take up a cause and lobby for it.

The girl becomes conscious of other people's feelings also. She is attentive to subtlety and the ins and outs of relationships. Glances, body language and feelings between people which may be ignored by boys are noticed by her.

Her active emotional life makes her mature more quickly than boys. She seems to know how to handle social situations, or at least so it appears, in comparison to the boys around her. She exudes self-confidence, although it is often only on the surface.

The girl's sense of ego not only is connected with her feelings but penetrates right into her gestures, including the angle at which she holds her head and the way she walks. Most of what she does is planned. She uses her body to elicit a particular response. She flirts and manipulates. Other girls see what she is doing and know how affected her behavior is, but the boys are impressed by it, although they aren't quite sure what is happening. The more socially mature boys react in a rather amused and controlled way, but others are either oblivious or confused by such shenanigans. Not content with gesture, the girls usually use make-up and clothing to express them-selves more fully and eagerly discuss the effect their 'look' has on those around them. A theatrical sense is all around them. A girl's preoccupation with appearance can lead to superficiality, but it also leads to an aesthetic approach to life.

The girls discuss and plan together. They share what they are going to do and what they will wear. After the social activity is over, they discuss what went on in great detail, including who did what with whom. They talk and talk and talk – planning, scheming, sharing. Their private life is usually out on display – in gesture, in notes that get passed around and in many conversations.

The girl's self-consciousness has an inner and outer effect. Outwardly, she is very aware of herself, how she appears to be. This makes her seem sure of herself, even arrogant. However, she pays a price inwardly. Her self-esteem is always threatened. She is always wondering what impression she is making on people, how they like her, whether she is being approved of. She never matches up to her ideal of herself. She is always too fat, too skinny, too tall, too short. Her hair is too straight, too curly, too thin, too thick.

The girl's challenge in her teen years is to calm her emotional life, to become more objective, to react less impulsively, and to accept herself. Slowly her ego separates from her emotional life so that she can take hold of and guide her inner life. There is a noticeable change around twenty-one, when a balance is achieved.

A particular challenge is presented to the young woman who is involved in a deep emotional relationship and marriage before she is twenty-one. She quickly connects emotionally with the other person without having had time to find her own identity. She will take on responsibility in her home, with her husband, and perhaps with a child. Yet, she still needs time to allow her ego to assert itself, to find out who she is by herself. If she is unable to do this, a silent war begins to rage within her. She may not become conscious of her feelings until her late twenties or early thirties: When she realizes that everything happened too quickly, before she had a chance to mature or realize who she is, anger and frustration result. Her initial excitement of love and family yields to a craving for independent experiences.

The emotional life of teenaged boys

The boy has a very different adolescent experience from girls. His emotional life is much less developed. His experience of his ego or identity does not become conscious so early. His ego remains independent and aloof, not as easily influenced by his feelings. He matures more slowly than the girl, and the independence of his ego allows him to be more objective. The boy's ego is so strongly connected with his physical body that he identifies with what he does rather than with what he feels.

He passes by situations, oblivious to undertones, unaware of the drama occurring in front of him unless his attention is called to it. When told about it, he may shake his head in amazement that girls can be so complex or that he could have missed it. Sometimes he is disturbed by the fuss and complications that girls bring to everything. Display of emotions is unnecessary and a waste of time, according to him.

He is more concerned with doing things, proving himself in rivalry with his friends, showing that he is not afraid – even if he is. He is interested in things of power – machines, cars, bikes, planes. He is fascinated with the way they work. He works out in a gym or lifts weights at home. He does gymnastics, runs, shoots baskets –enjoying a sense of confidence as he masters his body.

He is less in touch with his feelings than girls are. Feelings, often complicated and not easily controlled, are threatening, even frightening. He is afraid of being overwhelmed by emotions and avoids sentimentality.

He appreciates straight-forward comments that do not beat around the bush. He wants to know what to expect and what is expected of him. He has no patience with innuendoes and doesn't appreciate being talked to in circles. One young man described how his mother asked him to do the dishes. Instead of saying, "Ron, do the dishes", she took a deep sigh as she looked at the sink and said, "This is such a mess. Someone needs to clean up. Someone needs to do the dishes." She waited for the someone to volunteer. He was annoyed and amused at the same time. Another boy described his mother explaining the way he should do something. She went round in circles explaining it, and then when she was finished, she started all over again. He shook his head in disbelief.

The boy's patience also is taxed by his mother's asking him too many questions or wanting to know what is going on inside of him.

Boys do not easily open and share their private feelings – with their mothers, their friends, or anyone else. Especially in early adolescence, they creep into themselves where they can be in their own world – in a safe protected space. Parents often are frustrated because their sons have retreated into a shell, but it is healthy for boys to do that. They are protecting what is not yet ready to be exposed. Boys keep secrets in their souls. Of course, some boys share their inmost feelings and thoughts with a close friend, but they do not put them on public display as many girls do.

Adults need to respect a boy's need for privacy and not embarrass him by prying into his secrets. It is appropriate for a boy to show some reserve until he has a closer relationship with his feelings.

His romantic relationships tend to be less complicated. Girls become a part of his life, but they don't take over in the same way that girls allow their boyfriends to do. The girl builds a whole world around romantic feelings – including trying out his last name with hers to see how it fits. The boy keeps the relationship in balance.

Some see girls as conquests and approach them as they would a race or competition. The girl is there to be conquered – but not to change his life. They may brag about their exploits to their friends, but they don't share details.

If a boy's feelings are deeply touched by a girl, however, he is capable of the greatest devotion and love. He will forego many of his favorite activities to be with her. He will miss out on a pick-up soccer game and sit on the sidelines, holding her hand. He will leave his buddies to go for long walks with her. He will talk, letting out secrets he has dared to tell no one. His girlfriend is privileged to get to know a side of him which few others know. If he trusts her, she will be very helpful to him in exploring his feelings.

Boys may have moments of great loneliness, especially if they do not have a strong interest or hobby into which they can pour energy and from which they can gain self-discipline and esteem. This may be anything from weight-lifting to stamp collecting to working on cars.

Boys can too easily pass through adolescence being superficial and tough. They need time and experiences that allow feelings to awaken and mature. If this happens, they will have greater depth for the ego experience when it occurs around twenty-one. Beginning at about age sixteen, the boy's utter preoccupation with the outer world gradually – almost imperceptibly – gives way enough for him to begin to listen to his inner feelings and questions. Friendships and relationships deepen his soul-life by teaching him to share and understand. Matter-of-factness yields to greater sensitivity. As he becomes receptive to the needs of someone else, he also deepens his awareness of his own needs. This maturity also enables him to develop deeper, more sensitive relationships with girls.

The emotional life of the boy is crude by comparison to that of the female, Steiner said. While the female's is more highly differentiated and more delicately organized, that of the boy is not all that subtle. In the family, girls tend to be coquettish with their fathers, playing on their soft-spots while pursuing a subtle competition with their mothers. With boys, the reverse occurs as they compete with their fathers and charm their mothers. Rivalry between fathers and sons develops on all levels, from contests of physical skill to rivalry for attention from the women in their lives.

The teacher and the adolescent boy and girl

Differences in the emotional life of the boy and girl have an effect at school as well as at home. Boys and girls relate to their teachers in a similar manner to the way they relate to their parents. It is not unusual to see a girl flirting with a male teacher, trying to charm him into changing a grade or giving her special consideration, or simply looking for attention. The boys see rivals in their male teachers and feel that they have to take them on.

Teachers have to consider this difference in working with their students. Girls often are very astute and notice things about the teacher; they are quick to see weaknesses and contradictions. They are likely to make a direct offensive comment that hurts – in the name of being honest. Their manner is often arrogant and rude. Steiner advises the teacher to ignore most of it and to approach the girls with delicacy and grace. If the teacher can make a comment that refers vaguely to her behavior and then turns away, the young woman may take in the message. Head-on confrontations rarely succeed.

When a boy challenges a teacher's authority, he often does it in a way that conceals what's really bothering him. He will express his anger in terms of an unfair rule or policy rather than admit that the teacher has hurt his feelings. At all costs, the feelings must remain secret. The boy may lose his temper with the teacher, but if the teacher loses his or her temper with the boy, all authority is lost. What is more effective is humor. The boy's upset, however, cannot simply be dismissed with humor. Once the dust settles, the teacher does the necessary questioning, finds out what really was going on, and follows through.

At some point, the teacher also should step back and gain perspective. It doesn't hurt for the teacher to let the boy know that the action was not very serious but that it could not be ignored.

Another difference between boys and girls in school is that boys have much greater difficulty in initiating a heart-to-heart talk with a teacher – or even with a friend. The boys have feelings which are just as intense as the girls' but they would rather die than let them be known. The girl may blurt out her feelings in a flood of tears but the boy stoically holds his in. When he does venture out with feeling, the boy often makes a bad job of it. He hasn't the same knack for it as the girl. He says the wrong thing and ends up offending when he wanted to please. He is comical instead of impressive, crude when he needs to be smooth.

Yet another example of the boy's awkwardness at this age is the boy who has a serious comment or suggestion to offer but who can't do so without wrapping it in barbs. His self-image demands that he pose as the teacher's adversary, but his inner self actually wants to be helpful. The trick for the teacher, of course, is to acknowledge and honor the good impulse and to ignore the package it is wrapped in.

Guidelines such as these must be general. Each student is different and needs to be respected in an individual way. One cannot give recipes on how to treat disciplinary problems, but teachers need to develop intuition in their relationships with students. Nonetheless, I have found this approach very helpful as a teacher and as a parent.

Beauty, power and morality

During the teen years, youngsters are developing their attitudes to life; in particular, they are developing their sense of morality. Adults working with young people need to know that disciplining them is only a small part of nurturing their growth. It is more important to help them develop moral insights so that they will be guided from within rather than respond out of fear of punishment.

Young people, says Steiner, benefit in their moral development from certain images, specifically the contemplation of beauty – which deepens the youngster's moral insights – and the contemplation of heroic struggle in the defense of Good against Evil – which instills in the youngster a yearning to be courageous and noble. They still need explicit guidance on how to behave, but these images do more to develop a deep, personal moral sense than being told by an authority how to behave.

Both boys and girls need and respond to both of these types of moral inspiration, but starting in the pre-puberty years (sixth, seventh, eighth grades), he says, girls tend to be especially inspired by beauty. A refined aesthetic sense, says Steiner, inspires the girl to take morality and ethics deeply into her heart. Girls respond strongly to the sense that morality is beautiful and that the world is filled with the divine. This approach continues to mean a great deal to girls all the way through the high school years. The poetry of William Blake and William Wordsworth especially touches this longing in the girl's heart.

For boys starting with the pre-puberty years, the moral use of power makes a deep impression. Their ethical instincts are nourished when they see that heroic courage and commitment are at work in the world. They admire both legendary and historical characters who overcome enormous hardship to battle for a cause. They also are fascinated by the exercise of power through technology, which can be a fine moral image as long as the technology is beneficial to humanity.

Either of these fascinations can work against the young person's moral development if overdone. Love of beauty can become an undue concern for one's own appearance, and fascination with power can be harnessed to egotism as well as to idealism. Here, the skill and alertness of the adult comes into play to guide the young person with wisdom by his or her own example.

These generalizations about boys and girls don't always hold true, and the adult must be alert to those boys whose souls are deeply touched by beauty and to those girls for whom power is fascinating. In any case, the teacher or other adult should not concentrate too much on either beauty or power but should strive to be aware of the need for both to be present and in balance.

Complementary qualities in adolescent boys and girls

Complementary qualities in adolescent boys and girls draw them together and make their friendships a valuable preparation for understanding one another as men and women. The boys and girls can experience each other's strengths, at least vicariously. The girl envies the quiet strength and objectivity of the boy. His life is less complicated, and he does not get so carried away. She can depend on his judgment on outer things. He is more logical; she is more intuitive. She also resents his lack of understanding and feels that he is too cold. She wishes that she could change him. Maybe she can. His calm and aloofness are frustrating – but intriguing. She feels safe with him. He doesn't go off the deep end the way her girlfriends sometimes do.

He finds it difficult to understand her moodiness – but he's fascinated by her intuitiveness and envies her ability to express her feelings. He admires her social grace and her confidence, but her ability to get her own way makes him nervous. And why does she make such a fuss? How can she get so carried away by her feelings? He prides himself on being calm and uninvolved during her theatrical outbursts.

Of course, these are generalizations. Parents must remember that each person has a unique relationship of masculine and feminine qualities. We may prepare ourselves for a 'macho' son only to find that he is happier cooking or babysitting. Instead of a sugar and spice daughter, we have a girl in jeans who changes the oil in the family car. Everyone works through his or her specific sexual characteristics in an individual way.

Teenagers are intrigued by their sexuality and often express it in exaggerated forms, but as they mature, their sexual identities usually come into balance, and, as adults, they will establish a clearer relationship between individuality and sexual identity. However, that does not necessarily mean that they have resolved the problems. We live in such turmoil today concerning all areas of sexuality that there are more questions than there are answers.

Among these questions is the homosexuality issue. This question is complicated and I have no suitable answer. When I began teaching, homosexuality was only occasionally discussed, and very few students spoke openly about any experiences they might have had. Because the subject is so much more in the open, I recently have had discussions with young people who identify themselves as either bisexual or homosexual. They don't have easy explanations either. Having identified themselves as homosexuals, they are as confused as they were earlier by not knowing what they were. Because homosexuality is a sensitive issue, parents may not know how to deal with it when it arises in the family. Often, they treat it with silence.

What does seem clear is that we as parents and teachers need to accept the struggles that our young people are experiencing. At all costs, we must avoid isolating and punishing the adolescent for being different. Whether we are discussing a youngster who is still working out a sexual identity, one who has a well-balanced sexual orientation, or one who clearly seems to be homosexual, there are no firm rules to guide us. Understanding the general emotional make-up of each child is a help. Remembering that there are exceptions to every general statement is a help. Recalling our own relationships to our mothers and fathers, sisters and brothers, is a help. The overriding guideline, however, is to respect our sons and daughters as individuals and try to develop an intuitive understanding of the way they relate to life.

Chapter Seven

Introduction to the temperaments

What would the world be like without the temperaments – if people had only one temperament? The most tiresome place you can imagine! The world would be dreary without the four temperaments, not only in the physical, but also in the higher senses.

Rudolf Steiner[1]

One interesting aspect of family life is the collection of varied personalities we confront. Parents learn early that each child is different and must be treated differently. A trip is planned. One child is ecstatic. Another is upset because he doesn't want to leave home. Another wants to change the route to include only his favorite places. Yet another is agreeable as long as he can take his favorite toy and is promised that he won't miss meals and will have a daily swim. It's no wonder that parents sometimes throw up their hands in despair and shout, "We can never please everybody, so why bother!"

The traditional nature vs. nurture debate presents parents with two views of human nature:

Children come to us already formed. All we can do is feed, clothe, shelter, and educate them.

versus

Children come to us as a blank slate and are strongly shaped by us.

There is a third approach, however, which acknowledges aspects of the two traditional views but recognizes two additional elements: the power of destiny as a shaping force in human behavior, and the creative power of the human ego to transform itself.

Individuality develops from two directions, the spiritual and the earthly. From the spiritual side, the human being brings with it to this life its spiritual essence, its ego, which continues from lifetime to lifetime. It also brings talents, tendencies, and capacities that have been influenced by its own past. From the earthly side, it brings inherited qualities – family characteristics, race, and sex. On one hand, these inherited qualities limit and define the individuality. On the other hand, the individuality influences what has been brought by heredity. *The temperament is formed by the psychological space in which the individuality and heredity meet and influence each other.*

The temperament expresses the relationship of the individuality and the inherited nature. The individuality shines through the inherited nature and affects what has been brought from heredity. Rudolf Steiner calls attention to the study of the temperaments as a useful tool for understanding children. Although the temperaments provide a helpful clue, they provide only a partial picture. To gain a full picture of the human being, one must consider other aspects of the soul as well. It is tempting to stereotype people according to temperament, failing to recognize that the individuality is far more complex than any category can ever indicate.

The temperaments are expressed by psychological and physical characteristics shared by four broad groups of people: *cholerics, melancholics, sanguines,* and *phlegmatics.* In this chapter, we explore the four temperaments and show some ways in which they manifest in adolescence. First, however, basic laws concerning the temperaments should be stated. There is no good or bad temperament; each has positive and negative attributes. Each person has aspects of all the temperaments, although one temperament usually dominates. The temperaments come from deep within the human being and express themselves in outer life, coloring the way we react to life, forming our life gesture.

Temperament is influenced by the physical constitution, particularly the bodily proportions. Melancholics tend to be tall and slender, sanguines have balanced proportions, phlegmatics tend to roundness, and cholerics are usually of short, solid build.

The childhood temperament usually begins to emerge between the fifth and seventh years, and it shows itself clearly between the seventh and fourteenth years. The childhood personality reflected in the temperament is the foundation of the individual's behavior for all later years.

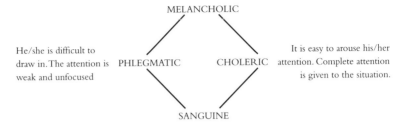

It is hard to get his/her attention,
but once gained, it is very strong.

MELANCHOLIC

He/she is difficult to
draw in. The attention is   PHLEGMATIC   CHOLERIC
weak and unfocused

It is easy to arouse his/her
attention. Complete attention
is given to the situation.

SANGUINE

It is easy to arouse his/her attention.
but it has little strength and disappears quickly.

The melancholic and phlegmatic temperaments are more inward, self-involved; the choleric and sanguine temperaments are outward or extroverted. In the first two, stimulation comes from within; in the latter two, stimulation comes from without.

The way adults react to a child's temperament strongly influences the child's self-image and way of approaching people and tasks. Hopefully, the positive qualities of the temperament have been nurtured. Where this does not happen, the youngster spends much energy during its adult life overcoming fears, anxieties, tempers, and so on.

During the transition from pre-adolescence to adolescence, the temperament gradually changes, one of many changes which children experience at that age. For example, the melancholic child often becomes a choleric adult, the choleric child often becomes a sanguine adult, the sanguine child often becomes a phlegmatic adult, and the phlegmatic child often becomes a melancholic adult. It is striking to see the new personality emerging and to glimpse the coming adult. The real individuality is taking over, and, year by year, this process becomes more stable as the temperament achieves a balance. Around twenty-one, the ego is born and is a major influence in the forming of the adult temperament and in the emotional maturity that follows.

A child simply lives with its temperament, experiencing it to its fullest. Children must depend on adults to understand and to bring out the best in them. Adults, on the other hand, consciously work on their temperaments.

The four temperaments

Each of the following chapters is a generalized characterization of one of the temperaments. No child will exactly match the description, but each child has enough recognizable characteristics to identify his or her temperament. The major temperament most strongly colors the personality, but the presence of supportive temperaments adds interest. For example, a choleric child with sanguine and melancholic undertones would be more excitable and more interested in life, more emotional, than a choleric with melancholic and phlegmatic undertones while the latter child would tend to have an inward and brooding nature.

The basic rule is: *Go with* the temperament, not against it. The child needs the opportunity to experience the world through the temperament and in that way to achieve balance.

Chapter Eight

The melancholic temperament

Nobody ever cares about me. Probably nobody will
even remember my birthday.

A twelve-year-old melancholic

Characterization of the melancholic temperament

Although his body is quite lean, the melancholic child often gives
the impression of heavinesss with a droop in his shoulders and face.
His limbs seem to hang with a heavy weight, and there is a general
sadness about the way he looks. His head is bent, his walk is measured and steady, his steps lack firmness and seem to drag him along.
He dawdles, closed-up within his thoughts, cut off from the world.
His voice is often soft and restrained. He holds back, either not
completing his sentences or mumbling the ends of them. When
confronted with decisions, his voice becomes toneless. If he is acting
stubborn, there is often a deep sigh.

He is very conscious of his body, sensitive to how things feel and
to the special clothes he wants to wear, complaining about tightness
around the neck or waist, the scratchiness of a fabric or an annoying
detail in the construction of the garment.

The melancholic child is serious and resigned, quiet and withdrawn, reflecting on what he has seen and heard, engrossed in the
past. He is convinced that a small insult or injury was meant to hurt,
and the event stays in his memory. He goes out of his way to look
for obstacles which then fulfill his prophecy that life is hard and
that people want to make it difficult for him. There is little hope
of convincing the melancholic child of anything; his viewpoint is
fixed.

He imagines all kinds of catastrophes, both in the natural world
and in his body. Every little ache is magnified. He often misses events
due to illness. The general lack of vitality gives support to his feeling

ill. He complains about not having enough sleep even though he may have been the last to awaken. If you ask how he is, you get a long list of discomforts. Sharing his internal misery gives him pleasure. Sympathy is sought and often received. He worries about everything, is self-involved, and seldom can hear what the other person is saying. Although he is very sensitive to any possible hurtful comments, he makes blunt comments and hurts other people. It is difficult for him to laugh at himself or to feel that he is the cause of anything. It is always someone else's fault. It is difficult for him to say, "I was wrong and I'm sorry".

On the other hand, the melancholic child tends to assume blame when it is meant for others. He is often filled with guilt and punishes himself when he is not at fault. This lack of objectivity gives him an awkward relationship to the world. Each reaction confirms the burden of life.

He is afraid of new experiences, prefers to stay close to home with what is familiar. He worries, "What will happen if I do that? What will I miss?" Making decisions is very painful. The child withdraws and is resentful if someone tries to draw him out. Even when a good time is had, what is remembered is the pain of the decision or a feeling of sadness. The child has to be reminded of what a good experience it was or how much fun he had. "Well, it wasn't all that good" or "It could have been better" is a common reply. This kind of response usually disheartens the adults until they learn how to deal with it.

One of the great problems faced by the melancholic child is that he responds to situations inappropriately or just too slowly. He is slow to grasp a situation, whether it be one of danger or the need for hurrying. The family may be rushing to go somewhere, but he moves slowly and deliberately – or he may not be moving at all because he has decided that this is the time to read or figure out a riddle. He is insensitive to the situation and even more insensitive to the angry feelings coming from others. In a situation of danger, he doesn't move fast enough. He is far more concerned with the poor construction of the tool being used or is indignant that the fire extinguisher doesn't work properly. The parent, of course, cannot take time to work with the situation at the moment and must deal with safety first and hurt feelings later.

When his sympathies are aroused, the melancholic child can be very kind and gentle. He is very thoughtful around an ill or injured person, but only after the person's situation has been pointed out to him. He responds easily to a hurt or sick animal and can spend endless hours caring for it in the most meticulous way. If it dies, he may brood for days and blame himself for the death. These feelings he will carry for years.

His memory goes very deep. His memory is very poor at first, but once he is helped to recall, many details will be slowly drawn out. Often he becomes lost in brooding over something and misses the main points. He hangs onto details but doesn't understand what is going on. This produces another exasperating family problem because he often has missed the main point of the parental explanation and then says, "But you didn't say *that*. You said ..." The child has heard the beginning and the end of a conversation, but has missed the middle because he was mulling over how the first statement would affect him. By the time he rejoined the explanation, much had been missed, which he genuinely did not hear.

He is not eager to meet new people at first and is more likely to be a loner in the family (except when it suits him). He is slow to make friends but often will become best friend of a similar child. He observes the world, but out of a lack of confidence often does not join in games, lingering instead on the edges. If he does join the game and the rules are not followed in the exact way they should be, he grows sullen and finds a way to get out of the game and justify his original feeling of not liking to play with so-and-so. It is safer to day-dream, read, build models, play solo games. He gets along better with older people who share a special interest, who communicate through thinking, or who indulge his fears and discomforts.

The melancholic can be a perfectionist who tears up his work because it does not meet his high standards, or he can stop halfway and quit because "it isn't going to be good anyway". When the melancholic child does finally trust someone, he is deeply loyal and does not easily transfer his allegiance to another.

He lacks humor in dealing with siblings and is easily teased and annoyed. Younger children learn how to antagonize the melancholic who, in his own way, asks for it. He takes the teasing from a younger child too seriously and, rather than laughing it off, responds viciously in the moment or awaits an opportunity to strike back. One way is through tattling. He experiences satisfaction in watching his enemy get into trouble. "All is right with the world, and I didn't have to risk anything to set it right. Justice is done."

In diet, he prefers sweets, often going to great lengths – including sneaking or manipulating – to get them. He is fussy about food and likes it prepared only in a particular way. New tastes are not easily acquired. An example of this need "not to be satisfied" was the child whose family had the same desserts every Wednesday, every Sunday, etc. His favorite dessert had just been served and he was crying because, "Now, I'll have to wait a whole week before I have it again".

The melancholic child is slow to waken and does not like to be rushed. He does not see the bright, new day as one to be enjoyed but as one to be tolerated. He sees the day as another possibility for problems, pitfalls, and the possibility of failure. It takes will power for him to face so dismal a world. This exhausts him. The weight of the world makes him old before his time.

The melancholic child is capable of thoughtful consideration of an issue. He ponders the pros and cons and is exhaustive in his research. He often is a thinker and gains respect for the attention he gives a problem. He often comes up with original solutions. He enjoys being responsible for figuring out details, such as the mileage covered on a trip, how much money is spent, what items are needed at the store. He is meticulous about following directions and is often interested in the thinking that lies behind the system or machine.

When the melancholic child chooses a hobby, much time and attention will be given to background reading, catalogue collecting, and comparing equipment. He can occupy himself for hours on end.

If someone shows interest in his thoughts, the child can be an excellent conversationalist about issues or events. He likes to share opinions and often has thoughtful and intelligent perceptions, but becomes nervous if he feels his inner life is being probed.

He takes impressions so deeply into his soul and right into his physical body that he may suffer stomach-aches and headaches. If the child has heard or seen a frightening story, program, or movie, it is good to ask him details so that he can bring the images out into the open where they do not continue to expand their importance in his inner life. Otherwise, it is easy for him to have fixed ideas or recurring nightmares.

Persuading the child to do something for someone else may mean building up the importance of the act – making it very special. The child receives benefit even if the adult feels too much is being made of it.

The key to the melancholic child is to find the appropriate way for him to bring into the light what lives in the dark of the soul.

Raising the melancholic child

The melancholic child is not easy to raise. It brings much soul-searching and guilt for the parents and few immediate rewards. With helpful support and understanding, however, the melancholic child can be nurturing and compassionate. His gifts of helpfulness and gentleness come from a deep source and, once awakened, can lead to sacrifice and committed service for others.

Parents need to be supportive but firm. They have to be careful not to indulge and at the same time not to ignore the child. This is usually the child who misses class trips or parties. Unless he really has a physical problem, the child may be covering up anxiety over any of a number of things. He may have borrowed someone's pencil and lost it, someone may have frowned at him or talked behind his back on the previous day, the teacher may have yelled at someone in the class and may yell at him today, he's sure that he won't be able to do the math problem. These are some of the things that may be blown out of proportion in the child's mind. Staying home is very appealing. Besides avoiding the problem at school, it is nice to lie in bed, sleep, dream, maybe have time alone with a parent. Parents have to be careful not to encourage escape from unpleasant situations. Often these children have difficulty completing their work on time anyway, and recurrent absences only add to the problem. Absences also separate the child from the rest of the class and increase the feeling of alienation. What is needed is sympathy for the discomfort but firmness that school or the event is still first priority.

The melancholic child feels that his experiences are not shared by anyone else. It is important to show him that other people have similar problems. He thinks that he is unique and cultivates the sense of separateness. Biographies help such a child break out of his self-preoccupation and take an interest in the lives and concerns of others. The child has to learn that all human beings have to endure. It is good for the parent to speak of the pain and suffering which the child will meet in the world and to share with the child great difficulties which the parent has overcome. This enables the child to sympathize.

One appeals to the *will* of the melancholic child – to hang on, to persevere. The parent should help him carry through by setting clear goals – "Do this for ten minutes". "Do this forty times". If the child knows the exact expectations, there is less chance of his becoming anxious. It is good to start with a small task and then extend it so that the child feels success at accomplishing it.

The melancholic child often has a strong artistic sense which, when cultivated, brings joy to others. Cutting flowers for the table, making cards for special occasions, making cookies for someone all are activities which may serve this end. Because some melancholics are convinced that they are not artistic, they need encouragement and special occasions as a reason to make things. This provides an outlet of appreciation and giving, balancing the egoism of the temperament.

Since the melancholic craves security, routine is very important. The melancholic child may make a fetish out of routine and has a difficult time adjusting to change. If there is an expected change, tell him ahead of time. Parents may avoid telling him, thinking he will be upset, but it is better if the child gets used to the change and is ready for it when it comes. Although it is easy to interpret resistance to change as negativity, it is actually masked fear.

The typical melancholic child waits order, both in his life and with his belongings. If a younger sibling destroys the melancholic child's things, he can be quite spiteful. Meticulousness over order can be extreme but some melancholics fall into chaos and don't know where anything is, looking each time for items that are misplaced. The child becomes annoyed that the world doesn't leave his things where they were put. The world disturbs his order – he is not at fault. If everyone would just leave things alone, everything would be fine.

The reactions of the melancholic are shallow and the parent has to be sensitive to catch the subtleties. Parents learn to read their children and know when there is unusually strong fear or great joy.

Serious family problems have an especially strong effect on the melancholic child. First, he wants to deny that anything is happening. He feels guilty and is sure that if he had done something differently, the death or divorce would not have happened. In the case of marital problems, the child often feels compassion for the parents, and it is very easy to put too much burden on the melancholic child. He feels that the world is collapsing around him. He is afraid and wants to know what to expect. He needs to be told about the situation just enough so that his guilt is softened and some sense of security can be renewed.

Trying to force the melancholic child to be merry does not work. It drives him further into himself, into gloom and reserve. The child cannot be talked out of inner suffering, but he can be diverted from self-preoccupation to concern with another person's pain and unhappiness. Reading can often be an escape for the child, but it can also be therapeutic, particularly if the child learns about great accomplishments made in spite of handicaps, as for example, in the case of Helen Keller. Humorous books also help the child to laugh at the world. Melancholic children often enjoy reading about or watching ridiculous, slapstick behavior which they would not do themselves but which they enjoy vicariously.

Changes in adolescence

During adolescence, the melancholic child typically begins the transformation into a choleric adult. Attention to details – so strong in melancholic children – becomes a positive aspect of conscientious leadership. Once the ex-melancholic's attention moves from within to without, he brings awareness of a situation to focus and takes charge.

Many attributes of melancholic children become very helpful when they become choleric adults. They may worry about how things will turn out, and they may feel the burdens of the world upon them, but they make responsible adults who carry their obligations through to the final detail.

During adolescence, the child's old temperament is fading and the new one is not yet there, however. For the melancholic, the insecurity of adolescence is intensified. Loneliness, cynicism, and a sense of rejection are aspects of the young adolescent's melancholic approach to the world. As the adolescent develops, the new temperament comes in more firmly. The wallflower blossoms into a sociable, confident young adult, but echoes of the old melancholic temperament remain as an undertone, providing compassion and sensitivity for others in need. When life is particularly difficult or when the adult goes through crisis, the melancholic undertone may become stronger, but the choleric temperament will usually help him through rough periods.

Chapter Nine

The sanguine temperament

I've been thinking about the way I do things. I try to do too many things and then I don't get to finish anything. But I like to be involved in everything. It makes life so interesting.

Eleventh grade sanguine girl

Characterization of the sanguine temperament

The sanguine child is usually slender of bone and muscle, well-proportioned, and supple of movement. She has a light, springing step. Inner happiness shines through her twinkling eyes. Her face is alert and expressive, and her features appear to change easily, reflecting her moods. She relishes her sense of well-being and delights in her fine coordination. Her gestures are quick and varied, adding to her general expressiveness. She bubbles, chatters, talks to anyone and no-one, enjoying the combinations of sounds and her own voice. She talks to talk. It is part of her joy of living.

She lives strongly in her nervous system. Impressions jump quickly into imaginations. She is quick to grasp and quick to forget. It is hard for her to concentrate on anything for long. Pictures come and go in her mind and in her feelings. She lives in the images rising and falling away. At times she is at the mercy of them. When she tries to remember something, she smiles but has forgotten what it was. Yet she is quick in her thinking, and her ideas cover many different areas in a few minutes. It is difficult for an adult to follow her train of thought, as it is so scattered. Because she is thinking of so many things at once, the inner connection is not obvious. She makes what seem to be random statements. She flits from idea to idea, loves the changeableness of life. Each new thing is greeted with an exclamation of wonder and acceptance, but this too passes when a new perception arises. She exaggerates freely, and, when this is called to her attention, she brushes it off and goes on. Sociability is her forte. She makes many friends – each person is an adventure.

The sanguine child is such fun to be with that life is never boring. She likes to meet the new child in the neighborhood or class and immediately gets her to play. She bounces back from minor physical ailments, brushing them off and springing back into the excitement of life.

At times, she runs into social problems because she lives so much in the moment. She tells a friend, "I love you best of all!" and ten minutes later says to another, "You are my favorite friend!" She means it both times – but is it true?

It is difficult to know where you stand with a sanguine. When you are with her, her sunshine envelops you and you feel warmed and charmed. Her smile is quite irresistible; before you know it you have joined her fantasy and are loping across the prairies or stalking in the jungle. She often has imaginary companions who are just as changeable as she would like to be in life. Sometimes fantasy and reality grow confused, and she is led astray. She sees goodness in the world and is easily duped. But she doesn't hold grudges and is ready for new adventures right away. Her manner is pleasant and accommodating.

She likes many foods, but she usually eats small quantities, nibbling like a bird. She often appreciates the trouble that the cook has gone to in preparing the meal and bubbles, "Oh, that was perfect! You are a wonderful cook". In addition to enjoying the meal, the sanguine enjoys the conviviality of the occasion.

It is difficult to establish habits in a sanguine child. She is open to any change; yesterday was yesterday, but today is a new day. She enjoys traditions, but they are not necessary. It is just as much fun finding new ways to do things.

She drops off to sleep without much problem – unless she is so sanguine that she has too many impressions flitting around in her mind, holding off sleep. Usually she falls into a deep sleep, gaining nourishment for the new day. She awakens early, dresses in an outfit that will provide her with an image – she'll be a ranger, a queen, a soldier, a ballet dancer. She lives in the fantasy of that personality for a while. She is vulnerable to fads of fashion. She wants to be in the center of whatever is going on.

It is difficult for the sanguine child to organize her room because she has so many interests. Most of them are short-lived, and remnants of each past interest are scattered around the room. The child likes her things but she does not have the attachment to them that the melancholic would. She treats them casually, expecting them to be available when needed, annoyed when they are not. When playing, she usually has several games going at once. She can read, talk, wind a ball of wool, and wriggle her nose. Her projects may look carelessly done, but her nimble fingers can be very skillful if her will is strong enough to ensure completion of the project – which isn't often. She is not perturbed if there are mistakes, and she merrily continues until the job is done, at least according to her standard.

You can imagine a birthday gift made by a sanguine. She likes many colors and cannot chose which one to use – so she uses them all! Her work is an expression of her temperament.

When the sanguine is the youngest child, she often is doted on, excused for being flighty, and enjoyed for her cuteness. As the child becomes older, however, her flitting about can be annoying, as when she doesn't finish her chores and leaves a mess for others to clean up, or becomes distracted and fails to complete her homework, or when the good shovel is left out in the rain, and unfinished projects are left in different parts of the house. Presents aren't finished, but a big smile and hugs come readily – along with promises to complete the gift.

If the sanguine child is older, she can bring to a family a love of life, of adventure, of zest. Good natured chaos surrounds the child. Emotional ups and downs are the keynote of her life. She's always on the move, going here, going there, constantly having friends over, surrounded with social life, but avoiding getting down to anything serious. She feels happy with her many friends, with whom she can spend endless hours on the phone. On those occasions when nothing seems to be going on, however, the sanguine child is easily bored.

The sanguine loves life and makes an adventure of it. Her enthusiasm and fantasy are contagious and an environment glows simply because she is there. A wonderful social partner, the sanguine is often the life of the party, a good joke teller, the happy person, the center of attraction. She puts people at ease. She enjoys sharing and is often overly generous. She would give everything away and have nothing saved for a rainy day. She makes you feel that you are the only person in the world at that moment, but she finds it difficult to maintain any depth in a relationship. She likes people and reaches out to them, slips her arm around theirs, snuggles into their arms.

She likes funny little things about people – Aunt Mary's odd laugh, Uncle John's gruff hug, Grandma's sweets, Grandpa's collection of wrenches in his garage. She embraces life and is adaptable to changes in routine, responding positively to family outings, events, and arrangements. Some notice, however, that she seems to let sorrow pass her by. We wonder if she has been touched deeply enough by the death of a relative or a marital separation, but she chooses to see the good in it, and she gets on with the adventure. There is the danger that her feeling life will remain shallow, lacking the richness of the melancholic child's inner life.

The sanguine's lack of persistence seems to leave much undone. Her parents can be led to think, "Such a sweet charming girl, but will she ever make anything out of herself?" or, "She's such a scatterbrain. What ever will become of her?" Despair sets in at the string of half-begun, well-meant deeds. Her ideas come and go, with little depth. She resists staying with things long enough to develop them. "Slap, dash, I'm done." She is impatient, forgetful, irresponsible. Her unreliability is nerve-wracking, especially because her charm tends to excuse her, time after time. It is difficult to sustain anger with her, but her forgetfulness puts a strain on people around her. She is often exasperating, yet her enthusiasm and good will balance the frustrations people feel. The sanguine child loves to please: "Oh let me do that. Pleeeeze. I'll help you". Her sense of play and fun lightens our lives, but we can get tired of the superficiality and wish for seriousness and responsibility.

Raising the sanguine child

Because the sanguine child lives so strongly on nervous energy, the parent should give particular attention to the environment. With the young sanguine, an attempt should be made to provide order and simplicity, to give the child's nervous system a rest. This is true especially in the area where she sleeps. Keep the walls, curtains and pictures simple. Rather than stripes, polka dots, and busy prints, I would suggest solid colors that let the light through, such as warm yellows and oranges that bring sunshine into the room. Rather than a dozen pictures and posters on the wall, a few special ones that nourish the child when her eyes rest on them would be beneficial. The more order and beauty in her environment, the more the sanguine child can relax. She will enjoy arranging shells, scenes of little figures, collections. A nice shelf for such arrangements gives her a limited area to keep changing things. A doll-house, a barn for model horses, and other models often serve this function.

Usually, a sanguine child has one serious interest underlying all the frenzy. If not, it is important for the parent to foster interests until a strong one emerges and stays for a long time. Once the parent finds a strong interest, everything should be done to support it. Suppose the child is sincerely interested in nature, for example. The parent can arrange trips, discuss animals seen, obtain books, and look up the animal habits, – i.e., find ways to keep deepening the interest. In that way, one works with the sanguine temperament in a helpful way. After a while, the child will experience pride in her achievements and knowledge. Sanguine children are usually very quick and enjoy knowing the biggest, smallest, longest, shortest river, stream, lake, country, etc. This kind of interest can also be quickened. The danger for desperate parents is that of pushing too hard to have one interest last. It takes patience. Parents can expose a child to an interest, but cannot impose it. The sanguine child is particularly unable to sustain something that does not touch an inner excitement. There may be a number of beginnings until a strong interest is found.

The sanguine child also taxes the parents' patience when it comes to discipline. Punishments and scolding have limited effect. Guilt may be felt, but fleetingly. The child accepts punishments and moves on to the next event. Parents do not experience the satisfaction that they are having any significant impact. The melancholic child may become sullen after a reprimand, but the sanguine brushes it off. The child wants to behave, but forgets. Her strongest motivating force is love for the people around her. The child will do things for a person rather than for the joy of the deed itself. You can tell a sanguine child how much something will please you, and she will find some way to bring you happiness.

Warmth and encouragement are necessary for the continued development of the sanguine child. If you lose self control, the sanguine child feels no sympathy for you, only lack of respect. Patience is the key attitude for the adult dealing with the sanguine child.

Parents can help the sanguine by putting before the child things in which she has to be involved for only a brief time, taking them away and hoping that the child will want to do them again. By doing many small projects, the child, out of herself, will crave to stay longer with something. Gradually the child improves her attention span. The parent may do a similar thing with a melancholic child who lacks confidence but the emphasis there is on skill. With the sanguine child, the emphasis is on completing the task, strengthening her will. There are many small household chores that fit into this category – setting the table, emptying the garbage, folding towels, checking the mailbox. It is particularly healthful if the task is rhythmical, occurring every day at the same time. After a while, the child anticipates the task, which helps her stay centered and not be as distracted.

Over a period of time, more and more emphasis should be put on doing the job well. In the beginning of the task, the motivation was to please the adult. As the child's will is developed, the motivation changes to getting the job done the right way.

Life is a game to the sanguine child, and much can be learned and attempted if the parent can keep a sense of magic and fun. Helping the child organize her room gives the sanguine a chance to bring order into her life, but it needs to be done in a light-hearted way if she is to sustain it. If the room becomes a pirate ship, for instance, and each thing has its place, or the room is a cave and the floor has to be kept clear for the dragon, or it is a beautiful palace being prepared for a dance, the child's fantasy will carry her arms and legs through the task, her eyes dancing every moment.

The parents need to trip lightly with the sanguine, much as with a younger child. The innocence of life is one of the key qualities the adult needs to keep in mind. At the same time that the sanguine child is a delight and a worry, she – or he – is a symbol of eternal childhood in man.

In school, the sanguine child is full of life and excitement. She is receptive to every new thing the teacher presents. She finds it difficult, however, to concentrate on the teacher's words and constantly is distracted. She responds enthusiastically to material, but can't remember it the next day. It is very difficult for her to hold on to anything, but she keeps trying. She's full of good will, and she calls out many answers, hoping one of them will be right.

The sanguine student struggles with assignments that call for depth. She tends to write all over the place, disregarding punctuation and capitalization. Wonderful ideas abound, but they lack form and development.

She is usually very cooperative and wants to run every errand – anything to keep from having to concentrate. Too many sanguines in a class can create chaos. Projects will not be finished, the students' desks will be a mess, yet they may all be having a wonderful time. Discipline is not easy because sanguines forget. They mean to control themselves, but can't help it if the answers burst out, their hands wave in the air, and they are jumping out of their seats. They want and crave lots of attention from the teacher. A class with a balanced proportion of sanguines can be exciting to teach – bursting with enthusiasm and full of life.

The sanguine child goes through adolescence

As the sanguine child moves into the confusion of adolescence, she experiences a slowing of the very life and growth forces that have sustained her sanguinity. Concentration becomes easier and she finds it more possible to focus. Instead of being distracted by everything that comes her way, she finds that she can take hold of one thing and stay with it much more successfully than ever before. Her cheerfulness stays, but it acquires an air of calm rather than of hyperactivity.

Consequently, sanguine children who were the despair of their elementary school teachers have a second chance in adolescence. They have to make up for many lost skills which passed by them in their butterfly days, but now they are grateful for the patience and support of teachers and parents who insist on form and order in their work. As they pay more attention to this, they come to enjoy the rewards of being organized and orderly. Their old sanguine self does not disappear completely, especially in the early adolescent years. As the ego comes closer, however, and organizes the soul life, the sanguinity is brought to rest and the energy is transformed.

It is not unusual for parents or teachers to compare notes and say, "I never would have predicted that scatter-brained Johnny could become so reliable!" or, "Janie never finished any of her work in the third grade. Look at how reliable she is at her job."

The changes of puberty, and especially the heaviness of the body that occurs, cause teenagers to slow down. They become preoccupied with the body and with the details of daily life. From their quicksilver childhood, they become solid adults.

Chapter Ten

The phlegmatic temperament

All things are timely done which are done well.

Octavius

Characterizations of the phlegmatic temperament

The phlegmatic child is good-natured, kind, thoughtful, a bit aloof, and easy-going. Not much bothers him. He likes to dream and gives the impression of being unintelligent, but that is very misleading. He needs time to work things out. He needs to put everything in order, look it over, and slowly come to a sensible decision. In fact, most things about the phlegmatic are sensible. He does not like being pushed to decisions. All things must be considered. The phlegmatic learns slowly but has a good memory. However, the images of past deeds are buried below the surface. When it is appropriate and enough time is given, the memory is stimulated and the image is brought forward.

The phlegmatic child is usually heavily built, roundish, and somewhat flabby. His walk is unhurried and easy. Usually his movements are clumsy. Everything about the phlegmatic suggests time; there is time to do everything, and there is resistance to any haste or compulsion. The child's eyes are somewhat dull, turned in to the self. This does not mean that the child is dull, but that he is asleep to much of the outer world. His look is calm, and he appears aloof. The child's voice is usually clear but without much modulation. The tendency for the phlegmatic is to go on and on in a clear and meaningful way, but without much drama in his voice. What he says is usually correct, but it is expressed in a boring manner.

The phlegmatic child moves slowly, lacks vitality and experiences life as a burden. He would much rather stay still and not be bothered.

It is much better to take it easy and not exert himself. In fact, the phlegmatic child is suspicious of or even sad for those busy bees who are always creating work for themselves. Physical satisfaction is felt in simply enjoying life in a sluggish fashion. This sluggishness has its own momentum. Just as it is difficult to set the phlegmatic going, once he does start, it is difficult to stop him. Give a phlegmatic child a task and he will keep on with it. He exerts his stubbornness and defies any change.

Often, he is a careful worker, his room is usually organized, pencils sharpened, toys neatly placed in the play area, blanket carefully folded. These things take time, and he considers this a good use of time. Other phlegmatics, however, live in total disorder. They are not affected by the chaos as long as their personal needs are met.

The love of order expresses itself in routines and habits. The phlegmatic child is comfortable about routine and likes life to be predictable with regular hours, large, full meals at the same time every day, regular bedtime hours. It is not a matter of insecurity or anxiety as with the melancholic child. The phlegmatic child prefers it this way because it makes sense and it is the way it is supposed to be. The phlegmatic does not like customs or habits of the family to change. What was good last year will be good this year. He resists change for change's sake, considering that to be a waste of energy.

A phlegmatic child is easy to raise, for his needs are the basic needs of life. He wants to be fed, given a comfortable place to sleep, and be cared for. This makes him happy. Generally, such children are well behaved and pleasant. They are amenable to whatever goes on as long as they are not made uncomfortable.

The phlegmatic is not the most exciting of friends, but he is very dependable, loyal, reliable, steadfast, honest, and truthful. He does not grab the limelight, but hangs back. He is not very self-confident; he often has good ideas, but is modest about bringing them forth. He does not want to stand out and will hold back an opinion if it makes him unpopular. Acceptance and respectability are important. The child is cautious and will not go ahead with new plans or take risks. The large middle of a group, whether it be a classroom or a scout troop, is often made up of cooperative, rule-abiding, pleasant phlegmatics. The phlegmatic children form a solid base. They follow orders and they enjoy doings things well. They enjoy the customs and rituals of life. As long as they are left in peace there are no serious problems. Jobs that have to be done well must be given time, for the phlegmatic child does not like to be pulled away from the job before it is done to its final detail. Changing to a new task is distasteful, and he will go to great lengths to avoid this.

The phlegmatic child will use his will power to resist. For example, if you ask him to do something he does not want to do, he will not challenge the request, but he will not respond. Nothing happens. His attitude is, "If I don't answer, maybe he'll go away". Nothing disrespectful is intended, but he is simply not interested in doing what is being asked. On the other hand, if the task is enjoyable to the phlegmatic, it is very difficult to get him to stop. He likes repetitive, fairly simple tasks that do not take much effort or thinking. The phlegmatic does not want to risk being rebuked so he will not express his opinion. If the silent response is not effective and the request is made more strongly, the child will shrug his shoulders and finally agree, letting you know how disagreeable the request is.

It takes a strong statement, perhaps a raised voice or direct eye contact, to move the phlegmatic child, and then he may become sullen and moody. But he doesn't let anyone see it because he doesn't want to create a fuss. A woman who had been a phlegmatic child told me that she experienced childhood through a dreamy sleep. When she finally woke up she realized all she had missed, and she was deeply upset. She needed the loving support of her teachers to help her through the next stage. She wanted me to be sure to let people know that the moment of awakening is very painful for the phlegmatic child even though it doesn't show much on the surface.

The phlegmatic child takes everything literally. He lacks a subtle sense of a situation. If you ask him to do something, he will do exactly what you have asked and nothing more. If you ask him to help you dry the dishes and you are called out of the room, he will usually stand and wait until you return. Seldom will he use initiative to finish the washing, or he will finish drying the dishes but not the silverware because you asked for help with the dishes.

The literal quality makes the child a butt of jokes, for he lacks the quick retort. Because he does not shoot back with a sharp answer, other vulnerable children in the group are drawn to the calmness and protection of the quiet easy-going phlegmatic who does not seem interested in bullying or being sarcastic. Often the size of the phlegmatic child promises someone who is strong and aggressive, but this is not often the case. The image of the bully bothers the phlegmatic who doesn't want to make waves. Other phlegmatic children, especially as they grow older, learn to use their wits to keep other people away. They make up names for people around them, become sarcastic (but usually not to another person's face), and use their size as an indirect threat to those who seem overwhelmed by them.

The phlegmatic child can be a wonderful listener but does not have much to say. There is very little that he has noticed that can be brought into the conversation so he listens happily to others. He likes other calm people around him who do not upset the course of life. Also he likes more excitable people around so he can vicariously experience situations, as long as they don't demand anything of him. He is interested in sleep and food. One phlegmatic child would sit in the hallway waiting to go to school. He would slowly unwrap his lunch, piece by piece, look longingly at each piece of food, and then happily and slowly wrap it up and put it back into the lunch box.

Raising a phlegmatic child

The phlegmatic child has a pleasant disposition. He usually goes along with what is happening, doesn't demand much of the family members, is likeable and usually well-mannered. His stability brings balance to the family. Shyness and introspection color his disposition. The child is happy to help (if the task isn't too demanding), enjoys spending the day quietly coloring, sitting, or playing quietly in the garden.

However, inertia can be a problem with the phlegmatic child who is difficult to get moving and difficult to stop once he is moving. Originality, creativity, and spontaneity are not as frequently expressed as with other temperaments.

Although the child is pleasant, he is not necessarily feeling deeply for the people around him. His pleasantness comes from a desire not to be disturbed. Family members can be very frustrated with the phlegmatic child because he does not want to take risks and express his opinion. "It doesn't matter" may really mean "I don't really want to do that, but I don't want to let anyone know, so I'll agree".

It is not easy to interest the phlegmatic child. He tends to be more practical than artistic and feels satisfied when everything has a rightful place and purpose. The child is easy to be with but not exciting.

If the parents have melancholic or sanguine children, how peaceful it is to have a phlegmatic child.

The phlegmatic child at school

Phlegmatic children often struggle with their memory. They take in the material presented by the teacher, and the material sits deep down beneath the surface. When the teacher asks what the young-ster remembers, he has a blank look on his face as if he never heard of the subject. Naturally, this can be very discouraging. Trying to get the phlegmatic to remember details is a chore. He tends to dream and finds it hard to focus. The teacher may have to resort to dramatic events to wake him up like occasionally dropping her keys on his desk. She has to be inventive to gain his attention.

Phlegmatic children work slowly and don't like being pushed. Because of their slow pace they have trouble completing assign-ments and showing what they know. They prefer fill-in assignments to essays, and they usually respond quite well to complicated but methodical arithmetic problems.

They are reliable about classroom tasks once they take them into their consciousness. Often they are the ones who remember birth-days and special activities that occur at particular times of the year.

If a teacher has a very active class of cholerics and sanguines, it is especially nice to have calm phlegmatics in the group.

Changes in the phlegmatic child in adolescence

The phlegmatic child often becomes the melancholic adult. The heaviness that was so much a part of the phlegmatic personality continues to act on the youngster, but the preoccupation with the inner world becomes stronger. His earlier enjoyment with comfort and well-being is transformed into concerns about illness and disa-bility. He becomes focused on himself. The physical body continues to be the predominant influence on his changing personality. As he moves through adolescence, much of what he has ignored earlier does start to bother him. He dwells on these irritations and takes them more seriously. He becomes concerned about the way people relate to him and wants to be recognized and appreciated. He responds well to praise, but finds ways to hurt those whom he sees as being on his case. He has little sense of how exasperating he can be. It is very helpful if ways can be found to work through his strength. For example, he may become an excellent discus thrower or wrestler which would bring him appreciation and attention.

The phlegmatic-melancholic adolescent is complicated. He may withdraw and do very little that is expected or he can be pleasant on the outside but scheming on the inside. During a time when teenagers tend to place much importance on appearance, this youngster suffers. He often transfers his frustrations onto those around him and experiences times of deep unhappiness. A special interest, once cultivated, is the saving grace during this difficult time of transition.

It is especially important to be aware of close and overly dependent relationships that may develop between mothers and their phlegmatic sons. The mother tries to protect him from growing up and facing consequences, and the boy finds refuge in the mother's doting. This does not help the youngster come into his own personality. Great patience and creativity are needed with phlegmatic children who can then bring many blessings in adulthood.

Chapter Eleven

The choleric temperament

> To be alive in such an age,
> To live in it,
> To give in it!…
> Look to the work the times reveal!
> Give thanks with all thy flaming heart –
> Crave but to have in it a part.
> Give thanks and clasp thy heritage –
> To be alive in such an age!
>
> Angela Morgan[1]

Characterization of the choleric temperament

The choleric child is usually well-built, muscular, and tends towards stockiness. There is a firmness and solidity to her appearance. Her body is filled with energy and she moves restlessly, not finding it easy to sit still for a long time. Her eyes, too, move restlessly about, scanning the environment. She stands firmly rooted to the ground. When she walks, she stomps on the ground, usually digging in with her heels. She is poised for action. She paces. She feels tension and restlessness in her body, and she feels caged when she has to stay seated too long.

Her gestures are short, assertive, confident, and purposeful. Her gait has a swagger quality. Ready for anything, she aims herself in a direction and moves with purpose through the room or down the street. She is not easily distracted. She knows her own mind and plows through anything that would deter her. Her voice is strong, often blustery. She easily commands, shouts, and fills a room with her voice and presence.

Her sense of well-being is strong. She takes pride in being healthy and doesn't understand why others are sick or weak. She stoically endures setbacks and is quick to taunt another child as a "cry baby". She doesn't show weakness or vulnerability easily and wants to appear tough and independent.

She is a bull in a china shop. She tries to step gracefully but it is difficult, and she often knocks things over or pushes into people. Her sense of self is tied up with what she does in life. She is self-centered, pushy, and demanding. It is important for her to be biggest, toughest, and first. Life is a competition either with others or with herself. She is always fighting toward a goal. If she has to intimidate others to get there, it is justified.

She is not fussy about food but particularly likes crunchy and spicy food. She eats heartily but does not indulge. When she arises in the morning, she wakes easily, plans the day, and sees it as a chance to prove herself, to succeed, and to complete tasks.

The choleric child feels mastery over situations and people. She has the sense that everyone relies on her – she is a natural leader. Her way is the best way and she has the energy to carry out her plans. Although she feels burdened by life, she is glad to tackle jobs and get them done. She is impatient with others who are too awkward, too slow, too fussy, or too contemplative. She tries to shape the environment to the way she knows it is supposed to be.

The choleric with a sanguine tendency wants to get things done in order to move on to the next project. Her pride is in finishing the task rather than in completing the details well. "There I've done it!" "At least it's done." She grows impatient when others talk while there is work to be done. She is more likely to take hammer in hand and start working, thinking about it while she is doing it rather than planning it out. She has the confidence to make anything work out even if she has to fix a few things along the way to make up for the quick decisions in the beginning. Itching to begin, she is impatient with those who want to discuss her plans.

A choleric with a melancholy tendency directs her attention to details. Everything has to be done perfectly – which means the way she wants it done. Everyone else is imperfect, but she does things the right way. She re-does what other people do, she re-organizes, and she checks up on other people's work. She worries about the low quality of what is being done and is convinced the world is headed downhill. Only she can set it on its course.

When people stand in her way, she becomes bossy and moves easily into a position of authority. When others challenge her, she trades insults, not letting their words touch her inner being. An argument between two cholerics is a loud, insulting, aggressive experience. When it's finished, they go about their business as before. Although they like the excitement of the encounter, they can have their feelings hurt and carry a grudge for a long time. The choleric with strong melancholic overtones has a particularly difficult time. She takes everything person- ally and exhausts people by demanding explanations, by lobbying for her position, and by finding it difficult to compromise. She also finds it difficult to take what she dishes out to others.

The choleric child challenges what people say and feels that she has to have something to say about everything. When she is not listened to, she pouts, but she overcomes it quickly and goes on. If her honor is attacked, she can be vicious, seeing herself defending the right and doing battle-to-the-death.

It is difficult for her to accept blame, and she is quick to put it onto someone else. She cannot bear to be criticized and will not admit being wrong. Later, however, she may see that she was at fault and try to repair the situation. She can be "big" and even apolo- gize for something in the past, but only when she has seen she was wrong. She has to think everything was her idea.

The choleric child is a good "ideas" person and makes many plans. She is a good organizer, but has no gift for details. She starts plans and then gets others to do the work. She has her fingers in many pies and feels happy with the resultant sense of power. She often attracts other children who follow her leadership and who bask in her confidence. She bullies them, but they like her sense of direc- tion and ability to handle situations. She receives the glory while they follow up on the little jobs. While she is clearly the leader, she enjoys being kind to her followers, but she does not share the glory well. She lets others have their turn, gives them presents, chooses the games, but she has to have the central authority.

The choleric child usually enjoys school. There is work to be done and she is happy to be doing it. She doesn't appreciate other students who detract from getting the work done. However, many of the difficult students are also choleric. Unless they get to do what they want, they bully and destroy the mood of a classroom. They want everything their way, so they throw temper tantrums and cause a ruckus. A strong choleric can be the power in a classroom, for good or for bad. Her leadership qualities are so strong she can sway the other children for or against the teacher without saying anything. Her leadership is unspoken. She can dig into her courses and work very hard, or she can become stubborn and argumentative, trying to argue with the teacher over every answer.

In the life of the school, the cholerics get things done. They organize projects and do most of the work. All they want is recognition from the teacher that they are indispensable. If they cannot find a way to gain attention in a positive way, they may vandalize or lead gangs of youngsters to do mischief. They seek glory and will gain it in whatever way they can.

When the class does a play, the choleric children hold it together. They speak out strongly, often dominating the chorus. They often know everyone's part and become self-appointed directors. Once they take on a task, they are generally reliable. If the director is opposed by the choleric students, however, rough times lie ahead. Stubborn refusal to bow to the direction of the adult may cause tension for everyone in the cast.

Choleric teenagers are the ones who organize fundraisers, take on projects, and follow through, riding roughshod over the others. A choleric seventeen-year-old president of his class was furious after some of his classmates had not shown up for a class garage sale. During the next meeting, he raved and ranted, intimidating some of the milder students.

The choleric teenager does not like to appear afraid. She will cover up her fear and get on with the task at hand.

Raising the choleric child

The choleric typically reacts in one of two ways. One is to say "yes" to everything and the other is to say "no". There is seldom an in-between. If she says "yes" all the time, she will become over-extended and burned out. It is not possible to stop the choleric from accepting responsibility, but a supportive adult can help the youngster set priorities. For the choleric, giving up a commitment is akin to letting a sinking ship go down. No one else can save it, so the choleric has to be reassured that the job will be done well by someone else. Sometimes, this involves promising her that she will be consulted from time to time by the new person taking on the task. That way, she will still feel that she has power without the day-to-day exhaustion.

The choleric who says "no" has to be treated differently. "No" is usually her first reaction because she does not like to be surprised. She needs time to integrate the request. Once she can envision what is being asked and comes up with her own ideas, she can often be very willing to say "yes". However, she has developed an agenda of things to do and how to do it. When a teacher or parent or friend wants to involve a choleric, it is best to mention it in passing first, then, after some time, mention it again. Once the choleric thinks that it is her idea, she identifies with it and feels involved. If she says no, don't be dismayed. Cholerics need time to change their minds, but they have to do it first in private. Saving face is important.

If a choleric has a temper tantrum or is overly aggressive, don't try to get her to see her behavior at that moment. Wait until the next day. Then, in a quiet moment, bring up the circumstance. Go over it step by step, quietly and objectively. The choleric then is able to see what happened and to look at her own behavior. This is very painful, but it works. At heart, the choleric wants to do the right thing, so she is able to accept the pain as well as the realization that she has erred. She is deeply saddened that she has hurt someone and will want to make amends. Of course, until she sees that she has acted inappropriately, she will stubbornly fight against all criticism.

If the choleric teenager feels needed, she can give her heart and soul. She will carry other people's burdens, both literally and figuratively. She can be very helpful because she wants more than anything to put her will to serve others. If she is not given enough opportunities to serve others, or if she is easily hurt, her tremendous energy can become self-serving.

Because cholerics are the movers and shakers in life, they need much space around them. They can stir up a room in minutes. They slam doors, glare at people, challenge, intimidate. They need to be stood up to or they go right on doing this. However, there can't be a confrontation over every issue, or life will become unbearable. Teachers and parents need to choose important issues to take on the choleric. This is exhausting, but it can be successful. Once the choleric realizes that she has met her match, she will begin to listen as Katerina did in Shakespeare's *Taming of the Shrew*.

Adults dealing with cholerics often put off confrontations because they require so much energy. This does not help the youngster at all. She needs people who care enough to stand up to her and who will spend the time quietly reflecting with her. When this happens, cholerics feel supported, and they can develop a wonderful sense of humor about themselves and be sensitive, generous people.

The change in choleric children during adolescence

Choleric children develop a sanguine quality as they pass through adolescence. Because teenagers are strongly influenced by the emotions that pour forth during this time, cholerics are easily pulled this way and that. They find it difficult to establish the control they had over their world in the past. Their friends also are developing stronger personalities and stand up to the choleric for the first time. In this way, the choleric experiences some of the hurt she causes other people and tries to rectify it by being more sensitive and aware of other people's feelings.

Her interest in getting jobs done develops into another sanguine-like quality as it expands to wanting to do many different tasks. The choleric's focused interest becomes quite diffuse as she tries to do too much. Earlier she had experienced success, but adolescence often brings one failure after another. "They didn't understand what I was trying to do."

In addition to fighting others, the choleric teenager is also fighting herself. All the new feelings stirring within complicate what she is trying to do. Some of her energy is diverted and becomes more scattered than before.

The choleric teenager with a strong melancholic quality has a particularly difficult time during adolescence. She can become self-pitying. Besides the troubles of the world which she has been taking on, she must deal with her own problems. If she is not helped through this, she can become a very bitter adult. If she is fired by ideals and supported by sensitive friends who truly care about her, she can become a devoted and loving adult.

However, she has to learn to give up control. When she is able to release the power she wants to have over people and things, a burden is lifted. This transformation is not usually accomplished in adolescence. The challenge goes on through the adult years.

When the choleric is able to achieve success with herself, the burden of life is lifted and she can step more lightly into the world. She often develops a delightful sense of humor, and most of all, she can laugh at herself.

Chapter Twelve

The development of character during adolescence

The whole object of the universe to us is the formation of character. If you think you came into being for the purpose of taking an important part in the administration of events, to guard a province of the moral creation from ruin, and that its salvation hangs on the success of your single arm, you have wholly mistaken your business.

Ralph Waldo Emerson[1]

Young people in their twenties are distinguished not so much by their physical looks or their temperaments, but by the kind of people they are. Their values, their motivations, and their principles speak to us more clearly than their keen intellect or their latest possession. If we are in a position to hire people, we want responsible individuals who can be trusted to work hard and perform their tasks well. If we rent a house to young people, we need to have character references. If our sons or daughters marry, the character of the intended spouse is far more important than how much wealth or prestige the person brings to the relationship. We expect good character in our elected officials and are constantly disappointed when they show themselves to be selfish and power hungry.

We can be temporarily impressed by wealth, position, cleverness, and skill, but in the long run, it is the character of the person that concerns us. We want to know whether the person can be trusted, whether the person has courage to face his or her deeds, whether the person lives an ethical life. In short, we are concerned with integrity.

Character develops slowly. In the first seven years it is the constitution of the child, the bodily form, that stands out when we meet the youngster. We watch the bodily form emerge over the years from infant, to toddler, to child, to youth. We notice that some children are solid and compact, others lanky. Some look like football players, others like wisps, barely touching the earth. However, beneath the physical surface the child is forming a picture of who he or she is. The attitude of the parents and other adults reflect the youngster's worth. Is the child respected and honored? Do the parents give the child the knowledge and assurance that he or she is worthwhile and important? Does the youngster feel secure within the family? Such an attitude becomes an important part of developing character.

When we meet the child in the years between seven and fourteen, we meet the temperament most of all. When we engage the child in conversation or activity, the quality of that engagement has a great deal to do with whether the child is choleric, melancholic, phlegmatic or sanguine. Unconsciously, however, children are continuing to develop their sense of identity. Are they easily pushed around? Do they stand up for themselves? Do they tell the truth?

Some youngsters are born with profound moral convictions which no outer force will dissuade. They have such strong character that other people feel uplifted with joy and hope when they are around such children; they experience the blessings of humanity because of the inner strength of such special young people.

However, most children do not have such a strongly developed character; they echo their parents' standards of morality and do not come to their own until later. After puberty they separate their beliefs from their parents' and decide for themselves what their values are.

During adolescence, the constitution and temperament move more into the background, and character comes to the fore. Character is mainly formed between ages fourteen and twenty-one, while in adulthood, especially between twenty-one and forty-two, the person continues to refine his or her own character. The ego consciously works with the hereditary tendencies and the cultural influences in developing the character. By the time adults are in the forties they have made themselves the people they are, and not many character changes occur after this time. They have become mature.

The character is an expression of the whole personality and evolves as the young person meets the world. It is shaped by experiences with people and with situations. The character defines the essential nature, the notable traits of that person, and includes moral and ethical qualities as well as the motivations that guide the person's life. The character is built from within the person by the moral decisions the person makes and by his or her standards of behavior.

Although character is influenced by a person's experiences, it is primarily an expression of the individual and not merely the effect of training or conditioning. Although you cannot teach a person character traits directly, you can significantly influence their development.

Character traits include loyalty, courage, compassion, honesty, commitment, steadfastness, attentiveness, fairness and idealism.

As the ego forms the character from within, it expresses itself in convictions which guide the person's behavior. The great religions and ethical systems of the world have described the force of character by many different terms such as the conscience, the still, small voice, the inner light, the Truth, the Spirit, the Christ force, the Holy Ghost, the Tao, or the voice of God. The development of character has been considered of prime importance by society, and in the past it has been considered the work of the family, church, and community to develop the character of young people.

As American society's respect for traditional institutions has wavered, so too has the importance of character. In the seventies and eighties we have seen ethical values become confused with super-patriotism and big business. Many young people have become suspicious of do-gooders and of those who stand for virtuous behavior on Sunday but act unethically during the work week. Two extremes of behavior have been expressed in American society over the last twenty years. One extreme is the very strict standard of behavior which leaves no room for the individual to disagree. The other extreme is the "do your own thing" mentality which holds that there are no objective values, and everything is left up to the individual's whim. These attitudes mislead teenagers and divert them from realizing the serious task of character development.

Character develops from within the adolescent as a response to what is going on in his or her community. As the adolescent faces dilemmas involving honesty, courage, and integrity, the opportunities for character development present themselves. But the parental attitudes and the social atmosphere have an important bearing on the way the young person develops. If youngsters feel secure in themselves they are not easily swayed by others. They are able to put off rewards and aim for long-range goals. These youngsters know what to do in different situations and are able to handle the challenge. The insecure youngsters have more difficulty handling new situations and making decisions that will benefit them in the long run. They want their rewards now, they need outer forms of recognition and status because they don't feel secure inside themselves.

All children make mistakes. However, the way the adults handle those mistakes reflects their moral values and helps the youngster develop character. This presupposes that the adult does care enough to deal with the issue at all. For example, I experienced two different ways of responding to a teenage theft.

A fourteen-year-old stole flasks from a chemical company. When the teacher took the youngster and the flasks back to the company so that the youngster could make amends, the teacher and student were told, 'Never mind, that happens all the time'. A valuable opportunity to help that youngster work on his character was lost. Instead, he was given the message that what he had done was common and acceptable.

During a trip to New York, an eighth grade class had dinner in Chinatown. As the youngsters climbed back onto the school bus they began comparing the ash trays they had taken. The teacher marched the class back to the restaurant and had each young person return the ash tray and apologize. The restaurant manager was very grateful for this and explained that although it was common for school groups to take things, no teacher had ever responded this way. This event made a significant impact on these young people, and several mentioned it years later.

We can help young people develop character by bringing them face to face with themselves and helping them set things right. By doing this we are communicating that there are objective standards of moral behavior and we expect youngsters to live up to them. If they are not able to do so out of themselves, we will help them do so. In this way we show them we care about the way they live their lives and we awaken in them a keener awareness of their moral nature.

Two girls used their lunchtime to do a "lawn-job", that is, to make deep ruts on a lawn with their car. The teenagers were identified and the owner of the property worked with the school and parents so that the youngsters replanted the lawn and did gardening for the owner. This was far more effective for their character development than being made to pay for the damage. The students felt much better afterwards that they were able to set things right.

Often when teenagers get in trouble they are calling for help, especially for the attention of their parents. If the parents focus on protecting the youngster from the punishment they often do disservice to their children. The important question is, how can we make the most of this situation so our youngster learns the right lessons from it? So often the wrong lessons are learned because the parents are not willing to look at what is happening in their family. Instead they place the blame on others. Then they seem surprised that their youngsters have trouble accepting responsibility for their own actions.

An example of the young person's inner desire to live a moral life is seen when youngsters have to decide their own punishment. They are often much harder on themselves than the adults are. Teenagers know when they are doing wrong, and although they may at first respond in a hostile manner and lie about what they have done, in the long run they are actually grateful for the adult's intervention and for the opportunity to learn a lesson. I well remember a young man who always seemed 'smooth'. He never actually got caught or received blame, but he was somehow involved with most behind-the-scenes activities that went on. When confronted, he put on the most innocent of looks and was in fact 'hurt' that he was accused of lying, cheating, bullying or whatever the situation was. Each meeting I called to discuss the problem was tense, and it took persistence to meet him each time and call him on his antics. As he got older we were able to speak about difficulties with a little more directness, and although he didn't acknowledge having been wrong, he did joke with me about it. After graduating, he wrote me, "First of all I can't tell you how glad I am that you have been my advisor. I know that might sound silly, but it's true … These past four years I have learned so much from you, not just academically, but about life and people. I'll never forget all the little conferences and meetings I had to go to with you. At the time I hated them, but now I realize how much they taught me. Thank you so much for everything, and I'll always remember you."

There are numerous opportunities in each community to help youngsters develop their character by facing their misdeeds and helping them set things right. However, it has become far more common for adults to ignore (either out of a lack of caring or out of fear) such actions, and teenagers are running rampant, destroying property, causing disturbances and even terrorizing adults. The greatest sadness, however, is that these young people are not only getting away with what they are doing, but they are doing nothing to develop their character. Unless adults make it a priority to confront errant youngsters with standards of behavior, it becomes harder for those adults who do care to do so. The result is a decreasing morality in society.

Character develops in other ways besides making amends for mistakes. For example, the parent can praise a child for owning up to the truth rather than getting angry because of what the child did. Such praise is a strong message of the parents' values. When the child gets the message and tells the truth, he or she is working on moral development. Such practice helps build character in the growing child.

Another example is cheating. In school there are many times the youngster comes face to face with cheating. "Should I cheat? Will I be caught? Is it right? How do I feel about my friends cheating?" The inner struggle the adolescent goes through in making such decisions is shaping his or her character.

Adults influence character development of a young person in several different ways – by personal example, by creating opportunities, and by setting standards for the adolescent to meet. When adolescents see adults making decisions in order to obey their own inner moral standards, it makes a great impression. Even though they may find it difficult to understand at the moment, teenagers are impressed by the effort.

Unfortunately, today, character is not valued very highly, and youngsters who choose to make moral decisions are often scoffed at and called goody-goodies. Because loyalty to the group is ranked higher than loyalty to the Truth, adolescents who make moral decisions are often unpopular with the crowd and risk being ridiculed.

As the adolescent begins facing existential questions such as "What will my life be like? What do I want to stand for? What will

I sacrifice for?" the young person is considering different values. He or she is deciding priorities. "Is service more important than money? If I have to go against my beliefs to work in a place, is it worth it? Do I want something enough to cheat for it? Am I being true to myself?"

For example, a nineteen-year-old college student had always planned to work in nuclear physics, but when she discovered that most of the jobs involved were connected with nuclear plants or nuclear weapons, she felt she had to give up that dream and choose another major.

Making plans for the future also confronts the adolescent with character-building opportunities. For example, "Should I continue my education when I would rather get a job and have a fancy car?" or "Should I choose a career that serves other people or one that makes lots of money? Should I take initiative or coast along? Should I help my family so my younger siblings can continue their education?"

Character develops as youngsters become separate from the adults and learn to make moral decisions on their own. It develops in freedom; it cannot be imposed by any other person. Youngsters struggle to live their own lives, often choosing values different from those of their parents. Many times, the young person sets a path contrary to all that is given to him or her, striking out to find his or her direction in life, often against terrible odds.

Despite what the parents can provide, youngsters want to make it on their own. For example, a youngster with outstanding intellectual aptitude may decide to work at a menial job to experience that kind of life. His or her life may be difficult because of it, but listening to inner principles takes priority over the easy way of life. Such a decision, rooted in the individual's ego, is not the same as rebellion. Such a decision is consciously made because higher values are at stake. When young people act out of such impulses, it is very difficult to talk them out of their plans. They are willing to risk loss of approval, financial security, and suffer isolation.

Here are some examples. A father was looking forward to his son's assuming his successful business. The son decided, however, to be a teacher. A young unmarried woman became pregnant. Her parents urged her to have an abortion. She believed it was wrong and assumed the responsibility of raising the child even though it was against her parents' wishes. A student spoke to a teacher about cheating in a class, even though he knew there would be pressure on him for reporting it. A young woman turned in her test to a teacher to be re-scored because the teacher had made a mistake and made the score too high.

Each of us has moments in which we are called upon to test our character, to be better human beings than we were before, to rise to great heights. Or we may give in to greed, we may not follow through on something important, or we may let a friend down. These experiences stay and often haunt us unless we are able to resolve them.

Youngsters need to contribute to their community. A part of character development is service. Is the youngster expected to contribute his or her efforts to the family or does every job come with a cash value? Does the youngster have an opportunity to help an elderly person or a handicapped person? These are wonderful opportunities which call out the idealism and good will of teenagers.

Opportunities to develop character occur during adolescence in leadership positions in organizations, in the family, and on the job. In these situations, the teenager has to deal with such issues as handling responsibility, dealing with the repercussions if the responsibility is not met, and denying himself or herself time for personal pleasure because of the needs that have to be fulfilled. The reward that comes is the satisfaction of a job well done. High school organizations offer many possibilities for such character development, and advisors to these groups should work hard with teenagers to develop priorities. Such development does not just happen.

Another important aspect of character development is the setting of standards for teenagers. Meeting expectations in the family, in the school, or in religious institutions, helps the adolescent to aim for the noble and to develop inner strength. To cultivate ideals, the teenager must be given a way to implement them. When standards are not met, the adult has the responsibility to reflect this to the teenager, however unpleasant it may be. No one likes to be told that he or she has fallen short, but it is a benefit in the long run. If the adult sees that the teenager has cheated or behaved irresponsibly in other ways, the adult should act upon this knowledge for the good of the teenager. It does not help teenagers for the adult to close his or her eyes and pretend it didn't happen. For teenagers to grow and develop their character, they need the courage of adults to help them face an unpleasant situation and to develop from it. The situation may be painful in the moment, but the youngster is setting a direction for his or her moral life.

To have a profound effect on the development of character means to do something over and over, to engage one's will, to build new habits and attitudes. Giving up a meal once in a while to remind ourselves of hungry people is a noble idea, but it only becomes part of one's life when this is done regularly, or actions are actually taken to help those in need. Visiting a convalescent home to cheer up the old people is a beneficial experience, but it only becomes part of a youngster's character development, if, for example, the youngster goes once a week for a semester or does something else to incorporate the experience into his or her life.

A part of character development is maintaining the balance between serving oneself and serving other people. It means using one's special talents to benefit other people and to avoid becoming egotistic and self-serving. Character development doesn't come easily. It takes effort, time and commitment. In this way a person influences his or her personal evolution.

Each of us has special qualities in our personalities. Whether we use these qualities to benefit others or ourselves is an expression of our character. For example, we may be very inquisitive, interested in details about people and subjects. If we are more interested in people, we might direct that quality in an anti-social way by being a malicious gossip. We might love to pursue a subject area by shutting ourselves up in our rooms and becoming lonely narrow-minded researchers, the image of the mad scientist trying to gain power. However, if our inclinations are to bring our talents to benefit others, we would move in a different direction. Our curiosity about people, rather than being used to turn one against the other could be used to bring about an understanding of people's needs, to understand how one youngster can benefit from one approach, how another responds best in a different way. Our curiosity or our interest in details then serves humanity. Along the same line, if we love researching subjects, we might discover wonderful benefits for mankind.

We might have the personality quality that wants everything to be in order. We know that when we are involved, things happen. If we are concerned with ourselves most of all, then we want to be the ones to decide how things should be. If anyone disagrees, we might fly into a temper tantrum or slam doors. We might feel unappreciated and frustrated. We want recognition but no-one is recognizing us, so we feel hurt and angry. However, if we are working to develop our character in a moral way, we can transform this quality so it benefits others. Our sense of order can help a group figure out what needs to be done, our leadership can inspire others to do what needs to be done without too many commands. This is described clearly in an ancient Chinese statement:

> The highest type of ruler is one of whose existence the people are barely aware.
> Next comes one whom they love and praise.
> Next comes one whom they fear.
> Next comes one whom they despise and defy.
> The sage is self-effacing and scanty of words.
> When his task is accomplished and things have been completed
> All the people say, "We ourselves have achieved it".
>
> Tao Te Ching

Another personality quality that often can be a blessing or a curse, depending on what we do with it, is flexibility. On one hand the person can be of weak character and keep changing to adapt to whatever comes. This person seems very easy going, but is actually rather spineless. What appears as flexibility is a disguised need to be accepted by the peer group, whatever its values may be. However, this can be a wonderful quality if transformed and developed morally. Such a person can keep things moving, sharing ideas and keeping things from getting too stuck. He or she can see what is needed and be able to change to make it happen. This quality then allows the group to heal wounds, to see new possibilities, and to proceed in a creative and constructive manner.

Each of us has many personality qualities that become the working material of our character development. Beginning in adolescence we become conscious of these challenges and begin the work to shape ourselves.

Steiner points out that there are special times in our lives when our inner voice speaks most strongly, usually in relation to our life's work. These moments occur in an eighteen-and-a-half-year rhythm, at about ages nineteen, thirty-eight, and fifty-six. At those moments, we face ourselves in a particularly direct way. We have an opportunity to evaluate what we want to make out of ourselves and see how far we have come. Sometimes we become ill, other times we face terrible loneliness, or we make decisions that turn our whole life in a different direction. At these times the work we have done to develop our character helps us.

Developing character is the great work of human life. We become what we will to become. Whether we believe that we are inspired by spiritual beings or that we develop out of rational ethical sources, the work is still left to our efforts to shape, to mold, to form what is truly human in each of us. This great work is set out during our adolescent years.

PART II

The Challenge of Adolescence

Chapter Thirteen

The needs of teenagers

When I was young, it seemed that life was so wonderful,
a miracle, oh it was beautiful, magical.
And all the birds in the trees, well they'd be singing so happily,
joyfully, playfully watching me.
But then they sent me away to teach me how to be sensible,
logical, responsible, practical.
And they showed me a world where I could be so dependable,
clinical, intellectual, cynical.

There are times when all the world's asleep,
the questions run too deep
for such a simple man,
Won't you please tell me what we've learned?
I know it sounds absurd,
but please tell me who I am.

Now watch what you say or they'll be calling you a radical,
liberal, fanatical, criminal.
Won't you sign up your name; we'd like to feel you're
acceptable, respectable, presentable, a vegetable!

At night, when all the world's asleep,
the questions run so deep
for such a simple man.
Won't you please, please tell me what we've learned?
I know it sounds absurd,
but please tell me who I am.

Rick Davies and Roger Hodgson[1]

Young children live united with the world in an unconscious manner; they have little awareness of themselves in relation to the world. As they develop, however, they become more conscious of this relationship and lose their earlier unconscious connection. They experience a shift in identity. They lose the earlier relationship to the world and feel withdrawn into themselves. We can say they lose the world to find themselves, and with this loss they experience loneliness. Then, out of loneliness, they reach out from the self to find the world in order to experience unity again – but a new unity, because they no longer are unconscious.

The tension that develops between the self and the world is a necessary tension of human existence. Because we live in two worlds – the physical and the spiritual – we feel at times pulled in two directions. Where the worlds of body and spirit meet, they create the realm of the human soul. Here, body and spirit weave the tapestry of individual destiny. Consequently, the soul-life is always in flux – a present moment hovering between past and future, the crossing point between inner and outer realities.

Adolescents live right in the middle of this tension, unable to find a secure place in the center. Their needs and desires swirl and storm within them – and sometimes sweep them away. It is only when the Ego develops at about twenty-one that most people gain the capacity to take hold of their soul forces and achieve balance in their lives.

Adolescents seek dialogue between themselves and the world. On one hand, if the needs of the world become too powerful, the youngsters lose their center. They lose hold of themselves in too much activity and intensity. Then they are at the mercy of what is going on outside and they can find little peace. If, on the other hand, the self dominates, they may shut out the world, retreat, and become self-indulgent recluses. All human beings have a tendency in one direction or the other, but most healthy people find a creative and tolerable balance.

I am grateful to have read *Beyond Customs* by the English psychologist Charity James.[2] Her list of adolescents' needs served as a starting point for this chapter.

In grouping these needs, it occurred to me that, on one side, the world dominates, and, on the other side, the self dominates. The needs having to do with the world are the attributes of the success-oriented Westerner who lives in the will (physical activity, intensity, affecting the world, belonging, being needed, needing facts), while the needs of the self are the attributes of the Oriental who lives in thought (stillness, routine, rhythm, introspection, separateness, community, imagination):

The Adolescent's Needs

physical activity	stillness
intensity	routine
to affect the world	to move inward
to belong	separateness
to be needed	need to need
facts	myth and legend

Just as there is tension between the Western and Eastern orientation to life, there is tension within the two sides of the individual's soul-life. A middle needs to be developed, where the strengths of the two can interact rather than confronting each other as opposites. The middle is the soul-life, the world of feelings, which mediates between thinking and willing.

The need for physical activity and the need for stillness

Teenagers are gaining mastery over their bodies, and their ability to feel comfortable in their bodies is an important element in personality development. In that sense, the need for physical activity and the need for stillness are really aspects of the same need. Some teenagers do not want to exert themselves any more than is necessary. Others relish the challenge to use every muscle, delighting in the strains and aches that result from heavy exercise. Others are afraid of physical contact; fear of being hurt causes them to avoid contact rather than meet it. One can see the differences quite clearly in volleyball games in high school PE classes. Some teenagers go to meet the ball, while others step aside to let the ball drop right next to them. Physical activity ideally embodies both graceful rhythm and style. Movement and stillness are in balance.

Physical activity takes many forms and has many benefits. For some, it may be frantic activity to fill time because the teenager is afraid of being alone. For others, it is part of the battle to keep from gaining weight. For whatever reason, teenagers should have opportunity for physical activity, whether it be walking, bicycling, running, playing tennis, or any other activity which strengthens the heart and lungs. The current fitness consciousness has encouraged many teenagers to work out and keep themselves in shape. If this does not become an obsession, it serves a valuable purpose. (Some parents, of course, have noted that they end up pushing the lawn mower while their teenagers spend hours at the gym.)

The need for stillness is a parallel need. It allows the body needed rest to replenish forces, to calm the nervous system. Stillness also is important because creativity is virtually impossible without it. Creativity tends to be born in silence. If our young people are going to have the resources to deal with the world that's before them, their creativity must be protected and cultivated.

Teenagers tend to operate on nervous energy, overdoing physical activity and experiencing emotions on the edge of catastrophe. Their lives become a dramatic contrast of ups and downs, and their nervous systems come under too much stress. No one can eliminate – nor should they try – the tragi-comic ups and downs of adolescent life, but the alternation between tragedy and comedy needs to be rhythmic rather than frenetic, gentle rolls rather than shock waves.

Time is needed every day when the demands of life recede, and teenagers can retreat into their rooms without the radio blaring, and experience quiet. Young people often use loud music as a hypnotic drug to shut out the external world and allow the youngster to retreat – but to what? Not to stillness, but rather to a chaotic and nerve-pounding sense-bombardment.

The attack on the adolescent nervous system has been exacerbated by the prevalence of the ipod with its earphones. Now people never have to be alone. Oblivious to the outer world, they can bicycle, ride, jog, or fish to the accompaniment of music.

Television isn't much better. Do we need to be hypnotized to be still? Television-stare is a stillness of sorts, and many people use television to slow down and escape from everyday tensions. Vicariously experiencing other people's troubles may help teenagers avoid their own, but it does nothing to heal the nervous system or to help them gain access to their inner life.

For some teenagers, the sole experience of stillness comes during those bedtime moments between waking and sleeping. Even those moments are endangered, however, thanks to radio earphones which enable the young person to drift off to sleep to a lullaby of restless, electronic throbbing while mom and dad sleep in the next room, peaceful in the illusion that their child is resting. There are better alternatives, however.

Activities such as hiking, walking, fishing, and sketching strengthen the young person's ability to be alone and enjoy stillness. During such activities, ears and eyes become attuned to the sounds of silence, to the "books in the running brooks", as Shakespeare tells us.

In our society, the need for stillness is ignored, and teenagers live in a hyperactive world of sense impressions. It is no surprise to hear about increased nervous disorders among a generation whose fear of silence is depriving it of stillness.

The need for intensity and the need for routine

Teenagers need to have excitement, new ideas, new people, and new challenges. They want to spread their wings and fly, to test themselves in many new areas of life. Telephone calls, time spent with friends and family members, and special activities contribute to the excitement of life. The young person craves new experiences and has trouble settling down to anything of a routine nature. However, too much intensity, like too much physical activity, leads to overstimulation and superficiality.

Balance is needed between stimulating activity – clubs, teams, jobs, social activities, homework, home responsibilities and family – and a steady, calming routine of everyday life.

Amid all the demands that accelerate their lives and leave little time to breathe, a family rhythm reassures adolescents that they can count on a few things in life while so much is in turmoil inside them. Rhythm is important because it provides a structure so that change can occur. Meals are especially important in the teenager's life, and it is important to keep some routine here. Even if teenagers know that they are on their own three nights a week, that constitutes a rhythm. However, when they have no idea when they are eating or whether they are preparing their own dinner, eating with the family, or heading to the nearest fast-food place, they lack security in one of the basic needs of life. They resent constant change (except when they are the ones initiating it). Of course, teenagers can deal with change and a break in rhythm, but it isn't fair to take advantage of their ability to fend for themselves. The older they are, the less they depend on the rhythm of their surroundings for support.

Teenagers also need routine, but too much becomes boring, and they feel that they are wasting away. They long for excitement, for changes of pace and place, for a more exciting social life. They daydream and imagine what other places are like and how wonderful their lives would be in other circumstances. Some teenagers long for routine. Others long to escape from it.

The need to affect the world and the need to move inward

Adolescents need to feel that they count, that what they say and what they do means something to people, that they have the possibility of expressing opinions and bringing about change.

They can be invited to participate and contribute ideas in family discussion and decision making, where appropriate. Learning to share ideas and express opinions in the protected space of the family is very valuable even if the parents make the final decisions. Being able to plan their room and arrange it so it expresses their interests and personality is a way of having some control over their surroundings.

School offers many opportunities to bring about change and affect their surroundings, by joining clubs, participating in student government, planning school events, and talking to faculty members about concerns. In the larger community, they can write letters to the editor, talk to people in responsible positions, make constructive comments at a job, and volunteer their services.

By evaluating their contributions and actions, they learn their limits. If they feel free to ask important questions, explore points of view, make statements, and contribute their energy to getting things done, they will be affecting the world. They need to know that they can put their ideals into action and make a difference.

The other side of this need is the inner side – the need to move inward. To offer the world something of value requires time for introspection. Reflecting, thinking about their aims in life, pondering values, wondering, comparing, musing, reading, drawing – all these offer the young person an opportunity to enter into a dialogue with his or her own soul. Such dialogue is the furnace in which ideals are forged. Who is it that lives within my soul? What is most important? What kind of person do I want to be? What do I want to do with my life? These questions can never be truly answered from outside. The inner side of the individuality is sensitive and private. It needs nurturing in a special way – unlike any other aspect of the teenage personality.

The need to belong and the need for separateness

For the adolescent, belonging to a group is extremely important and causes deep anxiety. Each group has its own goals and values, so adolescents need to consider carefully before deciding which to join. Joining a group tells the world what the teenager stands for. Once in a group, the youngster will find it difficult to change and still be accepted.

If teenagers do not find a group in which they feel comfortable or which accepts them, they can be miserable. It is easy for parents to ignore the teenager's frustration, but they must understand that a significant pressure is being experienced. Not to have a group is to feel either that you are alone in the world or that you are so special you will make it alone. Sometimes, however, a teenager chooses to stand alone, apart from a group. This choice is not made out of arrogance, but because the situation leaves him or her no options. Not everyone is a group person. Some youngsters are such private people that they are uncomfortable in a group. For them, adolescence can be especially difficult unless they find a close friend.

However, groups can dominate adolescents too much. They impose standards, ways of relating, likes, and dislikes. Adolescents may be undergoing critical inner changes, but they will be careful about showing it, especially if these changes include a shift in values or a change in groups. Teenagers know that leaving a group will mean instant, major adjustments in their social life.

Adolescents have as strong a need for separateness as they do for the group. They need to think about themselves as individuals apart from the group. They need the chance to take a look at themselves and see if they are satisfied with their activities, with the values with which they are identifying, and with the behavior acceptable to the group.

The struggle between the individual and the group is one of the major struggles of adolescence. The pressures which a group puts on the individual often determine how that young person will act throughout high school, and this, in turn, affects choices he or she makes concerning the rest of his or her life.

Adolescents struggle with self-esteem. Am I good enough? Why can't I be perfect? To feel good about themselves, they often depend upon a group's feedback. Yet that isn't enough, either. They gradually develop the inner strength to make their own decisions, but only after a period of painful insecurity. Anyone who has ever been around a teenager who cannot decide what to wear, what to do on a Saturday night, or whom to go out with, knows of the insecurity involved. Most young people overcome this lack of self-esteem, but some do not. To escape, they conform slavishly to their group or they escape into alcohol and drugs.

The need for separateness often is depicted as a rival to the need to belong, but both are needs and it is a mistake to think that one can choose one and exclude the other. Because of the pressures of society and the insecurity of adolescence, the need to belong is stronger for the early adolescent than the need for separateness. After the sixteenth-year change, however, the teenager can deal more effectively with individual decisions and group pressure.

The need to need and the need to be needed

Adolescents have an intense need to feel a part of their community, whether that is their class, their family, or their social group. Being part of a group lets them feel accepted and approved of. In addition to needing to be part of a group, they need companionship. The need to need, however, goes beyond friends or the group.

Teenagers need to feel that they can ask for help when they need it without being made to feel inferior. Because of the way they have been treated in the past, many youngsters feel that they must have permission to express their needs. In the family, there are many opportunities to reassure the youngster that his needs are important and appropriate. Obviously, when adolescents are doing projects in the house they will at times seek help. How that help is given varies from, "Why are you so stupid?" to "Here, let me show you and then you'll know how to do it next time".

Adolescents have to feel comfortable needing. If they feel inferior because they have admitted their needs or because they feel they have exposed their ignorance, they are learning a negative lesson: "Don't expose yourself. Don't admit your ignorance". Teenagers don't express their needs too often, and, if discouraged, they will express them even less.

Teenagers need support when in a frightening situation, but they often do not express the need out of fear of being called a sissy. The adolescent may be going into the hospital or to the dentist for surgery. It may be a driver's test or a competitive exam. Whether they ask for it or not, teenagers need their parents' support. They will be able to deal with the situation better if they know that their parents stand behind them. Of course, they will have their share of disappointments in life, but the way the adults respond to them may determine whether they feel they are a success or failure.

The need to be needed is a particular problem in modern society. In the past, teenagers were needed and valued for their labor. As teenagers assumed adult roles, they also received adult privileges. Today, however, we have denied adolescents many of the responsibilities they had in the past. They seldom have to leave home at sixteen, find a job, marry, and begin a family. Instead, childhood actually is prolonged into their twenties. What are their struggles during this time? They have the same struggles as the younger adolescent does – frustration because of dependence on parents, the desire to be accepted as an adult, wanting to make a mark on the world, and the need to get on with their own lives.

Despite the general shift in society, there is still a definite need for the adolescent's contribution to the family and community. However, many parents would rather pay someone to do a task than take the trouble to teach their youngster the skill. Too many teenagers – especially in suburban communities – have money on their hands which has been given to them rather than earned. They have no idea of its value and spend it foolishly.

Because society has been going through such radical change, it has been easy to ignore the need of the teenager to be needed. Roles are not very clear. Teenagers see adults acting like their peers, and this is confusing. Because adult expectations are cloudy, they are unsure where they are meant to contribute. Parents must become clear about their values and expectations.

It is important for teenagers to understand their obligations to their families. One seventeen-year-old girl told me, "I had to get away for three months in the summer to understand what I receive at home. I have more freedom now, but I am expected to do certain chores and a certain amount of yardwork. That's fair."

A family can have different kinds of needs. Chores are an obvious need, but if adolescents are paid for their chores, they themselves aren't really needed, since someone else could do the job as well. Parents should consider what they are doing when they pay their children for household chores. I am not saying that there are not times when a special project should be paid for, especially something that otherwise would be hired out. However, some work-contribution should be required, simply because each person is part of the family or community and there are tasks to be done out of love and responsibility.

If there is an aged person in the family or nearby, adolescents can do much to help. If they are given specific tasks to do for that person's well-being, it not only gives them something important to do, but it strengthens the bonds between the generations. A telephone call, a ten-minute visit, or other small gesture can mean much in an older person's day.

The need to be needed is especially strong around birthdays and holidays. If the teenagers are involved in the planning of a celebration, they not only fill a need, but they are storing up important experiences for when they become parents. If the adolescents are commanded to do things for a celebration, they may become resentful and sarcastic, and the purpose is lost. The task may be accomplished, but it is an accomplishment of bitterness. Similarly, it doesn't help to ask a teenager to bake a cake that evening if plans have already been made to do something else. It is a different matter, however, if the adult says, "Next week is Dad's birthday. What shall we do to celebrate it?" One child may volunteer to gather flowers, another to bake a cake, another to make his favorite meal. A wonderful attitude can grow when a family repeatedly is involved in this way over a number of years. Later, after the youngsters have left home, they experience great joy when they, too, are remembered in a special way.

The same holds true during the holidays. If the adolescents are brought in to offer their own ideas along with the established customs, they are usually happy to participate. For example, they may be thrilled to hide eggs for an Easter egg hunt although they feel too old to gather them. Rising early in the morning to be Santa Lucia on December 13 may bring special excitement if they are helping a younger sibling prepare to be the bringer of light. Older children can do much to help – selecting the tree, decorating, lighting the tree, supervising cookie-baking, and shopping. Even though they may complain at the time, they usually think back to that time with great satisfaction, if they had a meaningful contribution to make.

The world has so much need for the vitality and vision of our young people, and when this need is clearly conveyed to them, the response is outstanding. Young people today yearn to be needed. This generation is often criticized as apathetic, but I don't think they have been properly appealed to. The need for their help has not been sufficiently communicated. The need to help hungers in their souls. It is up to us to inspire them. We do them a great service when we find ways for them to demonstrate the compassion, tenderness, commitment and energy they have to offer.

The need for fact and the need for imagination

Adolescents crave both facts and imagination. Facts help them establish themselves firmly on the earth. They are relatively unambiguous and offer the teenager a way to know the world. Young adolescents often memorize lists of batting averages or words of songs. Holding onto facts provides a sense of power. Facts give youngsters something to talk about, whereas asking them to express opinions about something they do not understand intimidates them. Facts are safe – the person is right or wrong. Teenagers affirm themselves through the facts they know. Too few facts provide a very subjective view of life. Too heavy a reliance on facts deprives them of inner exploration.

Youngsters also crave the world of imagination. Fantasy is one level of imagination and offers an escape route from the greyness of the everyday world or a world that is emotionally too demanding. Adolescents, especially between thirteen and fifteen, hunger for fantasy. They soak up science fiction, mythology, and adventure stories (including romance), living in created worlds, on other planets, identifying with super heroes, or accomplishing amazing deeds. Adolescents yearn for excitement, for magic, for sensational escapes, and mind-boggling plots. Other youngsters dwell in the imagination of times past when good and evil were clearer than they are today, and they indulge in games that allow them to play roles and invent plots.

The human being learns in two ways – in a straight factual objective way and in an imaginative way. Each approach gives us a certain kind of information about the world which can be expressed in fact or fiction.

Youngsters enjoy the content of myths and legends even though they know the stories could not have happened exactly as described. Once they begin to see myths as veiled explanations of truths, they become involved in an exciting inner exploration. Even if they do not relate to myths on the metaphoric level, they may simply find them satisfying and exciting.

When adolescents experience the change of consciousness around sixteen, they also undergo a change in their relationship to fact and imagination. On one hand, they seek to expand their world of fact to include an understanding of world events, knowledge of the human being, and grasp of time and space. On the other hand, they see that facts alone are not enough to satisfy their questions. They crave archetypal images that appear in myth and have their reflection in the human soul. When they grasp the myth as metaphor, they can approach their own struggles as part of the human condition and see how it is part of a universality.

Fairy tales and fables previously met the needs of the child from six to eight. The myths and legends of the world, especially such legends as *Parsifal* and *Beowulf*, the imaginative works of Tolkien, Ursula LeGuin and others, and powerful imaginative dramas in such great books as *The Brothers Karamazov* and *The Divine Comedy* challenge and nourish adolescents.

Dialogue

The needs expressed in adolescence become the needs of the adult. In the dialogue between the world and the adolescent's own soul, the youngster experiences the dilemma of human life. Maturity, or integration, has to do with reconciling opposites or allowing polarities to meet in the middle, where a third possibility may arise. The mature adolescent allows for contradictions while the young adolescent bristles at opposites and labels their existence hypocrisy.

Adolescent needs are expressed in relationship to balancing physical activity and stillness, intensity and routine, making a mark on the world and introspection, wanting to give and wanting to fulfill a purpose, and craving both facts and imaginative fiction. The adolescent defines the questions and then, as an adult, travels through life trying to answer them. Thus our lives become quests and the visions of our adolescent strivings provide light on our journey for all our years to come.

Chapter Fourteen

Teenagers and the family

"Just having problems with my parents. They're yelling at me." "Don't let your parents get you down. They love ya, they do. I know that's hard to believe."

"Do you ever wonder if your parents are your real parents or if you got mixed up in the hospital?"

"What? Talk to my parents about anything personal? Are you kidding?"

"My mom and I are very close. We can talk about anything."

From various teenager conversations

The world of the small child is its family. In today's society, the family often is a more diffuse and variable group than in former days. Because of increases in divorce, the bonds of blood are loosening and new groups forming. Children need to be in a community in which there are people who have known them for a long time, who have shared experiences with them, who take care of them, and who love them unconditionally. Often, today's biological family is unable to meet these needs, but they are so important to the healthy development of the child that they must be met in some other ways.

Rudolf Steiner points out that families are not random combinations, that threads of destiny connect family members. The eldest child in a family usually has a special role in helping create the family. The other children come into an already formed family and have a different relationship to the parents.

As children reach adolescence, they relate to their parents in a variety of ways, two of which I call "The Volcano" and "The Mask". In dealing with the adolescent volcano, one senses rumblings beneath the surface and somehow knows that heat and energy are bubbling there. Spontaneously, the volcano erupts – all kinds of inner stuff is spewed out – and then the volcano cools as the adolescent explosion subsides. If the adolescent is not able to release pressure from time to time, the heat and energy move inward and the pressure is increased until it blows completely out of control.

The Mask is another way in which family members often experience the teenager. Adolescence itself is a mask, and teenagers present themselves to their parents and to the world in a series of masks, both comic and tragic. Parents sometimes look at their teenagers and wonder, "Do I know you?" or "Who are you today?" or "What will you be tomorrow?" Life at this time is a drama without an obvious director or producer.

The relationship between the teenager and parents becomes an arena for the emergence of the self, and the confrontation can be exhausting for everyone. Some parents see it as a necessary stage to be endured – "This, too, shall pass" – while many others find it an exciting and rewarding period of life.

During adolescence, the relationship between parent and child changes radically. Parents may experience the child as a stranger, an intruder, a rival – someone who argues about curfews, criticizes the parents' lifestyle, and doesn't like spending time with the family but prefers friends or even being locked up in a room with the radio, who conceals the confusions of life and turns to other people for consolation and intimacy. The parent feels empty and rejected.

Where are the long talks, the shared activities, the family feeling we had imagined would take place once our youngsters became old enough to share our concerns and interests? Where are the appreciation, consideration, and sympathy we hoped to experience from our soon-to-be-adult youngsters? Why, instead of running a home, do we find ourselves sharing a house – and car, refrigerator, telephone and limited income?

To the teenager, parents are fallible, inconsistent and unreasonable. They mis-manage money, time and relationships. They have lots of answers but are unwilling to discuss the questions. They concentrate on authority, yet they don't know everything.

There are long stretches in adolescence when the youngsters see nothing right about their parents, yet they still need them very much. Under all the outward turmoil, the most important question is, "Do you love me?"

Put another way, the question becomes, "Do you care enough about me to follow through on what you tell me, even if I fight you all the way?" For teenagers want the love and respect of their parents – even as they do everything they can to wear them down.

Friendships and romantic relationships come and go, but the parent-child relationship is a constant in the teenagers' life. In spite of all the tensions, it provides the anchor of stability.

As parents become worn out, they find it easier to give in, to let the youngsters go to the all-night bash, to hang around with whichever friends they wish, to choose whatever school, classes and activities they want. It is difficult for the parents to keep up the struggle when their hearts are full of questions: "Isn't that what teenagers are clamoring for – freedom? Then why are they so disgruntled? Why aren't they satisfied? Why do they fight for freedom and then slavishly surrender it to their group?"

Parents need to simply accept that teenagers want the impossible from their parents. They want the parents to guide them without forcing them, they want advice without commandment, limitations without punishment, and understanding without responsibility. They want adults around when they need them – but only as helpers, not as authorities.

What is so interesting is that the teenagers know this. They know that what they want is unreasonable, but they can't help wanting it. On another level, they don't want this at all. They want parents who talk with them, share their experiences, mean what they say, stand up for values, create family experiences, and limit them when they need to be limited. The problem is that most of them don't realize that this, too, is what they want. They see it only when they grow out of the first stage of adolescence and look back.

Siblings

For the adolescent, the family constellation includes siblings as well as parents. Teenagers do not only have needs and expectations of their parents, but also of their brothers and sisters. Different stresses are placed on the teenager who is the eldest of three than on the teenager who is the youngest of five. In his book, *Brothers and Sisters*, Karl Koenig examines the influence which the placement of the child in the family has on the developing personality.[1] The oldest is the first to test the waters, to find out what is allowed and not allowed, and to initiate the parents into the world of adolescence.

Compare the experiences of an eldest child with those of a youngest.

Is the eldest youngster constantly aware of being an example to the younger siblings? Is the teenager the ready babysitter and co-parent in a large family? Is the teenager given many more responsibilities and privileges because he or she assumes the role of adult earlier than the siblings coming up behind will do?

Does the 'baby' in the family find the teen years easier because the way has been paved by an older sister or brother? Has the age been lowered for certain privileges? Is he or she allowed to go along with an older sister or brother to see movies that the eldest never would have been allowed to see?

Of course, much depends on how the oldest siblings came through adolescence. If they were easy teenagers to raise, the parents may be relaxed and confident in their basic child-raising approach. If the oldest sibling had a difficult adolescence, however, the parents may be determined to do things differently. They may become much stricter, or they may feel that they were too strict and ease up a little. Younger siblings are very aware of how their older sister or brothers turned out and what the expectations are for them.

I've seen two patterns over and over. The first is the high-achieving eldest child followed by a younger sibling (usually of the same sex) who feels that he or she cannot match the achievements of the big brother or sister, so doesn't try. To avoid being measured by the achievements of the elder one, the younger cultivates a different image, choosing other activities, friends and interests. But the younger child never feels quite good enough. He or she secretly longs to be as bright, as athletic, as respected, but it doesn't happen. It rankles to have people saying, "Oh, you're so-and-so's little brother. Well, you sure are different."

In the other pattern, the oldest sibling is the weaker student, so embarrassed and intimidated by the achievements of the younger and by the competitive nature of the sibling relationship that he or she becomes withdrawn and leaves the family as soon as he or she can escape.

Divorce

There is no simple family pattern today. In a group of twenty teen-agers, you may find five living with both their natural parents, both still in first marriages. Nearly every family today has a different situ-ation – the combination of parents and step-parents, natural, step-, and half-siblings, grandparents, aunts, uncles, and various species of cousins creates an extremely complicated extended family with complicated emotional relationships. The effect of this on adoles-cents is different in every case, but the adolescent clearly must find some way to make sense of it all.

Because teenagers are trying to understand themselves, they must take into consideration all of the relationships which affect them. Adults often think that because teenagers are so involved with them-selves and their peers, they are not affected by the family constella-tion. However, the adults are models, and adolescents are trying to see whether they wish to emulate them.

The teenager's situation needs to be sympathetically examined. The youngster needs both parents and loves both parents. When one asks the child to be disloyal to one of the parents, the youngster is split. When divorced parents treat each other with respect, the children have a chance to develop positive relationships with each parent. They also feel relieved and thankful. They appreciate that their parents are making the best of a difficult situation. But parents who continually attack one another by word, deed, and innuendo, put their children in the impossible situation of feeling guilty whichever way they turn.

The parents' feelings about the divorce affect the way they treat their teenagers. If parents feel guilty, they often try to make up for it by letting the youngster have much more freedom than they normally would have. Parents also use the teenager as a way to make a point to the ex-partner. Children easily recognize and are quick to take advantage of the situation.

Parents often feel that teenagers can handle divorce, but the reality is that they have just as much difficulty as younger children.

Teenagers have told me that even though they had adjusted to the divorce when they were young children, during adolescence they re-lived the experience and it was much more painful. As they struggled to define their own identity and become independent, they were forced to come to terms with their parents' relationship and the divorce in a new way. They had to go back, re-experience, and re-examine their parents' relationship.

In some cases, divorce prompts one or both parents to experiment with lifestyle, confusing the youngsters' sense of stability and familiarity. As they work out their own values, teenagers often are confronted by sharply contrasting values held by their divorced parents. Once again, they feel as if they are in a tug-of-war.

Because teenagers are struggling with their sense of belonging, the divorce confronts them with additional problems. The question of what name they will use goes directly to the question of identity. They may choose to use a different name for a number of reasons. If they have been using a step-parent's last name, they may rebel against their mother or step-father by going back to the biological father's name. Or they may renew the relationship with their father after many years of minimal contact. The new relationship may be celebrated by the teenagers deciding to return to their father's name.

Children of divorce sometimes go looking elsewhere in the family for the love they no longer experience from their parents. They may yearn to be loved by the grandparents, or they may ask many questions about family members in an effort to find their roots. They want to be loved for themselves and not ignored because of their parents' divorce.

Divorce places an additional stress on the adolescent at school. In some cases, absentee parents show no interest in the student's schooling for months or even years, but then arrive unannounced at the school, wanting special attention. For the child, this piles embarrassment on top of the already existing pain of having been ignored. In other cases, a parent fails to show up for a very important occasion, such as a play or graduation. The youngster never knows what to expect.

Divorced parents may have conflicting attitudes toward homework and other school expectations. Parents commonly use school as another way to make points with each other. In the end, however, they only place additional stress on the teenager. If the divorced parents can possibly agree on what they expect of youngsters and stop fighting the lost marriage, they can offer support and clear boundaries to their children.

I have sat through dozens of parent conferences in which divorced parents discussed their child with the teacher. Tension, unspoken messages, and poor communication made these conferences difficult for all concerned. When the teenager was present, the parents' conflicting expectations for the student created additional tension. The possibility of having a fruitful conference often was better when the step-parents were included.

The most difficult sessions are those in which one parent attends with a new spouse while the other parent remains single. The single parent often is still dealing with the pain of the divorce while the new couple has begun to build a life together.

Another variety of divorce-induced stress on the teenager relates to money. Divorce often changes the teenager's life-style. The family home may be sold, the custodial parent and children may have to move into a smaller apartment, and the mother who used to be home now has to go to work. The family belongings are divided in two, increasing the youngster's sense of being split, and the family income has to be spread among two households and at least as many lawyers.

A sixteen-year-old girl who idolized her father saw him only a few times a year, but she talked about him between each visit. She was his "little girl". She looked at the boys on whom she had crushes in a similar way. They weren't quite real to her, and she had great difficulty establishing regular peer relationships with them. After graduation, she moved in with her father. She told me that she stopped idolizing him after about six months and began to appreciate him as a real person. After that, she also was able to develop more realistic relationships with males her age.

A seventeen-old-boy was very embarrassed because he had to help his father move out of the house. He felt terrible about having to do this because it made him feel that he was part of the separation.

An eighteen-year-old boy had hoped to go to a state university and had worked very hard to qualify. Yet, when it came time to ask his divorced father for financial help, he couldn't do it. He said, "I have to show him I can take care of myself".

Divorce involving children is a tragedy. There isn't any other word to express it. It may be the best of a difficult situation, and young-sters may even benefit from the divorce, but the trauma scars them. Teenagers are strongly affected by separation, the emotional dramas leading up to divorce, and the settlement of divorce – especially child custody battles.

At the very time when adolescents need to be working on their own relationships, they are absorbed in the destruction of the most fundamental relationship in their lives thus far – their family. During the time they should be breaking away from their parents as a way of gaining independence, they are doing the opposite. They are focused on their parents' problems, including having to choose which parent to live with.

One of the difficulties for teenagers is that they need parents who guide and limit, who are willing to be disliked, who are more concerned with the teenager's needs than with the teenager's approval. Divorce makes all this more difficult. Divorced parents are vulnerable. The parent with custody usually deals with the teenager in a nuts-and-bolts way, handling the everyday problems, sorrows and joys. The absentee parent often resents the amount of time the custodial parent spends with the youngsters and tries to make up for it by entertaining them and by avoiding confrontation. The custodial parent is weary under the load of house-keeping, chauffeuring to lessons and games, earning a living, and the loneliness of parenting, so that additional resentment builds when the absentee parent takes the teenager on a trip or buys special presents. The absentee parent wants to force intimacy that can develop only in time and without pressure. The custodial parent doesn't want the absentee parent threatening the kind of lifestyle followed in the home.

Teenagers are very sharp and see much more than one thinks. It is not surprising to find a teenager who tells the divorced parents to stop playing games and start acting like responsible adults. Or the teenager may step out of a ten-year loyalty to one parent, when new perceptions awaken and maturity arrives, and make amends to the other parent.

One in four US households with children is headed by a single parent – and that the figure is rising. Clearly, the one-parent family is not going to go away. We need to understand what that means to generations of children. We must find ways to help single parents. Some tend to over-protect their children because they feel vulnerable. It is easy for the parent to try to create a fortress against the world, trying to keep out hurt and strain. Other parents overload their children with responsibility to help carry the family. Under the burdens borne by so many single parents, it is not surprising when the single parent focuses on personal needs, becomes depressed, and loses track of what is happening in the teenager's life.

In spite of the difficulties, many single parents develop meaningful and nourishing relationships with their teenagers. Sometimes, the removal of strain from a difficult marriage frees both the adolescent and the parents to have a better relationship, which may provide some compensation for the loss of family life. In other cases, the mutual need strengthens the bond between parent and adolescent.

When single parents raise teenagers, special stresses occur. It is difficult enough for two parents to raise teenagers and to come through with dignity intact. In the single parent's case, the work is not shared. The burden falls on one adult. The single parent, as well as the teenager, is trying to recover from the wounds of the divorce. A family is needed and the parent is under stress to provide it. In the attempt to be responsible, the single parent is vulnerable to the child's criticism, spoken and unspoken, especially if the parent has come to rely on the child as a confidant. The parent may have no one else to share secrets and frustrations with, but this creates a gap between the teenager and peers, and increases the emotional burden carried by the youngster.

It often helps if single parents explore what resources are available in the community to supplement what they are not able to provide. They can invite the teenager's friends over, take them on a trip, or join forces with another single parent and teenaged friend. This helps foster a family mood in a relaxed way. Joining such organizations as Parents Without Partners may also be helpful.

Remarriage

After a marriage breakup, it takes about three years for the marriage partners to completely separate from one another. For the child, however, the bond to his or her parents continues throughout life. When parents remarry, they generally hope and expect that everything will be wonderful, that the mistakes learned from the past will not be repeated. For the child, however, the formation of a new family often conjures up memories of the original family and evokes anger and blame. Many children never give up hoping that their parents will come back together, but the remarriage of one of the parents usually ends that fantasy.

Step families

Remarriage has many effects on children. First, the child's natural place in the family is altered when two families merge. Let us look at some examples.

The oldest boy has been catered to, given in to. With his parent's remarriage, he experiences the loss of authority over his younger siblings. In the remarriage he becomes a younger sibling to new step-brothers or sisters. His long accustomed position of authority has been cut from under him and he reacts strongly. Where is his comfortable kingdom with his servants? He wants nothing to do with the new siblings. One of them is a girl close to his age, and he finds himself with a rival for the privileges he is used to having.

This child is youngest, a bit pampered, looks up to her older siblings, always reaching beyond, feeling that she must fulfill the expectations of those ahead. With remarriage, she finds younger children whom she barely knows looking up to her. Now, she must set an example and share space and time in the family. She is not overjoyed. On the other hand, she feels pride at being able to guide a younger step-sister.

So much depends on how the teenager feels about his or her position in the family.

A sixteen-year-old boy resented both his parents and his step-parents because every time he and his two teenaged brothers proved difficult, they were shunted off to the other parent. Neither set of adults would commit themselves to the boys.

A fifteen-year-old girl disliked her step-father so much that she could not bear to go to English class because the teacher so strongly resembled her step-father. She had no problem with the teacher, but, she explained, she could not have an objective relationship with him.

A fourteen-year-old boy was delighted when his mother remarried. His parents had divorced when he was a baby, and he never had met his real father. He enjoyed the companionship of another male in the household.

A seventeen-year-old boy resented his step-father's expectations. He could not compete with the outstanding academic record of his new step-brother and gave up trying. His step-father's attitude was "prove yourself", and the boy felt that he could do nothing right. He couldn't stand the conversation at the table which centered around "your children" and "my children".

An eighteen-year-old girl who never had been able to communicate with her father found an interested listener in her new step-mother. With her step-mother's support, she had a serious talk with her father and overcame years of hesitation. She told me, "It took me eighteen years for us to get to know each other, and I couldn't have done it without my step-mother."

In another case, two teenaged boys were having troubles. Their step-father's children had not turned out well, and he wanted his step-sons to "make it". They were treated very strictly. Their mother felt caught in between her sons and her new husband. The seventeen-year-old found it difficult to see his mother in this situation and wanted to move out. He said, "I don't want to make trouble for her".

I could go on and on with examples from step-families. Each is unique and has its own time of adjustment. As with single parents, remarriage is now a common part of our culture. We need to build support groups to help step-families survive in as wholesome a way as possible.

Where the parent enters a series of relationships which do not develop into a marriage, the youngsters go through the loss over and over again. Even if they are not completely pleased with the parent's partner at the time, they share with the parent the loss, the sense of starting again, and the vulnerability of being alone again. The children may celebrate that the man-friend or woman-friend is gone, but they still long for a permanent family.

Despite all that teenagers say in their moments of frustration, they wish to love and be loved by their families. They know that they have been influenced by their mother, father, and siblings, and they sense that they carry their family within them. The challenge they face is how to develop their own individuality in the context of being a family member.

Chapter Fifteen

Teenagers and friends

When you have a friend, life is worth living.

Ninth grade boy

When you have a friend, the sun is shining.

Ninth grade girl

"No," said the little prince, "I am looking for friends. What does that mean – tame?"

"It is an act too often neglected", said the fox. "It means to establish ties …"

"But I have made him my friend, and now he is unique in all the world."

And the roses were very much embarrassed.

"You are beautiful, but you are empty," he went on. "One could not die for you. To be sure, an ordinary passerby would think that my rose looked just like you – the rose that belongs to me. But in herself alone she is more important than all the hundreds of you other roses: because it is she that I have watered; because it is she that I have put under the glass globe; because it is she that I have sheltered behind the screen; because it is for her that I have killed the caterpillars (except the two or three that we saved to become butterflies); because it is she that I have listened to, when she grumbled, or boasted, or even sometimes when she said nothing. Because she is my rose."

And he went back to meet the fox.

"Goodbye", he said.

"Goodbye", said the fox. "And now here is my secret, a very simple secret: It is only with the heart that one can see rightly; what is essential is invisible to the eye."

Antoine de Saint-Exupery, The Little Prince.[1]

Friendship is important throughout life, but at no time is the need as desperate as during adolescence. As youngsters begin to pull away from their parents, they need another anchor, a place of comfort. As long as they have friends, they are not alone in the shaky transition from dependence to independence. While parents symbolize authority, one's friends symbolize acceptance.

Although friends are necessary, they are also replaceable. This gives the teenager a sense of freedom. The feeling that parents and siblings are with them forever makes teenagers feel secure, but it also makes them feel suffocated. They want to try out different friends: friends from school, friends from the neighborhood, friends who share a special interest, friends who make them feel happy, friends with whom they can discuss their problems, friends with whom they can be silly, friends with whom they like to go to the library, the movies, fishing, for a pizza, or for quiet walks.

I remember my own hurt feelings when my seventeen-year-old girlfriend said that she liked having different friends for different occasions. At the time, I saw none of her perceptiveness. Instead, I was jealous and thought, "Wouldn't real friends do everything together?"

Friends and identity

Because teenagers are in the process of finding out who they are, friends play a special role. Together, they can discuss what they like and don't like, whom they like and don't like, and why. Each learns something about life from the other, and each knows that he or she won't be judged. Together, they explore people, places, ideas and interests.

"I really like Jean. We have so much fun. We take out fashion magazines and plan all kinds of outfits. We laugh and have such a good time."

"You can't tell what Carol is like from the outside. She's really very sensitive and is interested in dreams and things like that."

"We call our group the 'terrible threesome' and we eat lunch together and read comics and talk about superheroes. No one else understands us, but we like each other."

An eighteen-year-old girl was describing her relationship with a classmate. "We understood each other very well. We knew we were completely different. As long as we stayed on certain topics, we could be good friends. But I never went to her parties or did things with her outside-of-school friends, and she would have been bored with my friends. We would never have become friends if I had gone to a large school. But here, we found how much we enjoyed each other as long as we respected the limits of the relationship. We laughed and joked and got along wonderfully with each other. We confided in each other, too. But that was as far as the relationship could go."

A sixteen-year-old said, "You have to be careful when you come to a new school who your friends are. You become identified with those friends and that could affect you for a long time. I wish I could have watched everyone from outside a glass window for a long time before choosing my group of friends. But it doesn't work that way."

Friends provide companionship which eases the loneliness of life. Having a very close friend is like having a special brother or sister. A twenty-one-year-old explained that he and his friend had been close for years because neither had brothers. "We became brothers. We affirmed each other's worth as males. We found we shared common views and could teach each other what we knew. For example, we learned from each other how to deal with girls. We learned to accept each other and to give mutual support."

When a teenager does not have an older sister or brother to learn from, friends are a fine substitute. Friends tell you what to expect and how to handle yourself. You don't have to pretend with a good friend, you can be yourself.

Friendships are like miniature communities. Teenagers have to learn how to reach out, how to understand, when to forgive, and when to be upset. In other words, many of the same lessons the youngster learned within the family now have to be learned again in a new context. In the family, the child can make many mistakes and still be loved, but a friendship is more vulnerable. If teenagers take their friends for granted or treat them as they sometimes treat their families, the friendships may well be over.

In the family, the teenager is one of many. The teenager's needs have to take their place with everyone else's. Attention is not focused on the teenager. If the teenager puts on a new outfit or cultivates a new persona, it is noticed but it doesn't always get front stage. Friends, however, notice everything and usually support the teenager in experimenting (within reason). The parents know that each fad will pass, but the teenager sees the fad as necessity and is supported in this by friends. When I was in high school, I had to have a dog collar around my ankle. It sounds ridiculous now, but it was necessity then. All "in" high school girls wore them. Friends tell the teenager if the jean cuffs are folded correctly, how the shoe laces should be tied or not tied, and what kind of make-up to wear. Friends form a mutual admiration society.

Friends also often act as surrogate parents. They monitor each other's behavior and get through to the friend as no adult can. Frank told me, "Rich is a creep. He acts like a real jerk. I don't even want to hang around him any more. People get mad at him because he's so arrogant and condescending. He deserves what he gets. I've told him that and he does listen to me. No one else can get to him. I'll try again."

Conformity

Friends help teenagers become independent from their parents, but they exert a new kind of authority – conformity.

Because teenage friendships usually center on school life, it is hard on the teenager when their friends attend different schools. Such youngsters have a circle of strong friendships in their neighborhoods and another at school. Others have separate circles of school friends and home friends even though they go to the same school. Neighborhood friends are almost like family members. Then there are friendships from religious training, which may become very strong if there is an active youth program at the church or synagogue.

In school, most friendships become competitive. To be friends with certain people you have to conform to their expectations. It is difficult to be your own person and have friendships unless the friends share your nonconformist behavior. Even if the teenager chooses not to conform to the group, the pressure is there. The teenager constantly has to choose, and this takes more energy than most adults realize.

In many schools, cliques dictate what is acceptable and what is not. Teenagers are concerned not to behave in such a way that they won't be accepted by the clique they want to be a part of. The need to be "cool" and not a "nerd" is strong pressure on both boys and girls. Dan may want to befriend Phil, but he won't, because of what the group thinks of Phil. Dan is afraid that the group may think he's like Phil. Only a very securely popular teenager can buck the often unspoken code of the group.

The friendships within the clique are insecure as well. There is always the chance that the position of one of the group will be weakened, or that he or she will be isolated and pushed out. Blackballing and back-biting can make life very difficult for a sensitive adolescent. This kind of political pressure in friendships makes it difficult for honest relationships to exist. However, even though many friendships are fickle, they still rule the social scene. It is not uncommon for teenagers to have only one or two close friends, even though they appear to have many.

In many large schools, the cliques are so strong that teenagers have to choose their extracurricular activities carefully to preserve an image. The activity has to be accepted by the group – certain activities are out, they are only for jerks. A twenty-one-year-old was reflecting on her experiences, first in a large public junior high school, and then in a small Catholic high school. "In a small private school, you are already making a choice to be different, and this affects your friendships. They are much deeper. You don't have to ruled by the cliques as much, and so you're not so superficial."

You have only to walk through a high school yard at lunchtime to get a feeling for the groups. In many schools, they are based on race as well as on lifestyle. Each group congregates in its own special place. There are the "jocks", the "burn-outs", the "preppies", the "aggies", the "intellectual jerks", the "cheerleaders", the "hoods", the "nerds", the "stoners", and the loners. The names vary from school to school, but the categories don't change much.

Boy-girl friendships

A platonic boy-girl friendship can be very nurturing for both. Without the complications of romance, the boy and girl can find this one of the most meaningful relationships they have. In a platonic relationship, each learns about the other sex; they find out the male

and female point of view. They often act as matchmakers, mother-
or father-confessors, and buddies.

The following note is an example:

Janet: So why are you so mad at me? You seem like you are.

Steve: No way Jay. Just having problems with my parents. They're
yelling at me. I'll start being real cheerful. The only thing is
the person who likes you, you don't like. So I feel bad for
him. Well, that's life.

Janet: Now, how do you know? Come on, you really don't know. I
could like Tom or Joe or Bill, and you really don't know. He
could even be not in this school, ya know. And don't let your
parents get you down. They love ya, they do. I know that's
hard to believe and you're goin, Wait, if they really love me,
why do they yell at me? Hey, Steve, if they didn't yell at ya,
you'd be lost, and life can't be all nice, but try to understand
them, OK?

Steve: You know, Jan, you might really like this guy, whoever he is, but
I know that there is a pretty nice guy out there that likes you.
Hey! he might not be a raving beauty but I'm sure he won't
treat you wrong. You know you've really turned into a pleasant
person to be around and now I guess I could say I've found a
friend who is a girl. I really thank you for this nice note. You're
so right, but sometimes I just feel like leaving the house.

Sometimes, the platonic relationship grows into romance, but more
often it acts as a stabilizing force in teenage life. If a girl hasn't been
asked to a big dance by her crush, or if the boy is not ready to step
out into the dating world, they can go together. It also works the
other way. If the boy has been turned down and the girl is not interested in any particular boy, the platonic date allows them both to
attend the event, and have a good time, without worrying about the
other's intentions.

Some of the most wonderful high school relationships are platonic
friendships. They are tender and affirming at a time when all else
around the teenager is unstable and threatening.

When girlfriend-boyfriend relationships develop, they often affect
friendships. The teenager can spend only so much time with friends
or sweethearts, and they have to parcel out their time. Girls tend to

be more jealous of their best friends' time than boys are. Girls feel let down, used, and dumped-on when their girlfriends leave them for a boy. They want equal time. Part of the reaction may be jealousy that they don't have a boyfriend of their own. One girl told how excited her friends were when she was beginning to get together with her boyfriend, but once the relationship began, they became sullen and complained to her, "But we never see you".

"I found I was under enormous pressure", she said. "No matter what I did, I couldn't win."

Boys seem to be more accepting of the changes without turning them into personal issues. Friendship between two boys can be strongly affected if they both like the same girl. In some cases, one boy steps aside for the other. Or one of the boys feels guilty because of his secretive behavior.

The boys are used to sharing with each other, but they can't talk about this, either because they know it will hurt their friendship or because they are not proud of their behavior. Or they can leave it up to the girl.

Friendship between two girls is also affected if they both like the same boy. Sometimes, a whole group will like a boy, and one girl will plot to make a friend look bad so that she herself will stand out and get his attention. Other times, the girls will celebrate the birth of a romance between one of their group and the coveted young man. All too often, however, the old maxim, "All's fair in love and war" takes over, and teenagers are left feeling betrayed and hurt.

Another element that has entered the arena of friendships is the accusation of homosexuality. The accusation may be true, but it usually is not, and it comes from lack of understanding or jealousy. Girls with a very close, almost sisterly relationship may be deeply hurt by being tagged lesbians. Likewise, boys who express affection for each other, even in a moderate form, can be isolated as "fags". Such incidents may cause deep pain and even lasting harm to the girls and boys who are maliciously labeled.

A special kind of friendship occurs between girls and the buddies of their big brothers. If the age difference is not too great, the girl may take on the mixture of friend and "crush". This may include teasing, camaraderie, long talks, and advice.

Friends vs. parents

One of the great issues in the teen years is whether parents approve of one's friends. Because friends represent the outer world, parents tend to judge them on whether they fit the image which the parents want their youngster to project into the community. I will always remember a day in which I had parent conferences with the parents of two close friends. The first parent said, "I don't think Jim is a very good influence on Ron". An hour later, one of Jim's parents said, "I don't think Ron is a very good influence on Jim". They were both right.

When parents look at friends, they are probably asking, "Does this represent my child's taste?" or "What effect will this friendship have on my youngster?" or "I really like this youngster. I hope the friendship lasts" or "What does my child see in him?"

Coming to know the friends is an important way of figuring out what is happening with the teenager. It is surprising to find out why a youngster chooses a friend. For example, Alice befriended a difficult, rebellious girl, Dana, who constantly was in trouble. Alice, of course, was constantly defending her friend. In a conversation between mother and daughter, Alice said, "I don't approve of what she is doing, but I feel I can support her and maybe change her behavior". From the outside, it looked as if the two were bosom buddies. Once the mother had this insight she trusted Alice more and she too was able to show appropriate concern for Dana.

As their teacher, I had a similar conversation with Alice. She said, "I'm wondering why she did it (break a very important rule at school) and how to prevent another occasion without making her feel like I'm just another person telling her how badly she behaves and all the things she does wrong".

Naturally, there are times when a friendship seems to be harmful and needs to be limited or ended, but parents should proceed gingerly. Teenagers understandably resent people telling them who their friends should be. This kind of sensitivity can be a sore point in family relations. Nonetheless, parents should trust their instincts. If they feel that the situation is very bad, they should have a frank talk with their son or daughter. (Their credibility, however, may rest on whether they have respected their teenager's other relationships or whether they have found something wrong about each friend.)

In some cases, the teenagers, especially the young ones, are grateful for parent restrictions. Thirteen-year-old Ellen was on the phone speaking to a friend who was describing a party planned for Friday night. Ellen said, "Wait a minute, I'll ask my mother if I can go". Ellen put her hand over the phone and signaled to her mother, "Say no". Then she got back on the phone and said in a sad voice, "Gee, my mother won't let me".

Parents can get to know the friends by inviting them in, sitting down with them and talking, inviting them for dinner or for an excursion. Otherwise, they may not have much basis for their opinions of their child's friends.

There is no question that teenagers can be adversely affected by poor friendships, and sometimes it is so bad that a major move is necessary. I have known parents who figuratively have picked up their teenaged sons or daughters and taken them, kicking and screaming, to a new school. The children hated the parents for doing it. In many cases, however, the youngsters were grateful a year later when they had gained a new perspective. In other cases, the youngster's anger sabotaged the parents' efforts and the new situation did not work out. Changing schools but keeping the old friends is a sure way to abort the new start.

I know of parents who changed neighborhoods to move their children away from a group. Some have gone as far as changing cities or sending the youngster to live with a relative for a year to break up a destructive friendship.

Teenagers generally move through a variety of friendships. As they mature, so does their taste in friends. They need support rather than criticism as they work through their friendships. Because friendships are such a major part of the teenagers' development, it may be very important if the parent can gain the youngster's trust enough to talk about these problems. Just as the friend provides a safe haven from parental problems, the parent can be an objective anchor in working through problems with friends.

No friends

Teenagers can be utterly miserable if they have no friends. They feel left out, unloved, and worth nothing. There are loners in every crowd, and their lot is painful. Wherever they go, they have trouble making friends. They may grow used to it, but it hurts. They may pretend they don't care, but they do. They may take on an arrogant air, but they are only protecting themselves. They may complain to their parents and teachers that they want to move, change schools, do anything that will bring them friends. They may try to buy friendship by inviting a classmate for an expensive weekend or by giving gifts. Or they may sell themselves and do what they really don't approve of – a sign that the situation is desperate.

In some situations, the youngster simply doesn't fit into the scene. Even when the fault lies more with the scene than with the youngster, the youngster suffers. In another place the young person would find someone with similar interests, and friendship would not be a problem. A new school may make a very big difference, giving the youngster an opportunity for a fresh start.

Once a group labels a teenager as odd, the youngster has little chance to make friends and be accepted. A fresh start, a group outside of school, a job, or a summer program are some ways to help the youngster start again.

If teenagers are without friends, they need their parents' support even more than before. Doing things together, having talks, finding common interests all will help them over the lonely period. Parents cannot take the place of friends their own age, but they can do a great deal to make life bearable and even happy.

Chapter Sixteen

Teenagers and the schools

We don't need no education
We don't need no thought control.
No dark sarcasm in the classroom
Teachers leave us kids alone.
Hey teacher – leave us kids alone.
All in all, it's just another brick in the wall.
All in all, you're jut another brick in the wall.
Pink Floyd Music Ltd. 1979, Lyrics by Roger Waters

A few months ago, I had an occasion to speak to a visiting graduate student from Nigeria. As he shared his observations about American society, he shook his head at the waste of talent and potential in students. "If the children in my country had the opportunities the students have here," he said, "they would celebrate". He found it difficult to believe the lack of interest and motivation in the young people he had met.

American education

It is no secret that American education is in crisis. It is commonplace to hear educators calling for reform. Does not every generation have its frustrations with the old views and the old ways? Aren't new ideas always calling out to be recognized and heard? Then what is new about the crisis today? It seems to me that the crisis is not about whether to have separate classes for gifted children or enough classes for minority children or stronger requirements for graduation. All these are important and legitimate concerns. More basic, however, is our fundamental approach to children, to human beings. Something is working at the core of our values that produces hostility, alienation between teenagers and adults (especially parents and teachers), causing teenagers to see adults as enemies. This view permeates television, videos, songs, and movies and, more than anything else, it permeates the way young people speak and think.

One of my strongest impressions from working with young people who have come out of large public schools is of lack of trust. They want to know what the teacher's "game" is. They don't believe that a teacher wants to help them. They are surprised and at first suspicious that a teacher will phone their home to speak to their parents or that a teacher will call them to talk about a problem or to offer help. They identify adults with punishment, and when the issue is not punitive, they are unsure how to react.

Another strong impression, especially with so-called "gifted" students, is that they have a narrow focus of thinking. Their minds are sharp – but closed. Having been identified as gifted, they are smug. Their training has not prepared them for social situations where doing and giving count more than superficial knowing.

When I speak with high school teachers who are teaching "cream of the crop" students in honors and advanced placement courses, they tell me how much they enjoy their work, how motivated their students are by pressure from home and by college requirements, and how much advanced material they can teach. They are concerned about the standardized exams that they are teaching toward and the college requirements that their students must meet.

They are less concerned, however, with educating for social change. The question, "Is there life after college?" seems not to come up. They are not involved in the rest of the school, and they don't associate with the majority of students who may also be bright but who are certainly unmotivated. They have carved out a safe niche for themselves and feel sorry for their colleagues from whom horror stories abound.

The underlying concepts of education today are materialistic, and the underlying motivation is self-achievement (although there are many exceptions to this statement, among teachers and students). I believe that the alienation we are experiencing stems from the lack of meaning in our culture, that it is a gut-level reaction by our young people to the picture that there is nothing more to life than chance and natural selection, and that our survival as a civilization has less to do with how smart some of us are and more with how we work together and understand each other. A society can go for only so long serving its young people stones instead of bread before they strike out in defiance and anger or withdraw into passivity or fantasy worlds.

In his book, *All Grown Up and No Place To Go*, David Elkind writes, "In our day, the American high school has become a school for scandal in a literal sense. As at least a half-dozen recent reports make clear, the majority of high schools in this country are doing a poor job of educating teenagers ... A less publicized but more serious scandal is the failure of our schools to provide teenagers with a protected place in which they can get on with the task of building an identity."[1]

It is not surprising that the schools are struggling. They reflect society's values in the setting of teachers' salaries and budget priorities. Responsibility has been placed on schools for all that is not going well in the home. The schools are supposed to deal with children suffering from parental stress, broken homes, lack of discipline, and lack of goals. In addition, the schools are in competition with television, drugs, suburban shopping malls, and jobs. Students often spend more time in front of a television than in front of a teacher. These diversions of society – television, jobs, shopping malls and drugs – provide a counter-classroom culture which undermines the authority of teachers and diminishes the importance of education in a teenager's eyes. The effects of television and drugs have become well known. But teenage employment has only in the last few years begun to be examined for its impact on teenagers' development and relationship to school. Whereas teenagers in the past tended to work to contribute to the family income or to pay for necessities, most of today's teenagers work for luxuries. These youngsters staff the counters of fast-food establishments, wait on customers at retail stores, or work in factories. They often work on school nights and on weekends. Their jobs interfere with their involvement in school and in the family. Homework takes second place to the teenager's reporting to work on time, school activities play second fiddle to job priorities, and participation in school assemblies, class trips and special family occasions are less important than serving one's shift on the job. In the past, jobs were seen as a way youngsters could assume responsibility and learn to appreciate their parents' efforts to support them. But that has changed. In an attempt to understand how adolescents have changed in relation to their jobs, researchers have turned their attention to teenage employment. Ellen Greenberger and Laurence Steinberg describe their findings:

"Among the most striking of these discoveries are that extensive part-time employment during the school year may undermine the youngsters' education; that working leads less often to the accumulation of savings than to a higher level of luxury consumer spending; that working appears to promote, rather than deter, some forms of delinquent behaviour; that working long hours under stressful conditions leads to increased alcohol and marijuana use; and – the coup de grace – that teen-age employment, instead of fostering respect for work, often leads to increased cynicism about the pleasures of productive labor … Stated more broadly, extensive commitment to a job may interfere with the work of growing up. In a society where it is possible to make a different life from that of one's parents, and where the diversity of choices that lie before most youngsters is truly staggering, adolescents need time for identity clarification."[2]

Whereas teenagers need time to find out who they are, involve themselves in a variety of activities in school and in the community, most teenage jobs concentrate on specific tasks that are repeated over and over again:

"Too much time in the adolescent workplace is likely to mean too little time for exploration – including exploration of better, more adult jobs that do not offer pay; for discovering academic and extracurricular interests that are satisfying; for testing out changing conceptions of oneself, and for reflection that leads to the meaningful integration of one's experiences. Sheer lack of time or freedom, for the sake of getting on the payroll early, may interfere with the important psychological work of adolescence."[3]

What are the choices?

Like most American adults, I am a product of public schools from kindergarten through college, and I believe that I had as good an education as was offered in the forties and fifties. School was a haven in the slums of New York City and in a small Florida town. I loved learning and I loved my teachers. Although the schools were large, I had many challenging and caring teachers. Society was stable and the schools were considered important and valuable in the community.

However, when someone tells me that public education protects the American way of life and that private or independent education is indoctrination, I differ. No school is values-free. Public education as well as private education has a view of the human being which is reflected in everything that is done, from the selection of a text-book and the choice of a song or poem, to a teacher's educational methods and the management philosophies of the school district.

When parents and students decide where the youngster should attend high school, many factors come into play. Most students move from year to year without giving any thought to changing, either because they are satisfied or because they are not aware of any alternative. Who are the people who do not accept the status quo? They fall into several categories:

–Wealthy or upper middle class high-achievement-oriented families who either move to school districts where the public schools have an excellent reputation and offer outstanding college preparatory programs or send their children to private preparatory schools to ensure their attendance at a prestigious university.

– Families for whom education within a context of religious values is very important. They choose a school that suits their religious orientation, be it Catholic, Jewish, Episcopal, Seventh-Day Adventist, Christian fundamentalist or other. In many cases, the tuition is a strain, but, because religious schools usually are church-subsidized, tuition often is adjusted to the family's income.

– Families specifically looking for an alternative educational method to the traditional school – public or private – which will prepare their children for college, may have a non-sectarian spiritual viewpoint, or may be based on some other view of the child. Such families turn to Waldorf schools, Montessori schools, "free" schools, private "basic" schools, or other alternative schools. Because these schools are not subsidized, they depend on tuitions but typically offer tuition assistance within their means.

– Families who move restlessly from school to school, within the public system or crossing over from public to private and back. These parents are unhappy with what their children are experiencing. They feel that their children should have more opportunities, should be better prepared for college, and should be more challenged.

Sometimes, they have children with special needs not being met in the present school.

Parents who move from public to private schools have to make basic life decisions. Because they are also paying taxes for public education, and they receive no tax benefit for private school tuition, they make a sacrifice. They set this kind of education as priority and other things must wait. Often, both parents work, and they forego vacations, a new car, new clothes, a nicer house and other amenities that many families have. Many other families would like the option of changing schools but cannot afford it, even with tuition assistance. For those families, the monopoly that the public education system has over tax dollars seems unfair and wrong.

For many of the families who leave the public system, changing school is an expression of their desire for something else. For many, it offers another chance. It is often a vote cast at tremendous sacrifice.

What is happening in public schools?

Although a growing number of students attend private schools, most young people are still being educated in public schools. What happens in public schools has such an impact on our society that we should understand and exercise some responsibility for what is happening. The public schools reflect the values, tensions and stresses of our society in many ways, such as in declining academic standards and increasing violence, drug abuse and crime. Schools once provided a safe place for teenagers to grow without pressure from the "real" world. However, teenagers cannot be naive in today's schools; they have to be always alert to protect themselves from danger while having difficulty relating to what is being taught. The schools have become large, impersonal factories where teachers and students often are alienated from each other and from the system and do not have much contact with each other. Students feel that they are numbers rather than people. How did the schools become such big institutions? At the turn of the century, about 519,000 students were being educated, 8.5% of the total youth population (ages 14–17). Those being educated constituted an elite minority. The rest were learning trades, working on farms or in cities, or home raising families. By 1981, the figure had risen to 13.5 million, over 94 percent of the youth population. The dropout rate, however, has remained steady at about 25 percent. The impact of the American high school on the general society was insignificant in the early 1900s compared to today where it exerts a powerful impact.

Because almost every young person in the country is enrolled in a high school, the schools provide a broad spectrum of courses to meet many different needs. In addition, during the 1980s, special-interest groups demanded that the schools provide for special situations, such as handicapped, gifted and minority students as well as for those who did not speak English. Neighborhood schools could not offer the advanced courses wanted by college-bound students, the diversity wanted by those who demanded more electives, and remedial classes for children of special needs. Consequently, school programs were analyzed in ways similar to the way factory production is studied and analyzed, and the answer was one that might be very effective for manufacturing but which is devastating for children – schools must become cost-efficient through consolidation – regardless of their effects.

The move to big schools

What happens when we give up small schools where parents and teachers know each other and where the youngster feels part of a community? What are the advantages? Children have more opportunities. They can have better equipment and a larger choice of classes. We can make more efficient use of facilities, teachers and classrooms. Larger athletic facilities can be provided because more students are using them. In larger schools, advanced science and language courses can be offered because there are enough students who want them to justify hiring the extra teachers. Slower students who otherwise would be incorporated into a mixed class now can go at their own pace in a special class.

We can have a more diverse population because students come from many areas. Students will get to know teenagers from other parts of the town or county. The racial mix can be more diverse than in small schools.

What are the disadvantages? Bigness in any institution breeds certain problems. Large schools require large administrations and supporting bureaucracy and endless papers to fill out. Administrators find it difficult to know every teacher and student. Relationships become more formal and impersonal.

Teachers are teaching many more students, but they don't get to know them as well. In a small school, one teacher may teach world history, US history, geography, and civics to a small number of students. In the large school, the teacher becomes a specialist, teaching fewer subjects to more students. The teacher has less opportunity to get to know all the students in the school. Teachers and students feel that they are in a factory. (Indeed, the architecture of many high schools resembles factory architecture, although some look like fortresses.)

When there is less intimacy between teacher and student, a very important person is removed from the student's life – the mentor. When students have an adult who gets to know them in a variety of activities, that person can help the youngsters create a picture of themselves. The adult is available for conversations, to share interests, to recognize their gifts, to see them outside of school. The student comes to see the teacher as a person and not only as an authority figure. Having a small group of teachers who know the student well helps the youngster gain insight, evaluation, and support rather than anonymity and lack of connection.

Small schools become communities. Parents, teachers and students see each other in the neighborhood, shopping, at church, at a movie. They have opportunities to see each other as people. In large, consolidated school districts, parents are less apt to feel a connection. There are more teachers to get to know, and the familiar neighborhood teenagers are absorbed into a large and unfamiliar student body. Because parents and teachers do not know each other, they are less apt to find their shared values. School policies and classroom practices become removed from the parents, who have little chance to voice their opinions except through cumbersome channels. In some schools, a special form has to be filled out if a parent wants to complain about something going on in class. Then the principal meets with the parent, and the complaint form goes into the teacher's file. It is considered inappropriate for the parent to call the teacher directly to discuss the problem. If each concern felt by a parent results in a form going into a teacher's file, it is no wonder that teachers feel threatened by parent involvement.

Discipline becomes impersonal and enmeshed in bureaucracy.

How often do parents in a large school have an opportunity to talk with a teacher about a child's problems either at school or at home before the problems assume major proportions, such as running away or suspension?

How is the student affected in the large school? When students go to school near their neighborhood, they still feel the concern of their parents, but when they attend a large school many miles away from home, they feel disconnected from parental guidance. They know that their parents have little chance of finding out what is going on. They are more likely to question rules, break them, or learn to get around them.

In a smaller school, it is easier for parents and teachers to find out who is doing what. By having more contact with the students, the faculty and administration have a better chance to discourage antisocial behavior and to attend to those causing the problems. In the large school, more students are breaking rules and behaving differently from the way they would at home. The more rules students break, the more other teenagers question the rules and learn to get around them.

When a youngster is absent from a smaller school, teachers have a better possibility of noticing and following up. In a large school, the teacher has so many students to be aware of that impersonal methods are used, and a child's absence often goes unnoticed. I have spoken to dozens of students who have been severely truant from many large schools before their parents ever received a call.

At the time in their lives when they need care and attention, youngsters do not thrive in large schools.

The charter school movement in the US has opened up new possibilities for teachers and parents to choose a different approach and curriculum and to have a smaller size school. Homeschooling has also offered new possibilities for parent choice.

What has happened to the curriculum?

Up through the forties most high schools had prescribed curricula. Ninth graders took certain courses, tenth graders took other courses, and so on. There was a limited number of electives, but for the most part, depending on which track you were on, your courses were laid out for you.

If you planned to go to college, you chose which language you wanted and whether you wanted elective music, art, or woodshop. You moved out of a prescribed course only if it was too difficult. During eleventh grade, some students took a full year of Algebra II while others finished after the first semester. When you took senior history, the teacher had a pretty good idea what history courses the student had previously taken. Behind this plan was the idea that an educated youngster needed certain courses either for the self-discipline of the course or for the specific knowledge and skills it taught. The teenager leaving high school needed to have certain knowledge in the humanities, sciences, and possibly the arts.

If you were not going to college, there were other kinds of requirements suited for the direction in which you were heading. Courses in secretarial skills, basic English, wood- and metal shop were offered. This system put students on a track which could be supplemented if they later wanted to go to college. Other schools did not offer tracks but had a program for most students with elective courses for those with particular interests.

In the fifties and sixties the high school curriculum became more and more fragmented. In addition, federal educational policy makers required that courses suiting special needs be offered. As David Elkind put it, "The aim of education – to provide young people with the basic skills, the fundamental knowledge, and the human values that will enable them both to realize themselves and to become productive, responsible citizens – has become enmeshed in a set of special interests."

Fragmentation influenced the curriculum. The integrated curriculum was replaced with a "smorgasbord curriculum". Students could now approach their education the way they approached a supermarket. They could pick and choose their courses regardless of the relationship of one course to another. What they wanted at the moment became more important than what they needed in the long run.

A separation occurred where there once had been a concern for the whole person, for the teenager's psychological and intellectual growth. As subjects became separated into compartments, so did the attitude toward life. Values, concerns, interests – instead of flowing from one area of life to another – became fixed in separate boxes.

With the growing emphasis on standards and accountability, teaching to the test has taken priority over teaching for learning. This has led to increased pressure on young children as well as on middle-school and high school students.

Changes in society

While changes were being made in curriculum and in the size of schools, significant changes also were occurring in society. The family as it had been known for generations in American life was changing.

As the divorce rate climbed, youngsters found themselves left without stability or family identity. The custodial parent went to work to support the family. More than ever before, American youngsters were filled with anger and alienation.

In many families, both parents took jobs to deal with higher costs and the desire for a higher standard of living, leaving the youngsters with unsupervised time on their hands.

Families moved more often, parents increasingly were transferred from one state to another, leaving behind their familiar roots and traditions.

Homes too often became empty soulless places from which youngsters fled to join their contemporaries in shopping-malls and street corners.

During the 1960s, drugs entered all areas of society and now are common in cities, suburbs, towns and rural communities.

Whereas television had previously been regarded as a supplementary form of entertainment in homes, also during the 1960s, television moved into people's lives, taking over time that had been given to conversation, family activities, reading, community activities, playing and chores. Teenagers now entered high school after years of television viewing, with passive acceptance of what came to them on the screen, the inability to discriminate real emotions from televised ones, and information coming from the television authority. Attention spans decreased and less time was given to homework and reading.

Crime and violence also increased in American society.

All these changes affected the adolescents. Since then, many other changes have occurred. Alternative life-styles have yielded to the more conventional lifestyles and attitudes, concern for jobs and money has become stronger. Students are more concerned with status and conformity than they were earlier. They are less concerned with social reform or ideals. Some of these changes have been reflected in the schools as well. More parents are concerned with basic education and with discipline. But the basic problems with the schools and with teaching as a profession have not changed.

The general standard of education has decreased, leading even the prestigious universities to offer remedial English to incoming students. Despite these negative influences, many idealistic young people are dedicated to positive changes in society.

The role of teachers

Teachers also were affected by these changes. In their own lives, they faced the same problems as other families. In addition, there was a sharp drop in their professional status. Education no longer was seen as an important agent in forming young people's attitudes, skills and thoughts. The problems in society came into the schools. Drugs, crime, violence, theft, vandalism, alienation, lack of motivation, lack of support and loss of traditions all were dumped into the schools.

As the schools grew bigger and as the connections between people became less personal, schools became frightening places to teach in, and the distance between teachers and their students increased. Salaries did not keep pace with those in other professions, teachers experienced increased stress from working with unmotivated students and from losing the support of parents and colleagues. Teacher burn-out became a major part of the American school scene. The stress on testing has discouraged teachers who had entered the teaching profession out of their love for teaching children.

As teachers became more specialized, pressures increased on teachers to be more attentive to a variety of new needs. Classes increasingly were interrupted for announcements or for students to leave for special classes, truancy increased, and teachers felt over-whelmed by the system and by the problems they faced in the class-rooms. Many teachers left the profession to take more rewarding and less stressful jobs. Others have been going through the motions, counting the days until retirement. Gifted young people are choosing other fields, leaving teaching to the less able.

As teachers become more discouraged, their own cynicism and lack of motivation are experienced by the students. When teachers do not put in the extra effort to correct homework or to speak to a student about a problem in class, the students interpret this as not caring. They then no longer care about what they are doing either. They see the teachers as lazy and indifferent, they resent it and feel hostile.

Teachers give less homework, either because they are so over-worked that they do not have time, or because they are so demoral-ized that they don't want to correct it. They feel less incentive to give challenging assignments because they are not sure the students will do them or because they don't want to invest the time evalu-ating them. They spend less time interacting with students because they do not feel appreciated. Homework gives the student a chance to work on self-discipline. It gives the teacher a chance to make comments on the student's work. When the student takes up the comments and improves the work, this communication strengthens the relationship between student and teacher and increases mutual respect. In the present situation, both students and teachers lose the opportunity of being emotionally and intellectually involved with each other.

When teachers work closely with students, many situations arise where, by showing interest or expressing confidence, the teacher can help a youngster correct inappropriate behavior or move in a more positive direction. The teachers can contribute to the youngsters' lives at a time when they need relationships with mature, caring adults.

When teachers become too specialized and too busy, they lose the opportunity to get to know a student in different capacities.

Adolescents need teachers who will talk with them, get to know their interests, recognize their gifts, and devote time, energy and skill to helping them realize their abilities. When a teacher works with a student on a paper, on a project, in a club, or on a camping trip, the student experiences insight, guidance and support instead of alienation and indifference.

In our current crisis, teachers lose, teenagers lose, society loses. It is not only in wartime that we can sing the song, "Where have all the flowers gone?"

Chapter Seventeen

Waldorf education

An alternative approach to schooling and teenage development

> To wonder at beauty,
> Stand guard over truth,
> Look up to the noble,
> Resolve on the good.
> This leadeth man truly
> To purpose in living,
> To right in his doing,
> To peace in his feeling,
> To light in his thinking.
> And teaches him trust,
> In the working of God,
> In all that there is,
> In the width of the world,
> In the depth of the soul.
> Rudolf Steiner

During the twentieth century there have been a number of attempts to develop an educational system based on a view of child development. Some notable examples are the Progressive schools based on the teachings of John Dewey and the Montessori schools based on the teachings of Maria Montessori. The free school movement has drawn its inspiration from the work of A. S. Neill and his experimental school, Summerhill. An educational approach which has been gaining recognition in many countries in the world is Waldorf or Steiner school education based on the view of child development put forth by Rudolf Steiner.

One of the important aims of Steiner education is to develop a curriculum which matches the stage of development of the child. The children's developmental needs in a particular class may evoke changes in the curriculum to suit those children. Steiner called attention to the need to understand the ideals of education and then to develop flexibility to deal with the practical situation. Thus life is a tension between the ideal and the real; learning to compromise is a necessary part of life. In this chapter I will introduce the reader to Waldorf education. Because this book focusses on adolescence, a brief introduction will be given to the scope of Waldorf education followed by examples out of the high school.

History of Waldorf education

Waldorf education had its beginning in Germany during the chaotic, post-World War I period. The centuries-old social order based on a fixed class system and privilege was being rejected in many countries, and a new social order, respecting the integrity of every human being, was emerging. Rudolf Steiner had been speaking all over Europe to thousands packed in lecture halls, to night school classes for factory workers, and to groups interested in spiritual science, of the need to transform culture based on a new view of the human being.

In the lecture, "Education of the Child in the Light of Anthroposophy",[1] Steiner laid out his fundamental ideas on education. He was deeply concerned about the need for cultural transformation in all areas of life, and he was given the opportunity to put his ideas into practice when Emil Molt, manager of the Waldorf Astoria Cigarette factory in Stuttgart, asked him to design a curriculum based on the anthroposophical view of the human being. Molt proposed to found a school for the children of his factory workers and he wanted it to be based on Steiner's ideas.

Steiner gathered a faculty of twelve people who had not been teachers but who were experienced and knowledgeable and who loved children and who were familiar with the ideas of anthroposophy. Over the next two weeks, he gave three lectures a day in which he described the psychology of the human being and laid out an education based on it. The first Waldorf school was dedicated and opened on September 7, 1919 in buildings of the Waldorf Astoria Cigarette Company.

The school for the factory workers' children flourished and soon was opened to other Stuttgart children at the request of people in the community.

In 1922, when the oldest students were preparing to enter the tenth grade, Steiner worked with the faculty to gain insight into the needs of adolescence. These talks, published as *The Supplementary Course*, and more recently as *Education for Adolescence*, are still studied as the basic principles of Waldorf high school education.[2]

Waldorf schools spread to other European countries, and, in 1928, the Rudolf Steiner School opened in New York City. During the 1930s, German Waldorf schools were closed by the Nazi regime, but were re-opened by the American authorities in Germany after the war. By 1947, there were four American Waldorf schools, and by 1972 there were eighteen. As of 2008, there were more than five hundred Waldorf schools worldwide, including more than eighty in North America. Waldorf schools (also known as Steiner schools) now comprise the largest non-sectarian, independent school movement in the world.

Each school is an independent organism, dedicated to the educational principles of Rudolf Steiner.

Basic principles of Waldorf education

> Every man passes personally through a Grecian period.
> R. W. Emerson

Waldorf teachers strive to understand the human being as body, soul and spirit. This view of child development, with its seven-year rhythms and critical periods of ego development, has been described in earlier chapters. The fundamental approach of the teacher is to develop educational methods based on this view of child development. Using this view as a guide, the teachers shape the curriculum and methods to meet the developmental needs of that age, since specific children or situations may call for unique solutions, and the teachers work together to try to find these solutions.

Steiner taught that the human being has passed through stages of evolving consciousness from ancient times to the present and that these stages closely parallel the psychological stages which a child passes through. This he called the evolution of consciousness.

The lower school

Waldorf education begins in the kindergarten years where the children enter into a world of play, colour, music, drama, festivals and practical life. When they leave the kindergarten they move into the lower school with a reverent and loving experience of nature and humanity.

Children in the lower school experience their learning through their feelings. The study of history, science, grammar, and geography evolves out of a feeling for the subject. The content is experienced in many sensory forms and in many mediums before the intellectual concept is formulated. In this way the youngster's experience of the world is multi-dimensional and has breadth and width. The children make their own books, they write stories and draw pictures exploring the subject of the main lesson.

Each subject develops from the first grade through the eighth grade, building on what has gone before and unfolding in a way that is interesting to the child of a particular grade because it addresses the inner changes that are going on.

The children in a class form a community and travel the journey from childhood into adolescence together with their main teacher for five, six, seven, or eight years. Their main or class teacher teaches them for the first block of time every morning in which they study one subject intensely for about three weeks before passing on to another one. The main lesson subjects alternate between the humanities and the sciences.

After the main lesson is over and the children have had a snack there are other lessons – painting, drawing, singing, playing instruments (recorder, lyre, violin, wind instruments), eurythmy (a form of movement working with tone and poetry), arithmetic, writing, reading practice, crafts (including knitting, crocheting, needlepoint, sewing and woodworking for boys and girls), gardening, and games. Here they meet other teachers who join them on their journey, sharing their special skills with them.

The children develop in a natural way through the grades. Some learn quickly and others need more time. Rather than being labeled or graded by how much they know or don't know, the emphasis in Waldorf education is on experiencing the wonder of the world, developing an appreciation of each other's gifts, working on skills, and being part of the class community.

First and second grade

During the first and second grade the child is still very dreamy, living out of imitation, and experiencing the world as unified. The Waldorf approach to reading, writing, and arithmetic has been treated in great detail in other books, and since we are concentrating here on adolescence, I will only mention briefly that the emphasis is placed on the oral approach, on developing a strong appreciation of language, vocabulary, and story telling out of which is introduced the alphabet, sounds, and words. Emphasis is placed on the children painting, drawing, and writing before reading (as was experienced in human history). A strong foundation of sounds, visual forms, and context is built so that reading is an experience of meaning rather than isolated skills. Arithmetic is taught in a very active manner, developing all four processes of addition, subtraction, multiplication and division using concrete objects and recognizing patterns that occur in number series. The children are active – moving and doing rather than being pressured to remember.

Third grade

The nine/ten-year-old has left behind the glow of early childhood when he or she experienced the world as perfect. Like Adam and Eve in the Old Testament, the child has been eating of the Tree of Life. But there comes the time when that is not enough. The child yearns to try something else. Temptation enters and the youngster eats of the fruit of the Tree of the Knowledge of Good and Evil. As children go through the nine/ten-year crisis and become self-conscious, their eyes are opened to the evil of the world. They leave behind innocence and are cast out of a Paradise-like state of being. Like Adam and Eve, they must go forth on the earth, learn to grow their food, clothe and shelter themselves, and experience the joys and the sorrows of being mortals.

As in the Old Testament, they go through many temptations and disobey the authority (God, parent), worshipping the Golden Calf and idolizing material wealth.

As part of the study of the Old Testament, children often learn Hebrew prayers and carry out the ritual of the Passover meal, complete with the proper questions, food and songs. In this way, they experience the customs and spiritual relationship existing between the Hebrew people and God.

The Waldorf teacher understands the change of consciousness which the nine-/ten-year-old is experiencing and works with the curriculum to meet the needs within the child. The nine-/ten-year-olds have left behind the experience of earth imbued with spirit. With the Fall, with the awareness of self, children feel separated from their spiritual origins and now have to become familiar with the earthly world – they must become earth-citizens. But it must go far beyond hearing and telling. They must grapple with the stuff that is the earth – so they study farming, house building, cooking and clothing. They work with the soil, plant seeds, cultivate and harvest. They gather what grows wild – apples and grapes. They cook and bake what they have harvested and "break bread together". If possible, they learn to milk a cow and make butter.

They learn about house building – the sturdy foundation, the walls, the roof, the plumbing, etc. Their teacher takes them to visit houses being built. They might mix mortar, make bricks, lay a pathway, or build a playhouse for the kindergarten children. One class made its own nails with the help of a parent who knew blacksmithing, another made bricks and then built a barbeque for the school, another built a rain shelter for the whole school. It is very important that they make something that is useful for other people, that their efforts are used to serve others.

In the clothing course, they learn about fibers and cloth – those that come from plants, cotton and flax; those that come from animals – silk, wool and leather; and those made by human inventiveness. They gather plants and make dyes and watch a sheep being shorn. They also learn stories and poems about the plants and animals related to clothing (such as "Little Lamb" by William Blake), learn to use a spindle – and perhaps a spinning wheel – and to card the wool and do simple weaving.

These are a few of the classes through which the third grade curriculum meets the consciousness of the third grade child.

Fourth grade

In the Norse legends, the fourth grade curriculum mirrors the Old Testament experience of the third grade. The twilight of the Norse gods is depicted. But a new type of character is introduced. He is Loki in the Norse myths (akin to the Trickster in the American Indian tales, Brer Rabbit in the Uncle Remus tales), who uses cunning and intelligence to win what he wants. Fourth graders are becoming aware of this quality within themselves and they relish stories in which the Trickster-type wins and then gets caught.

Now that the ninth/tenth-year change has occurred, the unified approach of early childhood gives way to more specific subjects. For example, in natural science the emphasis is placed on animals, in mathematics, fractions. Formal geography begins with the child's world at the centre – the classroom, school, neighborhood, community, city, and state. All the other subjects described earlier continue as well.

Fifth grade

The ten/eleven-year-olds pass from spatial consciousness to time consciousness, meaning that they no longer perceive the world as a random series of images, but begin to see it chronologically. As they study history, they gain an idea of what it means to speak of a thirty-year change or something having happened fifty years ago. The fifth grade curriculum bridges the historical epochs from ancient India, through ancient Persia, Mesopotamia, Egypt and Greece. It spans from mythology to history, and they hear about the lives of the great figures who brought the religions and cultures to humankind – the Buddha, Zarathustra, Moses, Osiris, Prometheus, Socrates and Plato. They learn about everyday life in these civilizations and about the way the people worked and played, how they built their homes and tilled their farms.

As with humanity during those epochs, the capacity for thinking develops in a new way. Out of the "still, small voice" mentioned in the Old Testament, conscience arises. Just as in each of the civilizations mythical thinking gave way to historical thought, ten/eleven-year-olds experience a similar transformation in thinking.

The Greeks were interested in why things happened, they were fascinated with thought, and developed the laws of drama, government, philosophy, mathematics, physics and music. They were the first conscious historians who went around interviewing people and recording the results. Fifth graders make their own books, filled with vivid descriptions of these historical figures. They make maps, trace journeys, illustrate narrations, make models of buildings, learn to measure in the way it was done in each of these civilizations. Their citizenry of the earth is more fully established and they learn not only to work on the earth as human beings, but to think as human beings.

The specialization in natural science is focused on botany; geography expands from the state to the country.

Sixth grade

In the sixth grade comes a deeper descent into matter as the youngsters approach puberty. Roman civilization is studied. Here, the youngsters trace the simplicity of early Roman life, the change from kingdom to the republic, the concern for honor and integrity needed to keep the republic pure, and then the decadence that set in as spiritual corruption took over the soul life. They study various aspects of the Roman Empire, such as the cosmopolitan unity that arose out of expanded citizenship, the *Pax Romana*, which made it a time of great accomplishments, and the disintegration of Roman character as the spiritual core of Roman culture dissolved. As slavery increased, laziness, cruelty, decadence and self-indulgence also increased and were experienced in gladiator fights and Roman orgies.

Sixth-graders are passing through similar inner experiences. The honor and purity of earlier years gives way to a fascination with grossness, with laziness, with self-indulgence. The golden age of childhood is passing, and the changes of pre-puberty cause the youngsters to focus on themselves. When they experience the mirroring of their changes in the descriptions of the Romans, they develop moral discrimination which helps them through these difficult years.

They study the rise of Christianity which occurred in the far eastern corner of the Roman Empire, the crucifixions and stonings, the slave uprisings, the persecutions of Christianity, the toleration of Christianity by the Emperors, and then the establishment of Christianity as the state religion as the northern tribes were making their way into the Roman borders.

In the sixth grade the teaching of science mirrors the new capacity of formal operations, as Piaget calls it, which becomes accessible to most youngsters of this age. They are able to grasp cause and effect for the first time. In the sixth grade curriculum science is formally introduced as the students study astronomy, geology, acoustics, light, color, heat, magnetism and electricity.

Seventh grade

In the seventh grade another very important change occurs. The development of the Renaissance period parallels the development experienced by thirteen-/fourteen-year-olds. Here the pre-adolescent shares with the Renaissance personality the questioning of authority, the fascination with exploration and experimentation. The Renaissance artists wanted to do their own work, receiving credit and recognition for it rather than being an anonymous part of a group. The scientists wanted to be able to think for themselves rather than relying on the ancient authorities. The leaders of the Reformation wanted to find their own relationship to God rather than going through the priest as intermediary. They began to see themselves as separate from the rich heritage of customs and traditions, and experienced doubt and questioning. Young teenagers, like their Renaissance counterparts, want to burst out from the restrictions that bind them. They will come to realize, as the leaders of the Renaissance and Reformation that freedom of choice, freedom of opinion, comes at a cost – leaving behind the familiar territory of security and stability.

Another aspect of the evolution of consciousness is the way the view toward authority has changed over the epochs. In the ancient world initiates guided the civilization. They introduced agriculture and crafts, gave the laws, established the first towns. About 3000 BC the leaders of the civilizations were figures who embodied three functions in one – they were the spiritually inspired priest-king-judges. Then came leaders who had specific functions. The priests guided the religious life, the kings administered the political life, and the judges made laws. After a while the memory of the time when the priests, kings, and judges were spiritually inspired faded and in their place came leaders who did not claim any spiritual guidance but were common people elected by the people.

The human being also goes through this evolution. In early childhood the adults seem to be like the gods, then around nine the adults are more like initiates who still have some higher knowledge. As youngsters come into early adolescence the adults are people with functions, and in later adolescence, around eighteen, the adults are viewed as people with more experience than them, but not necessarily wiser. The sixth grade science curriculum expands further as physics, chemistry and physiology are now introduced as well as world geography.

Eighth grade

The eighth grade consciousness is a continuation of the seventh, with emphasis on the modern world especially the industrial revolution and its effects on history. In most American schools, United States history is emphasized during this year. The science and geography introduced in seventh grade are continued; mathematical concepts are expanded to include an introduction to algebra.

The Waldorf high school/upper school

When the youngsters finish the eighth grade they pass over the threshold into the high school. Here many of the same subjects are taught but in a completely different way. In the lower grades the teaching was through feelings, through dramatic stories, through imagery. In the high school the subjects are grasped through presentation, discussion, reflection, and thinking, but the artistic is not forgotten. Teachers continue to deepen their artistic approach – to approach their lessons as an artist, to listen.

Rather than teachers relying on standard textbooks (although some may be used) they choose material that particularly relates to the students in the class. They describe biographies and events, create assignments that allow the student to explore the subjects in various mediums, and make evaluations based on the special nature of the ninth, tenth, eleventh, or twelfth graders. (Years 10, 11, 12 and 13 in UK.)

Instead of a class teacher to shepherd the class through the years, there is a community of specialists who teach the students out of their expertise. One or two faculty members act as class advisors or sponsors over their four high-school years.

The high school curriculum

The Waldorf high school curriculum is based on the understanding that each subject has a special place in the life of the student. For example, through science the adolescent learns to observe natural and mechanical processes. Through foreign languages the teenager learns to enter the thinking of another culture and to be able to communicate. In the study of mathematics the student experiences the wonder of form and pattern in number and nature. Through art the students develop inner sensitivity to living processes, through crafts they learn to bring an aesthetic sense to the practical world. In music the students develop an individual sense of tone and have a social experience of sharing musical works.

The subjects become the stuff of the world through which is woven an integrated view of the universe. In Waldorf education each child is seen as gifted, worthy of the enrichment from all subjects in the curriculum. It is only in the last two years of high school where some subjects will be electives.

The concept of the main lesson continues from the lower school into the high school, but the content and the form are different. After the main lesson time is over, the rest of the day includes a wide range of subjects such as mathematics, foreign language, English skills, litera-ture, choir, orchestra, art and craft, eurythmy and physical education. An attempt is made to work out the daily schedule so that the subjects that require the most alertness are placed in the morning.

The special nature of each high school year

Out of Rudolf Steiner's unique gift of the evolution of conscious-ness in relationship to education, the curriculum is related to each year of the high school and to the psychological development of the

students. Just as children in the lower school experienced the reca-
pitulation of cultures in their development, a similar parallel exists
in the high school. There is a key experience related to each stage
of adolescence.

The ninth grade

Ninth graders have left the second seven-year phase behind, and
as happens in most life phases, the first year of a new phase carries
with it something of the old. Eighth graders have arrived in modern
times, they have become contemporaries with others of their age.
As they come into the ninth grade there is a strong feeling of the
present. They want to be citizens of the modern world, but as of yet
they do not have much understanding of it. They are fascinated with
power and strength. The curriculum is woven around these themes.
For example, both in physics and in history power and energy are
addressed – in physics through thermodynamics and in history
through the study of modern times since the American and French
Revolutions.

At the same time ninth graders are focused on the physical body
and physical world around them. They are trying to understand
what things are all about. In History through Art the student learns
the way art was expressed visually from the Ancient world through
the seventeenth century. (Art, science and religion were united in
the ancient world and this was reflected in the art of most ancient
cultures, including Egypt. Most Egyptian art was created for the
gods and was not seen by the ordinary person. In Greek art we see
the perfect balance of heaven and earth. The gods were portrayed as
ideal men, their bodies based on the golden section, viewed as the
temple of the gods. Gracefulness, movement, balance, harmony lived
in Greek art.)

Art of the Roman, Early Christian periods, and the Middle
Ages, and the Renaissance are studied. The students draw and paint,
using the great masters as their teachers. Seeing and discussing the
different standards of beauty over the ages helps ninth graders see
that the present standard is not the only one. They learn that they
are capable of producing beauty and they gain confidence in their
drawing ability.

Rudolf Steiner felt very strongly that ninth graders should study history through art as a way of refining the crude emotions and distorted inner imagery they carry around with them. He said that such a study would go right down into their physical body and have a harmonizing effect.

In biology the ninth graders study the structure of the physical body, while in geography they study the physical body of the earth – the continents, the mountains, volcanoes, earthquakes and so on. They also study chemistry and foreign languages.

It is wonderful to see ninth graders working with wood, clay, drawing and calligraphy. Some ninth graders are trying to make an impact on everything around them. They have trouble being quiet and concentrating, and for them the arts provide a challenge. They have to learn to respect the medium and to work with it, to give themselves up to the process. Other ninth graders are still very hesitant, afraid to step out and make a mistake. For them the arts provide an opportunity to connect with the material. Instead of exposing themselves by talking, they can talk with their hands.

Ninth graders tend to be easily distracted, easily frustrated, and chaotic. By working closely with them, the teachers help them direct their energy while at the same time setting a foundation for the rest of the high school years.

The tenth grade

Tenth graders have come to the next step in maturity. Feeling fairly comfortable in themselves they become interested in process, in development, in metamorphosis. How do things happen, how do governments form, how did the Word come into being? Whereas the ninth grader needed stability, the tenth grader responds to that which is in motion. In geography they study the fluids, water currents and water power. In biology they study the fluids of the body, circulation, the endocrine system and reproduction. In chemistry they study organic processes of fermentation and distillation and so on. In physics the world of mechanics is studied. The idea of finding out how things work is very important in the tenth-grade year, and Rudolf Steiner was especially keen that the teachers develop what he called the practical lessons which would include surveying, first aid, typing or shorthand, technical crafts such as weaving and drawing.

In history the tenth graders now go back to the ancient world and see how rivers and climate affected ancient settlements; they trace the evolution of societies from ancient India to the Hellenistic period in Greece.

The study of Greece is of particular importance. It was during the time of ancient Greece that philosophers became conscious of the act of thinking. When the myths of the gods and goddesses, heroes and heroines no longer satisfied the early philosophers' questions, they turned to the world of phenomena and questioned what was the primal "stuff" from which the universe was made. This formed the basis of modern science. Socrates was put on trial for corrupting the youth of Athens because he questioned traditions and sought to find the meaning of the true, the good and the beautiful. His student Plato introduced the analogy of the cave – the imagination of spiritual reality and earthly illusion. Finally, it was Plato's student, Aristotle, who opened the gates of modern thinking with his emphasis on categorizing knowledge and seeking the laws of nature, drama, politics, and of thinking itself.

The tenth grader is experiencing many of the same changes. Out of the previous image-like thinking, pure concepts begin to be formed and grasped. Working with Greek ideas helps youngsters to bring form and order into their thinking as well as balance, movement and grace, that so imbued Greek sculpture and architecture.

In literature they study the Word – in the epic, lyric and dramatic poetry of the Iliad or Odyssey, of Greek drama and of the Old Testament.

Many other subjects are included in the tenth-grade year, and of course each school has its own special courses. For example, many schools in the United States include American literature that is appropriate to each grade. For example, I introduced 19th century American authors such as Hawthorne, Emerson, Alcott, Thoreau, Fuller and Whitman, and English writers such as Blake, Wordsworth, Coleridge, Byron, Keats and Shelley. In the tenth grade we enjoyed their language, their imagery and their exciting lives. Two years later we looked at Emerson and Thoreau again but in an analytical way as we traced the clarity and meaning of their thoughts.

The eleventh grade

Most eleventh graders have gone through or are going through a very important change, spoken of earlier as the sixteen/seventeen year change. The mysterious inward journey of the soul is mirrored in the curriculum through the question "Why?" In history the great religious questions are addressed in the study of the Roman Empire, the birth of Christianity, the development of Judaism and Islam, the development of the Roman Catholic Church and the Reformation. Just as the Renaissance personalities questioned traditional authority and asked "Why?" so do the eleventh grade adolescents. It gives them satisfaction and insight to see that the questions they ask are the questions of their age. It is exciting to know that to challenge the accepted customs is valuable and necessary for the development of civilization. Seventh graders respond strongly to the Renaissance because they are experiencing rebellion towards the physical authorities in their lives, but sixteen/seventeen-year-olds experience rebellion in their souls. For example, the doubt mirrored in the Reformation is not doubt of whether the authorities have vested power – more a seventh grade concern – but existential doubts such as whether there exists the soul, the spirit, God and eternity.

The emotional or soul life of the adolescent is going through a profound development during this time, and one of the courses taught is History through Music. One major aspect of music through the ages has been an expression of the meeting between the soul and the divine. Listening to music of the different historical periods and coming to appreciate and understand it helps the youngster develop an inner listening. Just as history through art in the ninth grade fed their craving for imaginative visual images, and history through poetry helped the tenth grader relate to language, history through music in the eleventh grade feeds their craving for tone.

In literature the study of Parsifal on its most apparent level mirrors the inner journey from foolish young knight to the Grail knight, from naivety to mature wisdom. There is great wisdom embedded in this story. The study of Shakespeare reveals to the eleventh grader the insight into the modern condition in characters such as Hamlet. Shakespeare's genius opens doors to many soul questions.

The world of the heavens is studied in astronomy, and the sub earthly power of electricity and magnetism is studied in physics.

The eleventh grade is a turning-point in the adolescent's Waldorf experience. Out of the richness of the courses teenagers are placed in touch with their inner resources and higher selves.

The twelfth grade

The theme of the twelfth grade is freedom. The main question asked is "Who?" meaning "Who is behind this doctrine?" "Who is working through that personality?" "Who is really speaking?" Through these questions young people confront questions of destiny, of good and evil, of meaning. Twelfth graders analyze and synthesize thoughts. They can look at an issue from many points of view, finding the common elements and the central issues. The Waldorf teachers bring example after example for the students to examine and think about.

Some examples from the literature studies are the great works of the nineteenth century Russians, Germans, and Americans. By reading Dostoyevsky's *The Brothers Karamazov* the student comes to understand how a Russian deals with the deep questions of life. In Melville's *Moby Dick* there is the struggle of the American soul with evil, and in Goethe's *Faust* the German approach. In each of these studies an understanding of the particular culture is aroused, but more than that is the realization that the issues addressed are universal. The greatness of these writers is that they have soared beyond their nationality and have given to humanity an artistic expression of questions facing human beings everywhere.

Twelfth graders grapple with the issues of their times. Before they leave school they step into the present. Their teachers examine with them the issues of the day, problems of economics, politics, social issues, nuclear chemistry, modern art, debates over evolution and so on. The history through art of the twelfth grade is the study of architecture in which the students examine the expression of thought in physical form. What is the gesture of an Egyptian pyramid, a Gothic temple, an Art Deco bank, or of a high-tech office building?

Everything twelfth graders study is done by the young Ego penetrating the world – reflecting, shaping thoughts, discussing, sharing. In mathematics the young adults have passed into the abstract world of trigonometry and calculus, in English classes they work with précis and research, synthesizing viewpoints, and analyzing a theme. In their foreign language study they delve into literature, exploring similar themes to their English literature studies – the battle between good and evil and the nature of freedom.

The twelfth graders can reach way back in their education into the imaginative first-grade world of the fairy tale and bring the powerful shaping forces into creative writing. They experience the sweep of history through thousands of years and see patterns and threads working in human and national biographies. They see the development of human life from the kindergarten children they pass every day to their teachers who are quickly becoming contemporaries. They are able to understand the paradoxes of life without losing sight of the ideals. Their eyes are on a distant shore while they prepare to leave their school-home and bid their school mates and teachers good bye.

Chapter Eighteen

The teenager and the arts

The poet, the artist, the musician, continue the quiet work of centuries, building bridges of experience between people, reminding man of the universality of his feelings and desires and despairs, and reminding him that the forces that unite are deeper than those that divide.

John Fitzgerald Kennedy

Art itself is the fruit of free human nature. We must love Art, if we would see how necessary to a full humanity it is.

Rudolf Steiner

We live in a world that is splintered. The spiritual life is separated from scientific and artistic life. We classify knowledge and experiences into neat compartments, but the soul of the human being fights against such fragmentation and cries out for unity, for inter-relationship. Because the newly awakened soul-life of the adolescent is open to all that works upon it from the environment, fragmentation is particularly painful. Art is the healing remedy for fragmentation.

The ancient Chinese character for art looks like:

I have often discussed this character with ninth grade students. We can imagine that the upper stroke is the heavens, the lower stroke is the earth, and the crossed figure in between stands for the human being, perfectly balanced between earth and heaven. If a person is too strongly connected with the earth, he or she is trapped. If the person is too connected with the heavens, he or she is "spacey". Art is the dialogue of the human being with the heaven and the earth.

In the following poem, Steiner describes how the arts are a gift to the human being who longs to be connected with the spiritual world.

> On a primeval day,
> the Spirit of the Earth
> approached the Spirit of the Heavens,
> pleading thus:
> One thing I know and that is, how to speak
> from out the human spirit.
> But now I beg to learn
> that other speech,
> whereby the great World-heart
> knows how to speak to human hearts!
> The Spirit of the Heavens, then, in mercy,
> bestowed upon the pleading Spirit of the Earth
> THE ARTS.[1]

Art becomes the saving grace for human beings cut off from their spiritual origins and suffering from the loneliness of the human condition.

Teenagers understand this image without any difficulty. They, too, feel cut off from the spiritual links they felt in childhood. By a living experience of art, they are able to reconnect with the celestial light which they once saw around all living things. When human beings feel whole once again, they are able to use their energy to enliven and transform social life. Lacking the feeling of wholeness, they feel empty and strike out at what is around them as well as at themselves.

Importance of the artistic process

When we are engaged in artistic processes, we have a conversation with our inner being. We are not so concerned with the product of our work as with the process, which puts us in touch with the spiritual in us. In most activities of daily life, we respond to the outer world, but art allows us to awaken our inner eye and inner ear to imagination and inspiration. It helps us understand our thinking, feeling, willing and to gain insights into who we are and who we are not. It helps us explore the qualities as well as the quantities of life.

As teenagers experience the many-textured levels of artistic process, the diverse ways of coming to an answer, the richness of metaphor in language, of rhythm and melody, of the living quality of form and space, their capacity for imagination deepens and their inner soul-space expands. A transformation of the common place stimulates their consciousness and sense of existence.

The inner life of the adolescent craves art as a way of connecting, of conversing, of creating. Out of the inner conversations comes judgment. When we create something artistically, we stand before a mystery, something unknown. We feel that something alive is present and that we are the means for it to come into physical form. As adolescents develop sensitivity to the creative process, they sense that they are the midwives to something that is being born. They partake in the mysteries of the universe. Although this is an intimate experience, it is also an objective one. As they work with stone or wood, tones or words, they must respect the laws of the medium. They must honor the material even as they impose their own will on it. In this way, they approach the artistic process as the philosopher approaches truth – as a beholder. When adolescent artists have a dialogue with their artistic work they come to love it so much that they become one with it. They experience the artistic process as a time of quiet contemplation and communication. It resembles a conversation between the lover and the beloved. This is the power of art.

Art and observation

Surrounding adolescents with works of art allows them to experience the power of creative expression. When they admire what is beautiful, they experience the creative powers that live and weave in nature and in creative activity. They develop an appreciation of subtlety and nuance. They feel uplifted by the creative energy that went into the work. When teenagers admire the beautiful form of a Greek vase, *The Pieta* of Michelangelo, or *The Holy Family* of Rembrandt, they develop a love of truth. It is not easy at first for young teenagers to appreciate the form and color of a painting or sculpture, but as they try, a new capacity is awakened that helps them see the beautiful. They exercise a new muscle which gives them soul-strength and endurance.

Drawing is another way of seeing. When teenagers are able to spend hours copying the works of the Great Masters, they come to know their works in an intimate way, and they never forget them. They take them, so to speak, into their inner being. As they explore their hidden talents, they find that they are capable of producing beauty as well as admiring it.

Even the most rambunctious teenager, if given an opportunity, feels calmed and awed by the grace and uplifting quality of great art. I have seen tough youngsters transformed by this process. It is as if the edges of a roughly cut gem are polished to reveal the glory of the human being – the higher self.

Teenagers should come to know about the artists' lives as well as about their works. The lives of the artists appeal to the teenager's fascination with the drama of life. The agony of Schumann, the magnificence of Beethoven, the sensitivity of Emily Dickinson, the quickly burning flame of Keats or Shelley, the persistence of Turner, the elegant simplicity of Georgia O'Keefe, the disappointments of Coleridge, the excitement of Byron, the tragedy of Melville, or the power of Dostoyevsky – all appeal at different stages of adolescent development. Because adolescents are envisioning their own destinies, they have a special empathy with the creative process and struggles of artists. Perhaps the extra sensitivity of the artist's soul-life is mirrored in the adolescent's own inner life.

Art and its relationship to feeling and thinking

When the teenager's life is permeated with the artistic impulse, the soul-life is exercised. Wonder, awe, fear, sadness, laughter, pain, happiness and compassion stimulate the breathing of the soul.

In their plays, the ancient Greeks applied this knowledge of the healing influence of rhythm by presenting three tragedies followed by a comedy.

Steiner tells us that memory is intimately bound up with feeling. An idea or concept enlivened by feelings is carried into memory. We remember those ideas best which are connected with strong feelings.

Because their souls are so receptive to the power of art, adolescents experience their own soul-life even through such elementary artistic exercises as color exercises in painting or vowels in eurythmy. The power of true art is so strong that even its simplest elements can transform. For example, when teenagers work with music and poetry, the ideal aspect of the art touches their souls; they feel lifted out of themselves and united with pure artistic powers. This is what lies behind the ecstatic smile and the big, awe-filled, "Wow!" they so often express after an intense, artistic moment.

Art helps us explore ideas in a non-verbal, non-linear way. Because it does not limit us by pragmatic do's and don'ts, we can explore the by-ways of our minds, and all things become possible. In this process, youngsters learn to take risks. Doing this in the artistic realm gives them courage to try it in the conceptual world.

A twelfth-grade girl was trying to express the difference between Western and Eastern thought. Finally, she came up with a fascinating way. She spent weeks creating a large urn, pouring her love and care into it. She fired it and glazed it, marking it with the Japanese character for life and glazed it again. She brought it to class where her classmates and teachers admired its beauty. She stood at the threshold of the room and said, "I will now demonstrate the attitude of non-attachment to things" and she dropped the urn. We sat in shock as the urn smashed. At that moment, she achieved a deeper experience of the concept of non-attachment than any research paper could have given her.

By working artistically, the adolescent's intellect is awakened and the will is activated. The human will is so strongly attacked by the overdose of sense impressions flooding in from the environment and by the impersonal nature of fast-paced modern life that many children instinctively protect themselves by withdrawing and becoming passive. Their will becomes weakened and they lose control over their own lives. When will activity is brought into the thought-life, however, it enlivens it. In this way, creative thinking can occur. The role of art in activating the will is essential. Teachers must give special attention to this by addressing the various capacities of the child – observation, memory and imaginative thinking. All of these are enhanced through the artistic process, and that is why it is so necessary that youngsters experience and understand art.

The artist does not progress in a straight line, but makes leaps in abilities and understanding. Moments of inspiration and insight are unpredictable and must be regarded with appreciation and wonder. We cannot plan for them, but once they occur, our lives are changed. The youngster who has this experience is put in touch with the inner sources of imagination and the unconscious world of archetypes.

The childlike forces of imagination do not continue into adolescence in the same form. At about the fourteenth year, the soul of the child moves inward to a protective inner space, safe from the onslaught of the new feelings, thoughts, impressions, expectations, and experiences. At about that time, the imaginative forces also withdraw. As in a cocoon, the soul lives in darkness until it is ready to burst its shell and emerge into the light of day as a butterfly. The forces of fantasy which previously lived in imagination had not been the child's own. They had come from the surrounding world and from the spiritual-soul sphere. They came *to* the child rather than *from* the child. In adolescence, these forces are transformed into forces of intelligence or into practical abilities. When imagination arises after puberty, it has a new quality; that of individuality.

The youngster arrives at an independent imagination from within the soul. When adolescents have an opportunity to work with art and to respond individually to it, their soul-lives are quickened and their imaginations stimulated. An atmosphere of individual freedom is essential if youngsters are to appreciate and enjoy art, and if they are to create artistic works. This does not mean the student is left totally free. The teacher should limit subject matter, but choices should be offered so that the adolescent helps shape the work. For example, if the class is doing water-color painting, the teacher may call for a scene including trees and water, but then let the students work out the placement and color. Or students may be asked to draw in the style of Michelangelo or Picasso, but they may choose from among ten or twelve of the artist's works.

Steiner made a great gift to education when he called attention to the arts as agents of healing, balancing and nurturing. Our utilitarian society sees art as frill or enrichment, but Steiner pointed out that art is essential to the well-being of the child, adolescent and adult. Because of this, art in its many forms constitutes the backbone of a Waldorf school and the central art is the art of teaching.

We have seen the growth of recreational art classes being offered as part of community education. Art classes are offered to the elderly, to the people with disabilities, to prisoners, to children and to over-stressed professionals. Art is so popular because it brings balance to our hectic lives, but it does much more than that. If we understood the healing aspects of art, we would honor it more in our daily lives, and art classes would not be the first ones eliminated when budgets are tight. Music, poetry, literature, speech, drama, movement, sculpture, painting, drawing and architecture allow the soul opportunities for expression, exploration and self-discipline.

The understanding of art and the teenager

When Rudolf Steiner introduced the curriculum of the original Waldorf school, it was built around those courses which lead to an understanding of art and those dealing with the study of the native language and history. These courses remain the core of the Waldorf high school curriculum.

In the ninth grade, art is understood through the visual arts of painting, drawing and sculpture. In most schools, the course includes art from the ancient world, Egypt, Greece, Rome, early Christianity, the Middle Ages, the early and late Renaissance in northern and southern Europe, to the seventeenth century work of Rembrandt. The youngster sees how art reflects the values and consciousness of the people in specific periods and places. The student learns, for example, that in the cultures of the Orient, the roots of art are in religion. In the West, however, art became more centered on the human being instead of on God, the understanding and feeling for the spiritual world diminished, and art became an imitation of nature. Finally, in the nineteenth century, art became a relative matter, a matter of mere aesthetic taste, a subject for the enjoyment of the senses.

As mentioned in the previous chapter, the unity of art, science and religion was central in ancient Egypt, but by Roman times there was already a separation. Art was no longer produced for worship but solely for decoration. The change between medieval art and Renaissance art parallels the change from group consciousness to individual consciousness, from art as a way of enhancing spiritual feelings through the icon or the catacomb sculpture to art purchased by businessmen to glorify the city of Florence and portraits commissioned by noble citizens.

Also in the ninth grade, many Waldorf schools (in some schools, it is taught in tenth grade) teach drama, focusing on tragedy and comedy. Ancient drama arose out of a celebration of the spiritual in life. In ancient Greece, for instance, drama springs from the mystery centers. Students study plays, see how the theater has changed, and see how modern drama deals with the everyday life of everyday people, and the anti-hero takes the place of the grand epic hero of old. This change in drama parallels changes in how people see their role in life.

In the tenth grade, the Understanding of Art course deals with poetry. Students work through the great epic, lyric and dramatic forms. They work with style, meter, patterns and imagery. They appreciate the contrast between the strong form followed by Homer and the other Greeks, who felt themselves inspired by the Muses, and the much freer forms of modern poetry. As they work with the structure of the language, they experience its genius.

In the eleventh grade, music is the vehicle to an understanding of art. Music is a more inward art than painting. It demands active listening, a more inward capacity than seeing. Therefore, it is taught in the eleventh grade, when the adolescent is going through the seventeenth-year change in thinking and is developing the capacity for inwardness.

In the twelfth grade, the students study architecture. They see the role of architecture in ancient cultures, where it was seen as a way to enhance the going-out of the soul from the body to the spiritual world, and how the forms of buildings have changed as Man's picture of himself has changed. They work with form and space, considering modern works as well as works out of past historical periods. In many schools, practicing architects visit to discuss what is involved in their profession. Students often are assigned to design and construct an architectural model.

In other courses throughout the four years, examples of art are woven into the subject matter so that the students experience examples of Romantic art, realistic art, modern art and so on, as well becoming familiar with the lives of great nineteenth and twentieth century artists in the fields of painting, architecture and music.

In addition to the powerful role of arts in adolescent life, crafts are also very important. When the artistic approach is applied to the everyday world, to the dishes we eat from, the clothes we wear, the furnishings in our homes, we imbue our surroundings with beauty and care. When teenagers become proficient in crafts, they develop skills, self-discipline, a feeling of purpose and a sense of worth. To make a well-formed plate from clay and take it through the entire process until it is ready for the table; to card, dye and spin wool, and then use it for knitting or weaving an article of clothing or household item; to make a bookcase or a chair; to print calligraphic invitations; to bind a book; to make a stained glass window; or to do any one of a variety of other crafts is a major accomplishment. Teenagers who have these experiences develop confidence, concentration, skill and appreciation for handwork. Their judgment is sharpened and their integrity enhanced. Appreciation for handwork also creates an understanding and appreciation for technology. Pride in craftsmanship and quality is needed in both handwork and technology, and certainly there is a need for improvement in the quality of mass-produced items.

The word craft once meant power or magic. It is not surprising, then, that those who take hold of a craft develop power in their lives. When adolescents feel that they have meaningful power in their lives, they are less apt to seek it in anti-social ways.

Music and the teenager

One of the most controversial areas of teenage life is music. Each generation has had its music, its songs and its singers. Fans have fainted at concerts and teenagers have been swept away in fan clubs in the past. Yet the music of today's youngsters has a different quality about it. This difference has to do with loudness and beat; it has to do with the effects of electronics; it has to do with the anger, drugs and violence that permeate the words, the album covers and the rock lifestyle. For many teenagers, listening to rock music is a way of identifying with the peer culture. They don't really know what they like, but they want to have group status. There is status in knowing the latest thing, and they don't want to be left out. They don't realize how insidious the messages of some of the songs are. They don't realize how much of a role money plays in determining the "popularity" of top songs; they don't realize the effect of electronics in music. All they know is that this is "our music". That is understandable, and we see as they grow older that they become more knowledgeable and more selective about the groups and songs they listen to.

Listening to radio, cds, or iPods (as well as the next new form of technology) is a very important part of becoming a teenager. To the young teen sprawled out on the bed for hours, each song has a special meaning. Listening through earphones brings the sound into a much more intimate relation than hearing it from speakers in a room. It feels as if it is coming from inside. There is almost no place a youngster has to go without being accompanied by music whether it be riding a bike, walking, running, or driving.

Music expresses emotions, hopes and dreams, losses and neglect. Lyrics that describe the teenager experience gives words to wanting a relationship, losing a relationship, feeling rejected, hoping for love, and wanting the future to be bright. Some music is politically focused, describing poverty, racial discrimination, and unfairness. Music expresses anger and frustration, loss and despair, loneliness, confusion, and yearning for the stability of childhood. Another whole genre of music expresses the rage of a generation of children who feel abandoned, angry about the break-up of marriage, of the father who walked out or the father the child has never known.

Just as music has an effect on teenagers, it also mirrors the teenagers' experiences. Reading the lyrics of many contemporary songs paints a picture of the challenges of present-day culture and its effect on the children.

A perspective on modern music

The big teen culture event of the sixties was Woodstock. People gathered from all over the East Coast, discussing life, protesting the Vietnam war, using drugs, singing and loving, and that set the tone for the youth culture for the next several years. The Woodstock experience was sought after and cultivated by young people from coast to coast. The typical rock lifestyle of the sixties involved parties, alcohol, marijuana and barbiturates. Performers were on very tight schedules and their lives were full of tension. They thought cocaine and speed helped them deal with the situation. After the deaths of Jimi Hendrix, Janis Joplin and Jim Morrison brought about a new awareness of the dangers of hard drugs, the use of hard drugs did seem to decline, especially among high schoolers. Marijuana, however, is still commonly used and cocaine has been fashionable in recent years, especially in the particularly dangerous form known as crack.

Heavy metal, pioneered by the group, Steppenwolf, developed in the late sixties, and was especially popular with bikers. An announcer filming the group said that the only way you could describe the music was as heavy metal. It pounds up through the body and gives a false sense of power.

Sex and drugs have been strongly identified with teen music since the late sixties. For the past decade or so, bodyguards of some rock stars have been told to give passes to certain people, allowing them to go backstage after concerts. These rock stars use their power over young women who come backstage and will do anything the rock stars want.

Many songs express sexual abandon and exploitation and prepare the fans for this special experience. Any parent who wants to experience what the rock music world is trying to convey to youth, can watch a late-night selection of videos. These typically range from Hollywood musical-type dance routines to sick and violent imagery.

Few young teenagers realize what big money is involved in the rock music business, stars and their agents often drive around in limousines, pass money around, and deal in drugs. Many rock stars are insecure, emotionally stunted loners who don't know how to interact with an audience unless they are on drugs, mostly cocaine, which they use to keep going throughout the concerts.

Rock groups project an image of being very powerful, and teenagers think that they can take on some of the power of the group they identify with. (A similar phenomenon occurs with fans of football teams, politicians, and the like.) This is referred to as the 'positive mania syndrome', reminiscent of primitive beliefs in which the tribal member takes on the power of a god by wearing a headdress or by drawing certain symbols. So, teenagers participate in "air bands", wear tee-shirts with grotesque pictures spread across their chests, and leave a trail of graffiti depicting the logos of their favorite rock groups on their books, school lockers, and in public places, enabling them to feel bigger and more powerful than they feel when they behold themselves as solitary beings. Heavy metal groups, bearing names with satanic imagery, convey attitudes of destructiveness, toughness and wildness. Drugs, sex and money are the three things the heavy metal stars seem to want out of life.

Other styles of music are also popular, especially rhythm and blues, New Wave, punk and reggae. Punk music, in part, arose out of avant-garde sixties music. Reggae has its roots in Jamaica and England. Punk and reggae have social messages, conveying the alienation of the nuclear-stalemate generation which felt that the world is on a collision course with death, with no hope and or reason for living. The music and lifestyle – expressed by the word anarchy – focus this message.

As music, these styles have a more mellow quality. Reggae is slower and less grinding than heavy metal. One can swing to it, and it doesn't take the toll on its listeners' nervous systems that heavy metal (sometimes called "head banging") does.

Rock stars have become an accepted part of our culture. Constant publicity makes us feel that we know them. This keeps records selling. Money makes it possible to buy drugs, and the drugs keep them going to make more money. Not all take drugs, however, and many rock stars today do not even drink.

Although drugs have played a very heavy role in rock music, there are singers who want no part of them. Some groups have a strong social message, warning about the direction in which life is heading.

The most outstanding feature of modern popular music is that it is polarized. On one side is a very decadent type of lyric, accompanied by obscene images and exaggerated beat. On the other side is music with idealistic lyrics and a melodic sound in which the beat is not overpowering. Once the beat becomes too strong and the musical element goes out of balance, it seems that balance also is lost from the message. Where the beat is not exaggerated, there also is less violence in the lyrics.

Effects of musical styles such as rock, hip hop, and heavy metal

Electromagnetic forces pulsing through rock music affect not only the listener's nervous system but his or her soul. Teenagers have said that the flooding of their senses by pounding, screaming music makes them feel drained and tired. This feeling bothers some teenagers while others like the sensations of being saturated by the music. They say that it feels as though they are being inwardly shattered, producing a euphoric sense of meaninglessness in the world – in the words of one common rock slogan, the feeling of "No future".

Imagine the deeply narcotic impact of such powerful images driving into the psyche of a teenager in a dark room with earphones on, drifting off to sleep in a warm cocoon of throbbing meaninglessness. How is this child to awaken the next morning, refreshed and ready to take on the world in a healthy way? The pulsing beat prevents restful sleep. In addition to hearing rock music as they go to sleep, many youngsters wake up to it, never giving their nervous systems a rest. Jurgen Schriefer, a distinguished musician and music teacher for over twenty years, has said that heavy listening to rock music even harms the quality of a young person's voice. According to Schriefer, the music hardens muscles in the back of the throat, reducing the quality of the singing voice.

In a distorted way, rock musicians understand something very important about our times, namely that the will is the key to the soul of the modern adolescent. If we work with the will in a positive way, we awaken devotion and service, but rock music cripples the will, making devotion and service very difficult. Allan Bloom writes about this in his recent *The Closing of the American Mind*:

> Music, or poetry, which is what music becomes as reason emerges, always involves a delicate balance between passion and reason, and, even in its highest and most developed forms – religious, war-like and erotic – that balance is always tipped, if ever so slightly, toward the passionate. Music, as everyone experiences, provides an unquestionable justification and a fulfilling

pleasure for the activities it accompanies … Armed with music, man can damn rational doubt. Out of the music emerge the gods that suit it, and they educate men by their example and their commandments.[2]

Teenagers are drawn to different styles of music. Teenage boys tend to listen to music highlighting frustration, rage, and despair, while girls prefer love, tenderness, and relationship. Some musical styles support resistance to authority, others describe personal problems at home or at school, loneliness, or feelings of inadequacy. Other stimulate relaxation, create a happy mood, calm insecurities, and provide rhythm to dance to.

Whereas the choice of music by itself will not cause a teenager to choose destructive behavior, those experiencing social alienation, disturbances at home, or a feeling of hopelessness are especially vulnerable.

Many examples of rock, rap, and hip hop music have made the use of alcohol and drugs popular and acceptable. Their use of graphic violence and sex promoting control over others such as masochism and sadism, and especially violence against women, are of concern. The lyrics, along with the heavy beat, exploit youngsters who are trying to figure out their behavior and their identity. Adolescence has always been a time when teenagers are learning behavior that will serve them as adults. While it is normal for them to feel a certain degree of alienation, they need to come to terms with acceptable adult behaviour as they mature. Explicit sexual and violent lyrics exploit their vulnerability and stimulate moods of depression, despair, and even self-harm.

A study was carried out by researchers by conducting a national longitudinal survey of 1461 adolescents, when they were 12 to 17 years old, and again 1 and 3 years later.[3] As a result they said there was a danger that children's opinions about the opposite sex would be affected for the long-term by constant exposure to the sexually degrading lyrics – many graphic and filled with obscenities. "These lyrics depict men as sexually insatiable, women as sexual objects, and sexual intercourse as inconsequential. Other songs about sex don't appear to influence youth the same way." Dr Martino added, "It may be that girls who are repeatedly exposed to these messages expect to take a submissive role in their sexual relationships and to be treated with disrespect by their partners … These expectations may then have lasting effects on their relationship choices. Boys, on the other hand, may come to interpret reckless male sexual behavior as 'boys being boys' and dismiss their partners' feelings and welfare as unimportant."

Another symptom of the huge impact of music on modern youth is the fact that teenagers today, far more than ever before, build their sense of identity around their music preferences. Until a few years ago, students grouped themselves into categories that had little to do with music. They were identified as jocks, preppies, etc. Those categories remain, but now there is an additional identity based on what kind of music a person listens to. A student is expected to know whether he or she is a New Waver, a punk, a heavy metal fan, or a soul music fan. There is the music of the inner city and the music of the suburbs. You are what you listen to. Only as teenagers become more self-confident can they buck this single identity and admit that they like different kinds of music.

Music and the soul

Music used to uplift the soul. Now, it is generally enjoyed for its sensual qualities. The introduction of radio strongly influenced the ways in which people experienced music, and phonographs, tape recorders, videotape players, iPods, and other technologies have made the change revolutionary. People once had to either make their music themselves or go to some place – concert hall, market place, or tavern – where others were making it. Music could not be experienced apart from the musicians.

Listeners no longer have to go to a concert hall or market square to hear music. They have music at their fingertip, at home, day or night, any type. A person can listen to music carefully or use it as background. Music has been almost entirely divorced from musicians.

One way to gain insight into what music is doing for the soul-life of young people is to watch the faces of people playing it or listening to it. Contorted faces, a wild-eyed look, angry fists, sexual gestures and orgiastic tension all contribute to an atmosphere in which the soul is pounded into the body and trapped in it. The soul becomes for a time a distorted caricature of a machine or animal. One can observe those youngsters who are caught by the music and those who are enjoying it but can let it go.

It is also possible to see which groups are on the positive side of the polarization. Anger by itself is not a simple indication. Anger against the frustrations of society has characterized folk music for generations. We must come to judgments only after we have listened to the lyrics and heard the sound.

Music and healing

An old saying goes, "Music alone with sudden charms can bind the wand'ring sense, and calm the troubled mind". Music has a very important healing task to balance the impact of technology and frenetic pace in our lives. To heal, however, it has to be healing music, music that brings harmony into our lives. Can we imagine music being so active in our lives that it would be possible to hear live, non-electronic music and not have to depend on records? Can we imagine hundreds of small orchestras or ensembles playing or singing together? Music, as the ancient Greeks pointed out, can change the psychology of a people.

What is most important is that parents learn to listen to the music which their children are hearing and distinguish the various forms, groups and styles. Some groups are trying to be socially responsible, while others try to exploit and poison young people. Parents have a duty to their children to listen to the music and lyrics. Then they can build a bridge with their youngsters by discussing the pros and cons of a song or group. It is not sensible to say that all rock music is bad and forbid a teenager's listening. It also is misguided to let the youngster play anything he or she wants on the principle that "every generation's music is obnoxious to the preceding generation". Parents should regulate the amount and kind of rock music a youngster listens to, and they also should introduce other musical experiences as a balance. If the parent attempts to appreciate some of the teenager's music, the teenager may be more open to the parents' tastes.

The parent has to stand on the thin line between being open-minded and being concerned for the adolescent's well-being. The parent, not the teenager, is responsible for deciding whether the youngster should attend a rock concert (or an R-rated movie). It is not a right of the teenager to do what is harmful.

Though we live in a splintered world, art is a bridge which heals the soul by uniting our spirits with our outer world and which heals our alienated young people. By sharing with them the Truth, Beauty and Goodness which true art conveys, we give our children art's greatest blessing: Hope.

Chapter Nineteen

Power and loyalty

Before I built a wall I'd ask to know
What I was walling in or walling out,
And to whom I was like to give offense.
Something there is that doesn't love a wall,
That wants it down.

Robert Frost[1]

As children become self-conscious, they experience themselves as one person among many. They feel the effects of other people's actions and they see the effects of their own. They learn early that a temper tantrum may get them what they want. They feel inner turmoil when two people they love are on opposite sides of an issue. In brief, they awaken to the fact that human beings live in groups, and this means there are times of stress as well as times of joy.

Social skills allow children to find their way into the whirlwind of human affairs. Inconsistency, mixed messages, and hidden expectations are among the obstacles that confuse them as they try to understand what is coming to them from their environment. They gradually become familiar with their family's and their culture's way of interacting. Whatever is around them, they assume is normal.

Young people must reckon with two powerful expressions of individuality: power and loyalty. Within bounds, these are valid means of identifying with the group and strengthening one's sense of self. However, getting stuck in the urge to power or in loyalty-at-all-costs to one's peers is very limiting. Working through these problems helps adolescents move beyond their personal satisfaction and thus gain a wider relationship to society.

The need for power: proving oneself

The adult and the adolescent have similar needs – to communicate with other people and to experience some degree of control over their own lives. In our society, these needs are often expressed in terms of power, which is even conveyed through body-language, by the walk and the gesture of hands. A carefully studied strut, for instance, is supposed to show confidence and strength. It says, "Look out! Someone powerful is coming". A studied look may also convey power, especially a look that challenges and tests. A tall boy may saunter over to a short one and say, "Carry this, Shorty". Shorty is already self-conscious about his height, and the last thing he needs is to be bullied. The more fear he shows, the more the bully lords his power over him.

Power is an issue in arguments with parents. When adolescents realize that their logic is as good as the adult's, the chin juts out, eyes shine, and the teenagers exploit the advantage they sense in the moment. Their sense of power merges with their sense of identity. Adolescents become what their point of view is. If the adult disagrees with their point of view, adolescents take this as rejection of them, and the confrontation ends up bigger than it seemed at first.

Girls use power more subtly than boys. The girl wins over adults, especially men, through coquettishness. She twists them around her finger. In addition to being flirtatious, she can be very aggressive. All obstacles fall before the onslaught of her self-righteousness.

When adolescents sense their strength, they are capable of consciously manipulating adults. In this situation, they assess the adult's weaknesses and attack. Adolescents also are capable of being rude and defiant one moment and sweet and gentle the next. Is it any wonder that adults become suspicious of the shifting approach and wonder what the youngsters have up their sleeves? Adolescents use their power to drive an adult into a corner to get the decision they want. Their energy is intense, especially when they gang up, and adults sometimes cannot withstand the intensity of the confrontation and back off.

During a ninth grade trip to Yosemite Valley, several students planned to sneak out and go drinking. When one boy asked if he and others could ride the shuttle bus that evening, I responded on a hunch and replied, "No". The conversation that followed went something like this.

"You don't trust me."

"I'm not discussing it. The answer is simply no."

"You're on a power trip."

"If that's what you want to call it, fine."

We stormed away from each other. He was over his anger in a few minutes, but my evening was ruined. I brooded over the unpleasant exchange late into the evening and again the next morning. I was annoyed at the way I had responded, yet I trusted my intuition. Years later, the student confirmed my hunch and sheepishly apologized.

Emotional scenes such as this occur in many homes each evening. Often, the apparent issue is quite unimportant, but the real issue is over who is stronger. Problems are bound to occur if parents feel that they must defend the position of authority above all else. The parent must sort out the issues and decide which ones allow room for compromise and which do not. The self-esteem of each individual is at stake, so once the battle begins, it is difficult for either to back off without losing face.

Parents often do not realize in the moment that they are over-reacting. Even worse, parents at times behave more unreasonably than their adolescents do. For parents, too, self-esteem and acceptance by friends, neighbors, relatives, or colleagues is important. The threat of losing acceptance because of a son's or daughter's behavior produces anxiety and causes parents to become angrier than they otherwise would. This happens especially when adolescents confront or defy parents in public. Parents feel humiliated. Instead of saying, "I don't want the neighbors, or friends, to see you like this because they won't respect me", they usually say something like, "It's for your own good", or "You are ruining the family's reputation", or "What you're doing is not decent or right". Parents don't realize at that moment they are afraid of the teenager's behavior as well as the possible loss of respect from their own peers.

Parents are frustrated at the shortcomings of the adolescent and fear that these shortcomings are being projected onto them by others. They may even feel that they have failed as parents. One father expressed his frustration because his son was withdrawn. He didn't feel that he could take his son where other fathers took their sons. His frustration was so strong that he lashed out and blamed everyone else for it. Finally, he broke down and wept, "I just want to shake him into talking to me. What have I done wrong?"

One way in which adolescents hurt their parents is by accusing them of caring more about their public image than about their children. There may be an element of truth to this, but adolescents over-emphasize the situation and leave the parents feeling unable to respond. These scenes are usually unproductive for both sides. If parents admit that they are embarrassed to have teenagers carry on in a particular way, the son or daughter is more likely to respond with understanding – even if it is years later.

I once became furious with my daughter because a group of her friends had decided to celebrate high school graduation with a picnic and baseball game at a park right outside the school gate. Because some of them had a few beers, I was humiliated by her involvement. I was concerned about her participation and felt it would embarrass me and the school. I expected her to be sensitive to my position. She explained that she had appreciated my situation and had influenced her friends to tone down their activities because of that. By the time she finished explaining, I was too emotional to give her much credit. We both ended up crying.

Having arguments with teenagers sometimes resembles a duel; the teenager's thrust can wound as deeply as a sharp sword. The adult can hardly match the directness and concentration of the attack. I have had this feeling many times in my years of teaching and have learned not to take it personally. A student once accused me of ruining his life by giving him a lower grade than he deserved. In his tantrum, he kicked the door and raised quite a ruckus. There was no point in my becoming upset, too, and two years later, he was much mellowed, matured, and humbled by life.

Sometimes, a power struggle is triggered by a misunderstanding or an unrealistic expectation on either side. Adolescents do not yet realize that the world is composed mostly of shades of grey. Instead, they see everything in black or white, good or bad, winners or losers. This makes them impatient and causes them to label many adult actions as hypocrisy. When youngsters come into their sixteenth or seventeenth years, greater tolerance and understanding occur. It then is possible to have productive discussions with compromise and benefit to everyone.

Many power struggles occur because one side or the other assumes that one view is good and the other is bad. A helpful way to avoid this is to present the problem and ask the adolescent to offer solutions for the parent's consideration. Problems with chores, curfews, and expectations, for example, usually offer room for many approaches. The young person's attitude changes when he or she is able to think things through from both points of view and to come up with a reasonable solution. Parents generally are surprised by the reasonableness of their childrens' proposals.

As defensiveness is reduced on both sides, the possibility of trust grows greater. Youngsters need opportunities to develop responsibility as well as to test their ideas. In these situations, the teenagers generally will accept fair punishment for serious mistakes in judgment. Self-evaluation is far more effective than grounding or loss of privileges. It is not easy, however, for parents to switch into this new mode.

All too often, adults need to prove that they still have power over the adolescents, and the battle lines are drawn again.

If we can remember that the soul of the individual is struggling for freedom, perhaps we can be more sympathetic to our young-sters. We can understand this if we can understand that they want freedom *from* rather than freedom *to*. Any limitation is seen at first as authoritarian or dogmatic, as a denial of their freedom. As long as adults issue final decisions without sharing the process of decision-making, teenagers will react, and their reactions are seldom gentle. To protect their need for independence, they protest, sometimes viciously. Later, they may apologize, "I didn't mean that. I just felt I had to gripe. It wouldn't be any fun otherwise".

Many power-struggle scenarios are played out daily. Here are a couple of typical ones:

After evaluating an unpopular decision, parents decide that they cannot give an acceptable or logical explanation because the decision is an intuitive one. The parents feel that what the youngster wants to do is inappropriate, and – as unreasonable as the decision may seem – they must stick by their position. No amount of crying or pleading, badgering or pressuring will change it, but the young person tries anyway. Eventually, both sides sense when enough is enough, and the contest ends. The next morning, however, the adolescent tries again, just to be sure there hasn't been a weakening overnight.

A sixteen-year-old girl relentlessly argues to do something that her mother is not comfortable with. Finally, the mother wears down and gives in. The girl tosses her mother a triumphant look and breezes out of the room, but that night, the girl is moody. When her mother asks what is wrong, her daughter replies, "It was terrible this morning when you gave in. It was as if you had died. I didn't feel you cared anymore".

If parents are to walk the narrow line between acting unreasonably and acting responsibly, they must be able to tell when they are simply protecting their own power and when they are acting out of conviction. If the adults give in whenever they are challenged by their teenagers, the adolescents never have a strong foil against which to test their own convictions. It is like pushing against marshmallow fluff. Nothing pushes back. Adolescents may be momentarily pleased, but in the long run, they experience the lack of resistance as a lack of caring. The parents did not feel strongly enough either about the issue or about the adolescent to take a stand. Teenagers do not admire weakness and will feel disdain as well as disappointment.

Parents are challenged most often over such issues as the choice of schools, responsibilities at home, summer activities, curfews and punishments. Some parents make it clear that certain areas are non-negotiable, such as health, education (through high school) and behavior within the family. This may mean, for example, that rudeness to parents, siblings and grandparents will not be tolerated, that the youngster's diet must be healthful, that a youngster won't be allowed to play interscholastic football because of the danger of injury, or that the young person is expected to maintain a specific grade average in school.

Teenagers may have some influence, however, in such negotiable areas as choice of friends, dates, interests, entertainment, clothes and arrangement of their room. Some parents would choose the reverse and would be uncompromising in choice of clothes, friends, dates. This is an individual matter. Whatever the situation is, adolescents should have a clear idea of which decisions are left to them and which are not. This enables them to know where their input is expected and even welcomed, and in which areas they must accept decisions even when they disagree with them.

During the early teens – through sixteen – it is especially critical for parents to stand firm. If parents give in too much to thirteen- and fourteen-year-olds, it is very difficult to hold back later. Young adolescents often disagree with their parents for the sake of disagreement, and they don't really know what they want. Disagreements with a sixteen- or seventeen-year-old are different, however, and parents should take seriously the adolescent's reasoning.

What seems to be a power struggle sometimes is really triggered by the parents' fear of letting the child grow up. The fear is genuine, and parents take an entrenched position. They may not recognize the capacity of the teenager to cope with the situation. They fear letting go of the child, and they fear being left alone. The growing independence of their child reminds them that they, too, are growing older.

All adolescents go through a period of testing their power against parents, siblings, teachers, and friends. This normal step in the development of the self becomes difficult when the parents cannot handle the challenge and either withdraw or react too aggressively. Both reactions end up cutting off communication.

In American culture, it is accepted that a young man shows power through competition, either on the athletic field or in academics. Young people are raised to be success-oriented and are taught to win. Pressure builds up, promoting a values system based on the ancient principle of, "Might makes right". Other slogans in this value system include, "Push 'em again – Harder! Harder!" and "Win at any cost". This attitude is especially transmitted in competitive sports involving young children whose parents confuse their children's win-loss records with their own egos.

Sportsmanship and cooperation are also dynamics of the competitive scene. If the parents, coaches, or school emphasize sportsmanship and cooperation, adolescents develop both appropriate pride and appropriate modesty. Youth sports then become the vehicle for character-building that they are so often said to be. The youngsters can enjoy winning, but their egos are not identified with being on top. They appreciate a good game if the team plays well, regardless of who wins. They share the joy of a teammate's achievement without feeling put down themselves, without feeling, "I hate him. He beat me".

When too much pressure is riding on a young person's performance, whether in a game or in a classroom, adolescents often develop a win-at-all-costs attitude that justifies cheating, giving someone else misinformation, or other devious means. Sometimes, they fail because they are too tense to function. They need to know that they are loved and accepted for themselves, regardless of their prizes. This issue leads us once again to the parents' needs. How much are they living through the achievements of their children?

Adolescents need ways of expressing and testing their powers because these experiences give them a sense of their limits. They need to set goals – and go beyond them. They need to feel the joy of accomplishment, of self-satisfaction. There are many ways this can be achieved without doing it at the expense of others, such as survival trips, backpacking, bicycle trips, orienteering, hiking, swimming, Outward Bound programs, volunteering at a hospital, becoming a camp counselor, taking first aid, being a lifeguard – in short, giving service where their strength and power will be helpful to others and will add to their own healthy development. Then their power and strength are put at the service of humanity. I have seen rambunctious teenagers transformed by the responsibility (and hero worship) that came with being a camp counselor.

The question of loyalty: where do I belong?

Another serious issue between adolescents and parents is that of loyalty. Parents generally assume that their children will feel loyalty to family values, family friends and to the social customs of the family and society. But adolescents' first loyalties are shifting to the peer group and often to the youth culture as well. A teenager's growing identification with the peer group and a growing-away from the family can shake up the family structure. However, this may be only a temporary shift, long enough to establish them in their contemporary world and also long enough to cause confusion.

Parents may not like the friends their adolescent chooses, but teenagers often are experimenting, trying on new friends as they might try on new clothes. Sometimes, they choose friends their parents don't approve of simply to shock them or show their independence. They may be trying to understand different kinds of people; they may be exploring values different from their own family's. Parents become nervous that the friend may be a bad influence on their child or that their sons or daughters may reject their values. They are concerned that the young person may shame them or make poor judgments concerning money or time.

Another aspect of loyalty is the youngster's commitment to the contemporary culture. Parents are usually still carrying the values and dreams of their own youth culture. The music, styles and heroes of their youth felt right to them when they were young, but they do not feel comfortable in the new youth culture. Usually, they don't like the way the heroes look or sound. They are not familiar with the language or jokes.

Some parents dive into the new youth culture as a way of communicating with their children. If this is overdone, it looks rather silly, but at least the parents are making an effort to be informed. This is valuable as long as the adult doesn't attempt to become one of the gang. That is embarrassing to adolescents who are trying to maintain a sense of distance from their parents.

Each generation produces some who stand apart to make a point. Adolescents struggle to identify what they are actually being loyal to – to a fad, a group, or a particular person within a group. There are subgroups within the larger teen culture. Teenagers know the characteristics of each subgroup, but sometimes they get into one without much thought. Just because of a dare, for example, they may join a gang. It can seem very important not to appear "chicken". Other times, this may happen because the teenager is friends with a member of the group. Each group has its own brand of elitism, and teenagers are soon introduced into a hierarchy. Some young people would like to explore a number of groups, but this is very difficult in a large school as the groups tend to get fixed. During the summer, however, teenagers often can explore new identities at camp or in a drama group or working on a ranch. They have a chance to try on roles, to see what it's like to be a "jock" or a "brain" without committing themselves for four years.

If teenagers give signs of wanting to change groups, they are accused of disloyalty. Once teenagers join a group, their identities are fixed and their social interaction limited. A youngster who is unhappy in a group suffers much heartache. This is one of the tragedies of adolescence, and sometimes a change of school or neighborhood or activities is needed to give the young person a new start.

It is far healthier when teenagers can express their talents and interests without becoming locked into groups. For instance, the youngster can show several aspects of his or her personality and abilities in such places as camps, church groups and small schools.

He or she is less likely to be simply labeled as a member of some group. Small size alone, however, does not insure open-mindedness, as cliques can exist anywhere.

Some teenagers identify so closely with their parents' values they are uncomfortable with many aspects of the youth culture. This can narrow teenagers' social options and prevent them from identifying properly with their own generation. Their need to break away from their parents will have to find a different form or wait until later. If the peer environment is too one-sided – either too loose or too tight, – if the adolescents are uncomfortable with the behavior or social attitude of peers, they may be left with the alternative of standing alone and relating mostly with adults or looking farther afield for contemporaries they like better. They are fortunate when they find such friends because this allows them to continue being connected with their generation without placing them in conflict.

This is not always possible, however, and some adolescents shy away from the youth culture so much that they are seen as "goody-goodies". They take no risks and never misbehave. Outwardly, they are model teenagers, but secretly they yearn for excitement. They may fantasize escapades or actually carry them out surreptitiously. By choosing a safe and narrow path because they are afraid of risks or afraid of their parents' disapproval, these young people may be missing their youth. For this reason, parents should be alert to their children's needs for new interests and new groups.

A teenager sometimes has to be caught doing something wrong in order to wake up the parents. Parents should appreciate the opportunity to open up communications and not become too involved with punishment. Very often, the embarrassment itself is punishment enough. It is important for parents to separate their anger or annoyance with the act from the support and love for the young person. If this can be done, there is a good possibility for increased growth and communication. Most adolescents appreciate the opportunity to tell their parents that they are in trouble before it comes from outside authorities. Giving teenagers the chance to do this helps them take responsibility for themselves and gives them a better chance to benefit from their mistakes.

Some teenagers have open communication with their parents and tell them about things they have done even if they haven't been caught. They are then open to their parents' advice and gain maximum benefit from parental support.

Many teenagers will speak to one parent and not the other. This puts a burden on the parent receiving the information. How should the parent handle this? Keeping it a secret from the spouse often backfires.

A sixteen-year-old girl was caught smoking marijuana. She asked that her father not be told. The mother agreed with her daughter and the punishment was given without his being told. He was furious when he found out, which doubled his sense of isolation and left him resentful as well as angry.

Adolescents feel divided loyalties, but when they are forced to choose, they generally are loyal to their friends rather than to the adult. When asked to give information about a peer, they want to tell the adult, but they are loyal to their friends. When confronted later with the lie, their response is plaintive, "You wouldn't have expected me to tell on her, would you? Would you tell on your friend?"

Young people have to live more closely with their friends than with the adults in their lives. We can make their lives miserable by turning them against their peers, and we have to respect the delicacy of such situations. Parents and teachers should be sensitive to the inner conflict that the young person is in.

During childhood, a similar situation occurs in regards to tattling. The conflict between telling on someone and telling in order to help is the main dilemma. A seventeen-year-old boy was in agony because his brother's life was threatened by heavy drug use. He was concerned about his brother and needed his parents' help, yet he didn't want to lose his brother's confidence. We decided to call his parents and the four of us sat down and talked. His parents responded very well, appreciating the possible repercussions and grateful for their son's concern and courage. They found a way to help their troubled son without implicating his brother.

Being able to confide in a family member can ease the young person's pressures. Older siblings may help by guiding the parents in the way they deal with their teenager. Often, the siblings see what the parents cannot, or they can offer help and support because they are less threatened by the youth culture. It is a lucky young person who has such an older brother or sister. Sometimes it works the other way. One sibling may side with another against the parent to get a decision changed. This is a difficult situation for the parent, and parents feel great stress when they have to deal with a double onslaught.

Adolescents do need a way to evaluate their loyalties. Parental understanding is a good first step. Loyalty to the peer group is likely to be a pro-peer stand rather than an anti-adult one. Adolescents themselves have to judge the importance of the immediate social group, their peers, and decide whether, in the particular situation, the peer group is the more important one in their life.

Power and loyalty are outer manifestations of inner attitudes. If youngsters feel secure in themselves, they will not feel a need for exorbitant power over their environment. If they feel appreciated in their homes and schools, they will be loyal without being slavish. Their identity in the group will be important but not critical.

An excerpt from Robert Frost's poem, *Mending Walls* began this chapter. When we build walls, we wall ourselves in and others out. An insecure adolescent divides the world into friends and enemies, feeling secure within a confined group of like-minded peers. People who are different are enemies and need to be walled out. They are labeled as weird and strange; they are put down, kept away or intimidated. Because these teenagers feel powerless, they seek ways to be more powerful than their adversaries. In showing their power, they feel big, but they shut out possibilities of growth. When Frost says, "Something there is that doesn't love a wall, that wants it down", we have a picture of the maturing teenager, who has reached the point where he enjoys camaraderie but not at the expense of others, and who is able to transform power and loyalty into capacities for courage and compassion.

Behind the struggle for power and loyalty lies a much deeper issue, namely, meeting another human being. When teenagers learn to accept themselves, respect themselves, and like themselves, if they do not have to prove that they are bigger, better, faster, or tougher, they can begin to glimpse the "I" that lives within them.

Respect for and acceptance of the other person, whether adult or peer, is the first step in "seeing the other". When adolescents develop emotional maturity, they are making progress specifically in this area of human relationships. On the other hand, if this maturity does not develop, and they relate to people in a highly competitive and overly aggressive manner, the scene is set for a chaotic and painful adulthood. In its essence, the question of power and loyalty is the social issue lying at the basis of relationships between people as well as between groups, such as nations. Many adults walk around with unresolved attitudes having to do with power and loyalty. These attitudes give rise to unworthy impulses, especially when the individual's "higher self" has been worn down by fatigue or stress. Because these attitudes are unresolved, unconscious and powerful influences are ready to jump out whenever the lower nature or "the double" rears its head. This occurs especially at times of stress. The biting, searing, cutting statements that flash out in an argument are the residue of unresolved power-loyalty conflicts which go on to haunt personal and professional relationships.

What began as an examination of issues between parents and children moves naturally into the greater issue of living in harmony with other human beings. This subject includes a variety of communication skills such as admitting one's mistakes, assessing one's needs and communicating them objectively, expressing hurts and disappointments when they occur instead of waiting for them to build up and explode, developing tact and honesty, and realizing that we do not have the right answers for every situation.

Dealing with the conflicts of everyday life teaches us that one person is rarely right and the other wrong and that there does not always have to be a winner and a loser. Both sides can win by discussing the problem and meeting in the middle. Learning to deal with conflict in this way enables teenagers to develop necessary skills for adult life.

The highest expression of human interaction is the I–Thou relationship. In this special relationship, one acknowledges the spiritual essence living in the other and respects the importance of the other's concerns as equal to one's own. One acknowledges that every human being has a task, and one honors the task of the other. Resolving the issues of power and loyalty that confront them enables teenagers to build a firm foundation for deep relationships in their adult lives.

Chapter Twenty

The role of love

What are we doing in love?
What are we doing in love?
I'm too young,
I am scared.
What am I doing in love?
The flowers 're still blooming,
The grass fresh and green.
What am I doing?
What am I doing, –

Ninth grade girl

"Mom, how will I know when I'm really in love?"

Love – is there any other word in our language with such a wide range of meanings? Is there another word with such power? Is any other word the subject of so many poems, letters, and songs? And is any other word open to so many interpretations and misunderstandings? Love is the greatest creative force in the world. It is the ideal of human relationships, and the basis of sacrifice between parents and children, husband and wife, friend and friend, person and God. Yet, it is also trivialized, cheapened, and denied its deeper meaning.

When children come into the world, they are an expression of pure love. They give total trust to those who care for them. As they grow and slowly separate themselves emotionally from parents, their love is extended to neighbors, friends, teachers and grandparents. And, of course, they have a special love for animals.

When children reach adolescence, a new experience of love is possible. From deep within the soul comes a new awakening on two levels – ideal love and sexual love.

Ideal love carries with it the qualities of pure spiritual love, total union, sacrifice and joy. The light of the higher self illuminates the journey of the soul. It is all-giving, all-forgiving and its radiance is wide enough to include all of humanity.

The impulse of sexual love comes from the newly freed soul-life. Feelings are kindled and warmed for a member of the opposite sex. In everyday life, these feelings are connected with instincts and desires, and they lead to an awareness of personal sexuality. Youngsters become especially conscious of their sexuality as they approach puberty, girls through awareness of menstruation, and boys through erections and wet dreams. They are both fascinated and embarrassed by the functioning of their bodies.

Ideal love lives in the mind and penetrates the soul. Youngsters form thoughts about the inner being of the person of the opposite sex, and they idealize the person. Some youngsters experience this around twelve, when they participate in the ritual of "going steady". Going steady involves careful preparation, usually a short-term relationship and speedy dissolution. For the eleven or twelve-year-old, going steady has a completely different quality from the going steady of sixteen and seventeen-year-olds. It may include the following sequence:

Step One: Thinking about it, planning with friends, asking others to find out if the feelings are mutual;
Step Two: Asking the question, usually in an offhand, awkward manner, probably by telephone or note rather than in person;
Step Three: Going steady. This includes sitting together, occasional hand-holding, sneaking kisses and endless telephone conversations;
Step Four: Breaking up;
Step Five: Gossiping about what did or did not happen. In going steady, the young teens are more in love with the idea of love than with each other. There isn't very much Going and even less Steady.

As adolescence progresses, the ideal of love intensifies, and romantic love blossoms. Ideal love is cultivated as the adolescent forms thoughts about the higher and finer nature of the other person. The feelings that emerge out of ideal or romantic love arise from such nurturing thoughts, whereas sexual love arises from the instincts and desires of the person. Of course, ideal love and sexual love together are part of the love experience.

The first love of the mid-teen years (15–17) has a different quality from the twelve-year-old's experiment with going steady. This new experience brings a deeper and richer range of emotions than ever before. They see life from a new perspective; life is bathed in a glow, and all the world is born anew.

Being in love with love makes lovers want to change the ugliness of the world caused by pollution, poverty, hatred, greed and pain. They want to help the poor, heal the Earth, give, share and love other human beings. The impulse for social renewal, which sprouts during this first love, grows throughout adolescence into the social conscience of their twenties, generating enthusiasm and idealism to make the world a better place.

These first experiences with love become the foundation upon which other relationships are based. While each positive experience gives confidence for the next one, painful experiences occur too, and the adolescent must overcome these to develop security and trust in a new relationship.

However, growth is often born of pain, and emotional maturity is a blessing even if it has a bittersweet quality. The ending of teenage relationships can make a youngster feel despair, yet how often we adults look back with gratitude that intense teenage relationships which seemed so perfect at the time did not lead to marriage! How thankful we are that the popular heart-throb of our senior year of high school or freshman year of college did not become our life's companion and the parent of our children.

For teenagers, love offers the same challenge it does for lovers of all ages – How to transform the intense and exclusive love for one's partner into love for humanity? As long as love is reserved for the loved one only, it is egoistic and possessive. "I want this for *us*" is only a slight variation on, "I want this for *me*". In teenager love, egoism is intensified by the adolescents' need to separate themselves from their parents and to find independent identities. Exclusivity is experienced as independence from authority, as two against the world. How often the drive to stay out late or sneak off to forbidden places stems as much from a need to rebel as from a need to be with the boyfriend or girlfriend.

The couple often feels singled out. On one hand, they feel that the world revolves around them. On the other hand, they feel that life's restrictions are aimed directly at them. They become a fortress, protecting their love from the world. They become so closely identified with each other that they find it difficult to function separately within a group.

A couple may enjoy these intense feelings for each other, but an antisocial element develops when they are with friends or at school. They find it difficult to participate in the group because they have eyes only for each other. Resentment builds as friends feel rejected and frustrated by the couple's lack of interest in the group. The parent or teacher who tries to penetrate the fortress must do so with tact. The couple is often so insecure and thereby defensive that any word from the voice of authority is reacted against rather than listened to. They do not see the inappropriateness of their behavior and accuse the adult of meddling, lacking understanding, of disliking them and even of jealousy. Their resentment often comes out in such comments as, "What's your problem?" or "Why are you on our case?"

Yet the fortress must be penetrated, and the young couple needs to wake up to what is fitting in each situation. Such a discussion, when it is successful, helps the young people strengthen their individual identities as well as their identity as a couple. Indeed, deep in their souls, they know what is appropriate and even appreciate the adults' nudging them out of their excessive dependence on each other. If the young people accept the advice of the adult and move back into the larger group, it very often helps their relationship move to a more mature level, allowing them as individuals to pursue their separate interests while nurturing their mutual love.

When adolescents experience love, they are setting out on one of life's most transforming experiences. If it is allowed to do its work, the teenager's narrow, indulgent love will blossom into the love of mankind which is the basis for human social progress. Love that is rooted in wisdom and understanding celebrates the spiritual in the other human being. Thus, the love of mankind that is needed for social renewal is a transformation of the sexual love prevalent in adolescence.

Sexual love, usually characterized by possessiveness and self-love, must be transformed so that it is freed from the body and becomes love of the *other*.

This love for the other usually takes the form of family love, for one's companion, husband, wife, child, or grandparent. It is a higher form of love than mere sexual love, but family love is still too egoistic to develop into a true social life.

The third stage is the love of the higher Self of another person, regardless of sex or family relationship. My husband likes to quote one of his early mentors who said, "Love is not blind. It's visionary". The person in love sees the highest aspect of the beloved.

When two people meet ego to ego, there is spiritual communion, and love arising from such a meeting nourishes not only the two individuals, but also the social life of the community. At this stage of development, each works to rid his or her self of egoism. The person becomes involved in outer things and the needs of other people. When this occurs, people experience a spiritual presence in the physical world, enhancing their own ability to experience love and sympathy. Such a deep soul-experience leads not only to understanding, but to feeling the needs of others as one's own. The task of modern man in the spiritual evolution of humanity is to develop the capacity for such love, according to Rudolf Steiner.

The capacity of love is with us at birth and never leaves us. Although sexual love comes early in human development, ideal love is placed side by side with it. Although sexual love is compelling in its demands on the present moment, it becomes a gateway to the transformation of the individual's feeling life if it is appropriately awakened.

Ideal love points to the future. It lights the way. Sexual love is necessary for the continuation of the human race and as a vehicle of tenderness and intimacy. It is the seed for a meaningful social relationship, for the renewal of society, but it is only a seed. Beginning by fostering respect and caring for the relationship, the two people need to extend their concerns over an ever larger community until they love all humanity. In this broad perspective, one can appreciate why adolescents need to understand love, sex, and relationship. To cultivate respect and to learn to listen, to nurture support and understanding, is to pave the way for developing new capacities of unselfishness in human evolution, expressed in the statement by St Paul, "Not I, but the Christ in me".

PART III

The Problems of Adolescence

Chapter Twenty One

Problems of self-esteem

Pressures, decisions and depression

> Despair is the price one pays for setting oneself an
> impossible aim.
> Graham Greene, *The Heart of the Matter*

About a year ago, I attended a gathering of teenagers who were discussing alcoholism. A few weeks later, I attended another discussion, and the topic this time was teenage sexuality. During both evenings, the recurring concern was self-esteem. It didn't seem to matter whether the teenager was male or female, the most popular youngster in the school, an academically outstanding student, a sports hero, or a shy teen who had difficulty speaking out in class.

Lack of self-esteem causes youngsters to demean themselves, to make dangerous decisions they do not want to make, and to walk around feeling, "I'm not good enough". Teenagers handle this feeling in diverse ways. Some become compulsive super-achievers; some withdraw; some take severe risks. Most teenagers experience depression that rises and falls according to their maturity, the strength of their self-image, or the affirmation they experience – or don't experience – in their relationships at school, at home and elsewhere.

What is self-esteem?

Self-esteem has to do with whether people regard themselves favorably, whether they feel good about themselves. Already in early childhood, youngsters form self-images based on how the family treats them. Children usually try to win their parents' approval. An unspoken question is, "How do my parents want me to be?"

During the seven-to-twelve phase, the teacher becomes a powerful influence on the child's self-image. Whether the child feels competent, stupid, brilliant, or mediocre is a reflection of the teacher's attitude. Now the child also asks, "How does my teacher want me to be?"

As the soul develops, individual identity becomes a major issue. Teenagers are fascinated with how they appear to others. They develop what David Elkind refers to in his book, *All Grown Up & No Place To Go*, as the "imaginary audience". Elkind writes;

> Because teenagers are caught up with the transformations they are undergoing – in their bodies, in their facial structure, in their feelings and emotions, and in their thinking powers – they become self-centered. They assume that everyone around them is concerned about the same thing they are concerned with, namely themselves. I call this assumption the imaginary audience. It is the imaginary audience that accounts for the teenager's extreme self-consciousness. Teenagers feel that they are always on stage and that everyone around them is as aware and as concerned about their appearance and behavior as they themselves are.[1]

They feel that they have to impress those around them, but they are not sure who *they* are. To find out, young teenagers put on many different masks. The response to each mask gives the teenager clues to the acceptability of one personality type and another. Thus, the youngster decides whether to adopt a particular way of behaving.

The teenager turns to peers to define behavior. The unspoken question to the peers is, "Tell me who I am", or "What do you want me to be?" Of course, advertisements, teen magazines, movies and songs have a significant influence on the way the peers form their evaluation.

As the youngster passes through the sixteenth-year change, the mask becomes less important. The teenager gradually gains greater control over his or her sense of person. Comments such as, "I've been thinking …" or "I'd like to be …" become fairly common. It is easy to become stereotyped in adolescence, and some youngsters have to leave home or change schools to start over again with a new image.

An eighteen-year-old who had been extremely withdrawn came to life in her senior year. She told her class, "I'm not sitting here quietly any more. I've got a lot to say, and you're going to hear me say it. I'm bursting out of the shell I've had around me for years."

Another girl, who had a traumatic relationship with her mother, could not feel good about herself. She said, "I can't figure out what I think of me until my mother accepts me. How can I accept myself if she doesn't accept me?"

For healthy emotional development, adolescents need a protective circle of support. This circle should include their family, their school, their religious leaders, and their community. However, with the breakdown of the family, de-personalization of the schools, weakening of religious ties and instability of the community, teenagers do not have a protective circle. Instead, they live in a world that limits and defines their acceptance according to narrow standards set by someone working on Madison Avenue or in Hollywood.

The expectations placed on teenagers cause stress and frustration. The youngster unconsciously asks, "What does society want me to be?" Advertisements, magazines and movies create an image of the acceptable male or female, defining how teenagers should walk, how they should socialize, what they should drink, what soaps they should use, etc. They define acceptable masculine and feminine behavior, and they set standards of beauty and style.

As sixteen-year-olds, my friend Debbi and I pored over an issue of *Seventeen* magazine, reading a quiz which told us our type. I never could figure out whether I was a gamin or a realist, but whichever I decided I was would determine the clothes I would wear and the way I would approach boys and school life, so some days I tried to look like Audrey Hepburn, and other days, I tried to look like Lauren Bacall.

Teenagers never feel good enough compared to the models in ads or to movie stars. Because teenagers can never measure up to these ideal figures, they are left with the feeling, "I'm not good enough. I'm either too fat, too skinny, too tall, too short, too flat-chested, too large-busted, too full-hipped, too lean. My hair is too straight, too curly, too long, too short, too fine, too thick." They fantasize that other teens are confident, look better, have an easier life, know what they want, feel o.k. about themselves. They are always shocked to find out that others feel insecure, too. Developing a sense of humor about oneself during this time is one of the greatest aids a teenager can have.

The teenager is in process of becoming a person. In his or her mind, the questions nag, "Do you like me?" "Does he like me?" "Does she like me?" At the deepest level, these questions are, "Do I like myself?" and "Does God like me?"

When the teenager asks, "What do I have to do to be liked?" he or she does not hear the same answers that a helpful adult might suggest, such as, "Be kinder, be more considerate, be more under-standing, give more time to other people, be more helpful, get to know more people, be interested in their interests and see if you can make someone feel more comfortable."

When the teenager looks to society for answers, the messages that come back are, "Wear your hair in the latest fashion, buy certain brands of clothes, walk in a certain way, flirt, put on a mask, hang around with certain people, avoid other people, count the times certain people say hello to you, identify the groups you want to stay clear of and which ones you want to associate with, don't put yourself out too much, don't be too smart, don't be a do-gooder – and then you'll be o.k."

The dreams that teenagers carry in their hearts don't seem greatly valued by their community. They soon learn what is acceptable and what isn't. The teenagers' place in society has become tenuous. Instead of being needed, instead of feeling that they have a place in the community, youngsters do not know where they fit. They are not children and they are not adults. Most of what they want to do when they are fourteen, fifteen, or sixteen is illegal or unadvisable, yet they are being urged to do it anyway.

They find out that their dreams are not as attainable as they thought. During the senior year of high school, many teenagers are naive about what they'll be able to do in life. One idealistic young woman said in October of her senior year, "Life for me is like a candy store. There are so many things that I can have, I don't know what to choose." By April, after college acceptances and rejections, her candy store had narrowed its offerings. Six months later, after being exposed to the job world and to college, her choices were even fewer. She was more realistic and more disappointed than she had been twelve months earlier.

Adolescents find out that the road to their dreams takes longer and requires more preparation than they had expected, and that there are more and more limitations along the way. While they are students, their identities become merged with the school's. How often a young person feels, "I've got it made because I got into this school", or "My life is finished – I didn't get in." Or someone thinks that a youngster is special because he or she was accepted by or attends a prestigious school. When a youngster is rejected by a college because of very stiff competition, he or she often interprets that as, "I'm not good enough. They didn't want me".

As a high school teacher, I've come to resent April – that dread, yet exciting month when the mail brings thin envelopes that mean rejection and thick envelopes that mean acceptance. If the results aren't what the youngsters had hoped, they feel, "I have failed. I haven't lived up to their (parents', teachers') expectations". Depression sets in.

A similar series of disappointments occurs in the job world. The youngster lands a job and is treated in an impersonal way. Schedules are changed around, the interests, sensitivities, or values of the youngster are of no concern to the employer. The youngster soon sees himself or herself as just another anonymous body in the job market. A sensitive vegetarian finds himself pounding meat in a hamburger joint. If he doesn't want to do it, he loses his job. A young woman is told to set up the salad bar in a particular way. Out of interest, she asks, "Why?" She is fired for having a bad attitude. Youngsters are promised thirty hours and given fifteen. Their lives are messed up because they had one expectation and the reality is something else. They find themselves running between jobs. They cannot question or they lose their jobs, and there are many more teenagers waiting to take those jobs if they become available.

Most teenagers' dreams of ideal family life already have been dashed, either by the dissolution of their own family or by that of a friend's family. Insecurity in relationships combines with the tentativeness of the youngster's sense of belonging to leave him or her feeling alone. Panicked by the sense of isolation, teenagers join groups, become part of a pack, become "we" and "us" in order to feel safe. Paradoxically, they worry about finding friends, they find them, and then they are afraid of losing them. They worry about being rejected. If they don't have the friends they want, or if they lose their friends or are rejected by them, they become depressed.

Adolescents with strong self-esteem know who they are and what they want; they are not easily influenced by peer pressure. Self-esteem, of course, offers no protection against misguided experiments and other forms of poor judgment.

The lack of self-esteem, however, exposes the adolescent to additional hazards. Over and over, I hear teenagers speak of getting drunk, getting stoned, playing chicken with cars, or getting pregnant, because they wanted to feel accepted, because they didn't want to look like a "jerk", or because they wanted to show they knew their way around. Had they strong self-esteem at a particular moment, they might have said, "No".

With strong self-esteem, a youngster may choose to avoid a bad situation but do it in a way that does not buck the group. One sixteen-year-old, for instance, knew that his friends were planning a bash that Saturday night, and he didn't want to be part of it. He created an excuse that his parents had something else planned. He didn't confront his friends, but he also didn't lose their friendship. Other youngsters just don't show up and simply make the excuse, "I couldn't get away".

Excuses can't be used often, however, without causing resentment. At some point, the teenager who has grown uncomfortable with the crowd's behavior will have to take a stand or leave the group. Surprisingly often, if the youngster has the strong affection of the group, taking a stand can awaken their consciousness as well and turn the whole group around.

Most groups will accept a person who makes his or her limits clear, as long as the teenager has a secure position in the group to start with and doesn't preach to the rest of the group. "Whatever turns you on", seems to be a motto among many teen groups; "If you want to do it, cool. If you don't, cool." The typical teenager assiduously avoids judging his group-friends with the implicit attitude, "I'm not taking a stand and I won't be influenced by anyone else".

Depression

Depression, disappointment and despair are a normal part of human life, but problems arise when a teenager suffers such prolonged depression that it affects his or her ability to respond to life's challenges, especially when the youngster feels that there is no way out of the problem.

Depression may result from feelings of rejection, loneliness, loss, isolation, or from a change in family life, or a move. The cause can also be something as vague as a lack of direction or simply being overwhelmed by the experience of being an adolescent in today's world. The reason can be something as seemingly simple as a loss of a stuffed animal or a cancelled appointment. Sometimes a combination of things triggers depression – a friend moves away, a pet dies, a parent is hurt – and the youngster feels overwhelmed and helpless. At such times, it's especially easy for the young person to turn to alcohol or drugs.

How to recognize depression

It is difficult to tell if teenagers are deeply depressed or whether they are simply moody. The everyday frustrations of a sensitive adolescent may look very much like depression yet are completely healthy and normal feelings.

It seems strange to be on the alert for adolescent depression. We can understand a forty-five-year-old being depressed, but don't teenagers have everything in front of them? What can be so bad to discourage them at this young age? Psychiatry once claimed that true depression could not exist before the age of eighteen, but we now know better. Children and even infants can become depressed when they experience separation. Youngsters of all ages and from all classes of society experience deep depression.

Symptoms of depression are usually not directly related to the problem. They may be psychosomatic – headaches, stomach-aches, or chest pains – or the youngster may stop doing homework, fail school, become truant, take drugs, change eating patterns, lose interest in hobbies, or become listless and generally torpid. Because they feel lonely and isolated, they may seek escape in sex, pregnancy, truancy, running away, or suicide. Other symptoms of depression may be trouble at school, drug or alcohol abuse, repeated abortions, or violence.

It is always better to be concerned than to ignore symptoms of depression. If youngsters have the symptoms mentioned above, especially after a significant loss, the situation should not be ignored. Parents should talk with the youngster, with a doctor, a counselor, a minister, teachers, a psychologist – anyone they have confidence in to help determine the situation.

Stress and depression

Depression usually arises from stress or a combination of stresses. Common stresses are change, loss, and high expectations. The adolescent responds to them by feeling grief, guilt and/or anger.

Change and loss

Change means leaving something behind and moving on to something new. Inwardly, the adolescent experiences the leaving as loss, as a death, and goes through a period of mourning or grief.

Growing up means leaving childhood behind. Children must adapt to new feelings and new ways their body behaves, such as the awkwardness of their legs and arms or the changes in their voice. Losing confidence in the physical body creates tension, frustration and melancholy. The onset of menstruation is a significant cause of depression in adolescent girls. The adolescent grows moody. "What am I supposed to do? How am I supposed to act? I'm not ready to grow up. Why does it have to happen to me?"

Growing up also means losing childhood innocence. Youngsters hear and see things of the seedy side of life, destroying the purity they once felt. The grapevine of information brings them all kinds of information and mis-information. As they "fall into matter", they become fascinated with the grotesque, the sick, the gross. Lust, violence, or perversions may flood their imagination while part of them longs for the time before they knew what life was like.

Growing up means losing dependence upon parents. New freedoms and privileges create stress on teenagers. They are concerned with knowing how to behave in new situations, how to do the right thing. They fear making fools of themselves or giving the wrong impression.

Along with the general loss of childhood come specific losses, and the adolescent is more vulnerable to them than parents imagine. At a more stable time, loss would not cause the same stress. For example, if the family moves, the youngster's familiar boundaries are lost, and everything changes at once: friends, home, social rules and lifestyle. My family moved from New York City to a small Florida town when I was beginning the seventh grade. Each new experience produced anxiety – riding my bike to the new school, getting lost, registering for classes, trying to understand the Southern accent. My dress was wrong, my speech was wrong. I didn't know anyone, and we were in the middle of hurricane season. How could life be so miserable? Instead of experiencing adventure, I experienced stress.

Changing schools or neighborhoods even within the same city or town creates stress. "Whom do I talk to? Will I be accepted? Which group should I try to get into? Will they like me? What if I eat lunch alone? What are the teachers' expectations? Where is the restroom? Will I get pushed around? How do I impress people?"

Adults who make changes also experience stress, and adult depression is common, yet we rarely take adolescent stress seriously. I recently attended a week-long conference at a prestigious university. Having come from a struggling immigrant family, I do not have a prestigious educational background. I felt anxiety building in my stomach. I didn't know if I was wearing the right thing. I didn't know whom to sit with. I abhor cocktail hours, but each meal began with one. As an adult, however, I have learned to deal with new and threatening situations. The new situation was uncomfortable, but because I know who I am, it was not as threatening. To an inexperienced and insecure adolescent, however, such stress can be overwhelming.

The pain of separation which accompanies loss is like a death experience and causes deep grief. The loss of a best friend, the loss of a romantic relationship, divorce, or the death of a pet, a friend, a parent, or a grandparent may be a major turning point in the teenager's life. The combination of several losses can cause an adolescent to withdraw into seclusion or strike out with hostility. The youngster feels helpless and abandoned.

In the case of divorce the teenager not only feels the loss of the parent who is no longer living at home, but the loss of a family-centred life. Even though some stress is reduced by diminishing the tension between the two parents, the change is resented. New stress comes to take its place, and the loss of familiar routines and expectations shakes the adolescent's feeling of security.

Expectations

One of the major stresses in a teenager's life is the inability to live up to high parental expectations. Adolescents are caught in the tension between hyper-sensitivity and hyper-criticism. Parent criticism makes them feel vulnerable and rejected. They feel unappreciated, unnoticed, and unloved. Yet at the time they are insensitive to the fact that they trample on the feelings of their parents, criticizing and rejecting as they please. They are quick to point out hypocrisy in others, but they can't help living it in themselves. It doesn't help to point this out because it only aggravates the situation. What does help most is to have conversations in which the adult expresses appreciation and understanding for the youngster.

Parents are not conscious of how many goals and expectations they set for their children. When these goals cannot be met, the youngsters feel insecure and unworthy. If the expectations were unrealistic in the first place and cannot be met, the teenager does not experience the fact that the expectations were unrealistic, the teenager experiences the failure. Here there is much the parent can do. Expectations should be discussed and arrived at together. The teenager should have a chance to question the expectations before they are set. If teenagers can agree that the expectations are fair, or if they can come up with their own which the parent approves, they not only have established a working relationship with the adult, but they feel they have some control over their lives. The older the teenager, the more expectations should arise out of joint agreement and less from the parent's wishes.

A temporary form of let-down after high expectations comes during the senior year of high school. The successful students have achieved their goals, done very well in high school, and have been accepted at the college of their choice. What is next? What about the reactions of other people? A best friend did not do as well. Another friend is jealous of the teenager's accomplishments. The successful students may feel isolated from friends. The honour has distinguished them, but it has also separated them from their friends.

Or they have plans made for a job after graduation. Or they have plans to travel. They feel ready to go out and meet the world. But do they feel ready? They are not sure. They are itching to get out of high school and challenge the world. How can they get through the daily routine for the next five months? They become moody, restless, bored, irritable. But 'Senioritis' will pass and it does not give most parents or teachers concern.

When I was not able to give a top grade to a young man who felt under pressure to succeed, he lost his self-control and yelled, "You have ruined my life." When he didn't get into schools of his choice, he went into a depression. Since then he has worked through those early feelings and has been a very effective student and worthwhile young man.

Similar experiences of feeling let-down after success is felt by athletes. After attention is focused on them, after they have been cheered and paraded, what comes next? What can compete with the sense of exhilaration? It is not unusual for depression to follow.

Many youngsters do not understand how natural this pattern is in life. They try to keep the high and avoid the let-down through drugs and alcohol. Adults can help teenagers by discussing this pattern with them, by preparing them for the experience, by lending them support and not just praising them when they are succeeding.

It is not unusual for teenagers to see the future hinging on one small event. When that event does not turn out as expected it seems tragedy is just around the corner. Most teenagers can absorb temporary depression as part of life. Dealing with disappointment helps the youngster come to terms with reality. What is the fine line between temporary appropriate depression and a serious depressive state? This depends very much on the individual person and situation.

Lack of trust

Another weakening of self-esteem comes when the adult sends out a clear signal – I don't trust you.

I have sat through parent conferences in which a parent dominates the discussion. Whenever the teenager tries to speak, the parent interrupts and fields the question, explaining how the youngster feels, what his or her hobbies are, what school activities are preferred, and so on. Is it any wonder the student feels intimidated? When teenagers feel that what they say is not important, when the parent interrupts to explain what the youngster is trying to say, this experience is a blow to his or her shaky self-esteem.

Teenagers are more receptive to criticism if it is given in small doses so that it can be discussed rather than as direct confrontation which is taken as a personal attack and against which they feel they must defend themselves. Teenagers want to be respected and listened to the way anyone does. When adults hold back this respect, when teenagers feel that what they say is not important – their self-esteem suffers.

When teenagers feel their parents do not trust them to make decisions, they feel suffocated and the crisis builds. When they feel every decision is being made for them they feel little power over their own lives and this sense of helplessness leads to depression.

Parents are busy, working, trying to keep their lives together. Teenagers feel the loss of time available as loss of caring. The adolescent internalizes this as rejection. Because teenagers need their parents so much, when they interpret the lack of time as lack of love they are left feeling unloved and unwanted.

Specific family problems can also cause depression. Arguments and physical fighting, alcoholism or drug abuse of parents or siblings cause the teenager to feel helpless.

If the parents do not communicate well, with each other or with their children, the home feels empty and cold. Feelings are suppressed, and everyone goes through the motions of daily life, but there is no joy.

Examples of teenage depression

In spite of all the media impressions of how much fun sex is, how "everyone is doing it", many young women feel a sense of loss. An eighteen-year-old woman described her feelings when she lost her virginity. "After I had sex for the first time, I went for a walk and sat on the shore of the lake and stared into space. I felt grey and empty. I loved my boyfriend, and my unhappy feelings did not have anything to do with him. I just felt different. I felt older and alone. I knew my childhood had passed and I could never be innocent again. I spent hours sitting and staring. It was one of the saddest days of my life."

A sixteen-year-old girl was very confused about her sexuality. She desperately wanted friends as well as a special boyfriend. She attracted friends quickly and lost them quickly. She drained their energies. Insecure in her family and jealous of a very talented sibling, she would fall into dark moods and then further alienate those who reached out to her. At the core of the problem was a lack of self-esteem. On one hand she did not feel worthy; on the other she was furious when she was rejected.

A seventeen-year-old boy was preoccupied by his lack of growth. Concerned about both parents who were alcoholics, he felt rejected and a failure. It was easier not to try in school in case he might fail there too.

A fifteen-year-old girl went into depression because she didn't feel accepted by "the" group. She tried everything, yet whatever attention the group gave her wasn't enough. She was jealous of their homes, their families, their clothes, the "right" way they dressed, and their confidence in the social scene. She finally left that school because she could not shake the depression.

A seventeen-year-old boy felt rejected by his girlfriend's parents. Under pressure from them, his girlfriend wanted more space in the relationship. She asked him to relax his intensity. He wanted her. He said his life would never be the way he pictured it. He had to have her. No matter what was said to him, he stared at the ground and repeated, "But I want her."

A thirteen-year-old girl became ill, yet no symptoms could be found. She couldn't get out of bed; she felt sad all the time. She was part of a triangle of girls and felt left out most of the time. She wanted the other two girls to reach out to her more often. She felt sorry for herself and wanted them to feel sorry for her too. So she stayed in bed unable to face the day.

A fourteen-year-old feels unlike the rest of the family. Convinced they don't understand him, he asks "Why was I born?" He retires into his room, eats by himself, runs away, fantasizes being adopted by a family that understands him. His depression confuses his family, but they don't know what to do about it. His minister tells him he must respect his mother's wishes. His mother tells him he has to be part of the family, and he cannot spend so much time alone. He feels trapped.

Why do some teenagers get depressed while others who have reason to do so, don't? Many depressed teenagers have one or both parents who are depressed. When the teenager needs support, the parents are lost in their own problems and not available to help.

Adults usually show their depression by being withdrawn. But teenagers often show their depression by getting angry, by being rebellious. They don't know how to handle the frustration and rejections so they strike out and attack.

Because teenagers lack knowledge or experience, they see the world in black and white – it's terrible; it's wonderful. Even though adults often feel depressed, they also know that time heals. They know they will wake up one morning and the world will look better. But teenagers feel hopeless when they experience loss or frustration. The epidemic spread of suicide attempts is related in part to teenage depression.

Many of the situations described in this chapter would not in themselves cause depression. Usually there is one situation that sets off the depression as a reaction. The symptoms that may alert adults to depression in the teenager are:

lack of interest in food
unexpected weight gain or loss
the inability to sleep
sleeping too much
difficulty in waking up
sadness, listlessness
boredom
little interest in past enjoyments
no friends
sudden change in behavior
conflicts
running away
becoming sexually promiscuous
shoplifting
truancy
extreme self-esteem
feeling ugly
feeling a failure
feeling of being unpopular
feeling of incompetence
risky behavior including drugs, alcohol, reckless driving
suicide talk or behavior
self harm

Suicide

We should not leave this chapter without reflecting on the increase of teenage suicides since the 1950s. Youth suicide is now the third leading cause of death amongst adolescents (fifteen to twenty-four years old).

According to Education Week, October 31, 1984, the US Department of Health and Human Services notes the rate of adolescent suicide is 12.3 per 100,000 young people. The Center for Disease Control in Atlanta points out that the "increase in youth suicide is due primarily to the soaring rate in young males." From 1970 to 1980 the rate of male suicides increased by 50 percent, while that for females rose by only two percent. This means roughly five male suicides for every one female suicides. However, these figures can be deceiving because more females attempt to commit suicide, but the attempts fail because they often use overdoses of drugs or of poison and can be saved. The males use more violent means and are often successful in their attempt.

The warning signs of suicide include most of the same signs as depression. If a youngster comes to an adult to speak about suicide, the adult should always give this serious attention. Talking about problems often helps to make the problems become less important.

Suicide is a mystery. Not all youngsters who commit suicide exhibit signs of depression. Not all youngsters leave a suicide note or give clues. What is left in such cases is a big question mark that the survivors live with the rest of their lives.

Perhaps the central message that needs to be communicated to youngsters is that committing suicide is no solution for the problems. Although pain can seem so intense that at the time the only way out seems self-destruction, it is not a way out at all. All the options are then taken away to resolve the problem. It is a solution that is no solution at all. The people who care about the youngster have no way of helping, the youngster loses the opportunity of maturing beyond the problem, and the precious experience of life is foregone. As one young friend of a boy who committed suicide said, "He had so much to *live* for. Look at all he'll miss." Another friend of the same boy said, "I am so angry that he could feel so alone that he could not have reached out to someone to share the problem."

There is no way to avoid stress and loneliness in the process of growing up. Everyone has problems. But some youngsters feel their problems are more severe, more painful than those of others, and they cannot bear to go on. Whether they actually contemplate the repercussions of their deed or whether they are acting out of the moment is a question we will never be able to answer.

We must reach out to support our youngsters, we must take their concerns seriously, but we cannot insulate them from the feelings of inadequacy, frustration, or loneliness. We can hope they have the strength to bear what comes to them in life, and we can tell them and try to show them how much we love them. Sometimes, even that is not enough.

Chapter Twenty Two

Pregnancy and the teenager

I thought if I had a baby I would feel needed and
have someone to love.

16-year-old girl

"Mom, I'm pregnant." Have you ever wondered whether your teen-aged daughter would say those words to you? If other parents in your circle of friends have had to deal with teenage pregnancy, what has your reaction been? You may have breathed a sigh of relief, glad that it wasn't happening in your family. As with other difficult life situations, we are confused and frightened when they actually happen to us, no matter how many times we have thought about them. Most of us carry mental images of the way we hope our lives and those of our children will be. When something disrupts those hopes and dreams, we are disoriented and scared.

How one handles a teen pregnancy depends on a number of considerations, such as the girl's age, how the pregnancy happened, the nature of her relationship with the father, and whether marriage is an option.

Although pregnancy doesn't fit neatly into the normal picture of adolescent life, much joy and closeness can come of it, if the family supports the young couple. The father of the coming child should be involved in decision-making as much as possible. Ultimately, however, the young woman must decide whether to have or abort the baby and whether to keep and raise the child. It is her body, she will carry the child, and she will be chiefly responsible for it for at least the next eighteen years.

Why is this happening? We don't have any quick answers, but the situation poses many questions for parents. Is abortion being used as birth control? When there is so much information available about contraception, why are American teenagers ignoring it and choosing instead to eliminate the fetus and possibly harm themselves as well? What does it mean for us as a society to have so many thousands of teenagers living with the consequences of abortion? How will this affect this generation of youngsters as they become adults?

That is not the whole problem. In addition to the large number of abortions, the percentage of teenagers who have their babies is as high or higher than all the pregnancies (aborted or carried) in similar countries. Does this mean that American teenagers are more sexually active – or that they are less willing to take responsibility for their sexual lives? These are questions to ponder.

However, when a teen pregnancy comes to your own family, statistics fly out the window and you must deal with the problem at hand. Teen pregnancy is one of the most challenging problems a family can face. You, with your daughter, must consider the possibilities. If abortion is an option, time becomes a pressure. You cannot ignore what is happening.

Even though teen pregnancy has become common, it still is not completely accepted. As your daughter advances in her pregnancy she will become the object of gossip. How will the family deal with this? Trying to make decisions, feeling insecure, and feeling pressure all affect the young woman's ability to cope unless she has the strong love and support of her parents.

Every human being is a spiritual individuality – a miracle – the product of the weaving together of physical heredity and spiritual individuality. The young woman has to decide whether to welcome this being onto the Earth or to block its incarnation. If she decides on an abortion, she then must bear the decision within her own conscience.

If she marries, the question will be, is there deep-enough love and caring to sustain the challenges that face all marriages, and especially teen marriages? If she decides to give up the baby for adoption, she again will have to live with the unfulfilled yearning of not knowing how her baby is, what kind of a person her baby has become, and whether she will ever again see him or her.

No decision is easy. The family should consult friends, religious leaders, a doctor, a social worker, or anyone who will help the family think through the choices. Advice is very helpful, but, in the last analysis, the young woman must decide in the intimacy of her family and in the privacy of her heart and conscience. Whatever she decides, parents have an opportunity to give their youngster love and support, guidance and clarity, all of which she will need in this situation.

What are the options and what is involved in each?

The first reality is that young teenagers and mid-teen youngsters, with all due respect to their nascent sophistication and experience, are still children. They are not yet ready to assume the responsibility that comes with parenthood. Because they are preoccupied with themselves and are still learning to be responsible, they have difficulty making the shift to taking care of a child.

Keeping the baby

If she keeps the baby, the young woman has two possibilities, marriage, or raising the baby as a single parent. In either case, she will need proper pre-natal care. She should see a doctor, find out how advanced her pregnancy is, and receive advice on diet and health care.

What about her schooling? Will she remain in school until she is ready to give birth? Some schools have special programs, which include classes in child care as well as pregnancy counseling and support groups for pregnant teenagers. Some teachers are threatened by having a pregnant girl in classes, and some parents feel that a mother-to-be serves as a poor model for their daughters, that the school is implicitly condoning the pregnancy by allowing her to attend school. They are concerned about the attention she receives, and they confuse support and friendliness with supporting premarital sex. (When I was dealing with such a situation, I was surprised that the parents who were most upset about having a pregnant student in class were the mothers and fathers of the more sexually active youngsters. Was the situation coming a bit too close?)

What about the girl's friends? Will they continue to support her? She needs their friendship very much at this time. And her friends' parents? Will they allow their sons and daughters to continue friendships with the pregnant girl? Frightened parents have been known to forbid their sons and daughters to be too close to a young, unmarried, pregnant woman. Needless to say, the youngsters found ways to see their friend and assure her of their loyalty. Through the shock of the parents' reactions, I learned how threatening teen pregnancy can be to adults who otherwise are stable and sympathetic to the needs of young people.

What will the role of the father be? Will his family be involved? Will the couple continue seeing each other? It is not unusual for the girl's parents to forbid the couple to date, or to allow them to see each other only in certain situations. Does this not remind us of the old proverb about locking the barn door after the horse is stolen? Pressure will be placed on both the young man and the young woman because fear and anxiety are inherent in such a situation. The young father's anxiety is heightened because he is legally obliged to support the child until it is eighteen years old or legally adopted. This may be a hardship. Who will pay the costs of medical care and delivery? Will the couple be able to live together if they wish to? To what degree will the parents make decisions about the young parents' lives? Often, the young mother is still a minor.

A teen mother may have many reasons for keeping the baby. If the reasons are not sound, or if parent support is not there, even the young mothers who keep their babies may decide to give them up for adoption after they are born, sometimes even two or three years later. One young friend told me that several of her girlfriends had been pregnant at the same time she was – all around fifteen years old. After the excitement of the delivery and the cute baby days were over, the girls were overwhelmed. Two of her five friends eventually gave their babies up for adoption, after the babies were a year old.

Often the teen mother is emotionally immature and she is not willing to accept responsibility, yet she is assuming the most significant responsibility of her life. She often is frightened and unable to cope with the situation by herself. Regardless of how parents feel, they must consider what their daughter is experiencing.

A good prenatal care program is essential for teens, and parents should be sure the young woman participates. With diet and medical guidance, the young teenager can have a healthy and successful pregnancy. Without guidance, however, problems can and do occur, such as birth injuries, infant death, illness, or mental retardation. Low birth weight often is a result of drugs, alcohol, smoking, and poor diet. Anemia and toxemia also are common when the mother does not receive proper medical care. A higher death rate exists for younger mothers who do not take adequate care of themselves.

Everything possible should be done to help the young woman prepare herself physically, psychologically, and spiritually for the birth and care of the child. If the young woman can appreciate the wonder and awe of the incoming being, she may be able to prepare herself to receive the child in quite a different way than if she perceives childbirth and childraising as purely physical responsibilities. Experienced and loving mothers in the community may be able to help her by inviting her to their homes, talking about the care of the child, sharing hints, and welcoming her into motherhood.

Getting married or not getting married

The decision to marry because of teenage pregnancy is very sensitive. Clearly, it would be better for the mother and the child to be in a secure, protected, and nurturing relationship if that is what the marriage would bring. Unfortunately, most teenagers have enough trouble handling the complexities of boy-girl relationships and would be unable to carry the seriousness of marriage. The question of marriage should be considered very carefully. The scars of divorce may be as traumatic as the scar of being a single parent until one is mature enough for marriage. Teenagers who are at least seventeen have a better chance of developing a mature relationship.

There are many alternatives. In one case, the parents insisted that their fifteen-year-old daughter live at home, continue going to school, and have her baby. She and her boyfriend could continue their relationship, and, after graduation from high school, could marry. The young woman followed through in this way, despite some difficult times, and the couple married and began their life together. They have been married for over six years and have two children in what appears to be a stable and happy marriage.

In another case, the pregnancy was the result of a summer romance. After much consideration, the couple decided to marry.

They received strong support – both financial and moral – and have become independent and solid as a family. They, too, now have a second child.

Another young woman wanted no connection at all with the father of her child. She moved in with her parents, who were saddened by the situation, but supported her and received the grandchild with loving attention. They have helped the young woman stand on her feet, continue her education, and be a good mother. As she said not long ago, "Even with all the support I've had, life has been very hard".

Most young teen mothers who return to high school drop out unless they have a strong parent, sibling, or friend standing behind them. It is difficult to be a high school student and then go home and deal with a tired or sick baby. In addition, being out of touch with high school life may result in alienation from peers.

School friendships tend to drop off and new ones made with other young mothers. The young woman now is more concerned about colic than about solving the quadratic equation.

Teenaged mothers who are punished by their parents and made to live with the consequences of their actions often haven't enough education or income to take care of themselves and their child. On top of that, they bear terrible isolation. Whom is the parent punishing? And what lesson is really being taught? The young mother often ends up on welfare or marrying prematurely for companionship and security – and soon after, pregnant again and possibly abandoned by the husband.

Marriage may be the right decision for the young couple, but it should be made only after a great deal of careful thought and with sensitivity to the couple's age, the quality of their relationship, and the kind of support the two will receive from their families.

Adoption

If the pregnant teenager considers adoption, she has to think about dropping out of normal life for a year, usually losing a year of school, changes in her social life, and a change in her self-esteem. As she carries the child, she comes to feel a connection with it, yet she knows that she will give it up. She may feel guilty about giving up the baby, but, on the other hand, there is a serious shortage of adoptive babies and large numbers of couples yearn to adopt a child. These people offer care, love, attention, security and a home. In such cases, adoption may be a choice that solves the predicament in a selfless way – assuring life and love to the child she is carrying, and offering the opportunity of parenthood to deserving people.

With the liberalizing of regulations concerning the confidentiality of adoption records, many biological parents and children are finding each other, years after the adoptions. These reconciliations can bring embarrassment (as in cases where the mother has not told her husband or family), but they can also resolve guilt and bring joy to all.

Adoption is a great sacrifice; it is also a responsible way to resolve the situation of the young woman who is not ready for marriage or for motherhood. About twenty years ago, a family friend sent her pregnant daughter to live with our family for a few months. The young woman gained support and warmth by being in a family during that lonely time, even though her sense of loss was great whenever she thought of giving up her child. After the baby was born and the adoption proceedings complete, she returned to her home, resumed her job, and, after several years, she married and had a family of her own. As far as I know, she has had no connection with the child she gave up for adoption. When she married at twenty, she was mature and ready for a deep relationship – much more than she would have been at sixteen.

Abortion

Once a youngster learns that she is pregnant, she usually has trouble believing it. More than anything, she wishes the whole situation were a dream and would go away. Taking the life of the fetus is not what she wants, but she may feel that it is her only option. Abortion for most young women is seldom chosen without serious thought and feeling. Her dilemma confronts the young woman with her actions – she cannot be sexually active without consequences. For those young people who have been having casual sex, the actual experience of having an abortion usually shocks them into seeing the serious consequences of their behavior. Regardless of why the young couple did not use birth control, the reality of an abortion may force them to look at it. The issue between parent and teenager boils down to responsibility and communication.

If a youngster uses abortion instead of contraception as a regular means of birth control – and some do! – she is being completely irresponsible. She is not considering the moral issue involved in abortion with appropriate seriousness. If she continues to be sexually active and does not take precautions, she is developing a calloused attitude toward life which will affect her relationships in other areas of life as well.

The considerations are legal, physical, psychological, moral and spiritual. The physical danger is especially acute for young teens. Girls under sixteen are more likely to suffer damage to the cervix than women over twenty because the cervix in younger girls tends to be small and inelastic. Many teenagers make the risks greater by waiting until after the thirteenth week before seeking abortion. This is especially true of younger teens who often are slow to recognize that they are pregnant, and who are most likely to stall about telling their parents. Younger teens also are less likely to seek help from an agency or a doctor.

Abortion is an intimate matter, deserving serious consideration and weighing of responsibility. The decision to abort may not seem all that grave at the time, but, as the young woman matures, she is likely to reach a deeper understanding of its gravity.

We have been concentrating in this chapter on the young woman's situation with pregnancy. What about the teenaged father? If you are the parent of a son, some important questions should be asked. Have you been as frank with him as with a daughter? What has he been taught about responsibility, about consideration and respect for girls? Do you feel that it's the girl's problem if your son gets her pregnant?

Boys tend to get less involved in the pregnancy decisions – especially if the relationship has been a casual one. Few boys for example, accompany girls to find out about birth control. Society stereotypes the man as the provider and the woman as the one concerned with bearing and caring for the child. Should that stereotype continue? Is birth woman's business only?

Girls become aware of their passage into womanhood rather dramatically, through the onset of menstruation. For boys, it is not as clear. Rarely does the ability to have an erection confront the youngster with images of fatherhood. The models presented to young men show them as conquerors or controllers far more often than as caring, feeling partners. One common image is the conqueror who leaves the woman – who takes, uses and discards. Is it any wonder that many young men feel no responsibility when a pregnancy occurs? One teen father told me that his parents resented the young woman, felt she was responsible for the pregnancy, and did not want him to marry. They felt that she had trapped him. He did not want to marry either, and he didn't. At his construction job, other seventeen-year-old fellows made remarks about his being "caught". When he visited the baby at the girl's house, he felt ill at ease. He was the baby's father and had to support the child, yet it was difficult to feel that the baby was really his. He wasn't a member of the family, and his relationship with the girl wasn't the same any more. He felt intensely isolated. When he thought about continuing in this way for years, he became depressed.

Some young men have babysat or have taken care of younger siblings, but many are far removed from little children and intimidated by them. The prospect of fatherhood leaves them feeling trapped and scared. The young woman has the advantage of being able to work out of instinct, but the young man does not. He is not ready to settle down and give up dreams of adventure. The adjustment varies with each young man, but, with support, he usually comes to appreciate and make the best of his new situation.

Teen pregnancy is a complicated and serious problem. Whatever decision the young woman makes carries consequences. Decisions are often made at such times solely on the practical level, without considering the spiritual at all. Courage and vision are needed at this delicate time, and considering the spiritual aspects can add another dimension to the decision-making.

Chapter Twenty Three

Teenagers and alcohol

It's OK not to drink.
Bumper sticker

I recently attended a meeting with teenaged alcoholics, and some of the statements they made are still buzzing in my mind.

"I was afraid of everything. When I drank, I wasn't afraid."

"I don't know how I drove home. I was drunk, but somehow I got the car into the garage."

"I got really scared when I realized I was losing my short-term memory."

"When the teacher asked me if I was on something, of course, I said I wasn't. At that particular moment, I wasn't. I thought I was so smart!"

"I got to the point where I felt I was dying, and I begged for help."

"What really bothered me was when one of my high school drinking friends said, I'm worried about you."

Teen drinking is a national problem. The use of hard drugs reportedly is down, but the use of alcohol among preteens and teenagers has increased. It's commonly said that drinking has been part of the teen culture for generations, so why are parents so concerned? How do parents know when their child has a drinking problem and what should be done about it? Let's look at an ancient Hebrew legend cited by Chaim Ginott in his book, *Between Parent and Teenager*.[1]

When Noah planted grape vines, Satan revealed to him the possible effects of alcohol. He slaughtered a lamb, a lion, an ape and a pig. He explained: 'The first cup of wine will make you mild like a lamb; the second will make you feel brave like a lion; the third will make you act like an ape; and the fourth will make you wallow in the mud like a pig'.

Unfortunately, when most teenagers drink, they have something else in mind than this legend. They don't see themselves wallowing in the mud like pigs; they see the pleasure of being in a group and having feelings of sophistication, maturity, and status. More available and cheaper than drugs, alcohol "is the drug of choice" among teenagers.

Alcohol and judgment

Alcohol is especially seductive to teenagers. At this most insecure time of their lives, alcohol promises security – but doesn't keep the promise. It makes them feel mature – while hindering their maturation. They look tough and strong and are accepted into certain in-groups – but they risk becoming weak and possibly even outcasts. They feel independent of authority and deliciously rebellious – but they are flirting with a dependency much more demanding.

Drinking with a group makes them feel accepted. Alcohol is all around them, and it is neither as dangerous nor as expensive as other drugs. They feel that they can handle its effects and are certain they won't become alcoholics.

It generally is agreed that alcohol affects judgment, exactly the area in which the teenager already is weak. Even without drugs, the teenager swings to the extremes of the emotional pendulum. Wanting to be accepted already renders the teen vulnerable to risks and dare-devil feats. Alcohol gives short-term bravado. With alcohol, teenagers can drive without putting their hands on the steering wheel, they can have the courage to jump off a bridge into a river, they can have sex without thinking too much about it.

If they depend on alcohol to socialize, to dance, or to face new and frightening social situations, they never develop real social skills or a sense of appropriateness. Using alcohol deprives them of the experience of coming to terms with life and leaves them emotionally immature.

If teenagers do dangerous or foolish things under the influence of alcohol, they can delude themselves by thinking, "That wasn't me. That was the alcohol". Projecting blame and not taking responsibility for their behavior becomes a life-pattern which, in time, so weakens their will that they no longer have the courage or determination to do things or face situations. That kind of courage cannot be gained from alcohol.

Adults help teenagers develop their budding egos and wills by involving them in decision-making. If they are spared having to make decisions, their egos are dulled, and the opportunity to develop consciousness and character has been forfeited. The young person is left directionless, at the mercy of whatever the group does.

Alcohol and its effects

Alcohol is made from fruit or grain. There are two types of alcoholic beverages. One kind includes wine and beer and is made by fermentation, in which yeast is used to change sugar in the fruit or grain into alcohol. The second type includes various hard liquors, made by distilling the alcohol from a fermented liquid and aging the distillate. This produces a more alcoholic beverage than wine or beer. Beers range between 2 percent and 8 percent alcohol. Wines range from 8 percent to 21 percent alcohol with the so-called dry wines having the lower alcohol content. Vodka, gin, whiskey, rum, brandy, and liqueurs are from 40 percent to 50 percent alcohol.

Alcohol does not have to be digested. It is diluted by stomach juices and enters the blood very quickly through the walls of the stomach and intestines. The rate of absorption depends on which beverage was drunk and how full the stomach is. Absorption takes longer when there is food in the stomach, especially fatty foods. Carbonated beverages, however, speed up the absorption rate. The blood transports the alcohol to the organs of the body, including the brain.

Alcohol affects the brain in two ways.

First, it is a depressant on the central nervous system. As the concentration of alcohol increases, the depression intensifies, leading to sedation, passing out, and coma. It puts to sleep some of the cells in the hypothalamus, a part of the brain having to do with the regulation of vital processes, such as breathing and heartbeat. Consequently, *the person cannot react as quickly as usual because the alcohol has slowed the body's reflexes.* An intoxicated person is unable to use full intelligence or exert self control.

Second, alcohol is a stimulant which causes the person to feel exhilarated, lose control, talk excitedly, change moods and become hysterical.

Ninety percent of the alcohol is disposed of by the liver. The rate at which the body can dispose of alcohol is limited. An average-sized man can dispose of one-half ounce of alcohol per hour. That is equivalent to an ounce of whiskey, a twelve-ounce bottle of beer, a four-ounce glass of dry wine, or 2.4 ounces of fortified wine. If a person drinks more than his body can burn up, the alcohol accumulates in the organism, resulting in intoxication.

Teenagers and intoxication

When youngsters become even mildly intoxicated, their perceptions are affected and they cannot make clear decisions. As they go on drinking, their awareness also affected, they are unable to see clearly, and their reflexes grow sluggish.

As far as we know, small amounts of alcohol, even when taken regularly over a long period, have no pathological effect. In the case of occasional drunkenness, the body returns to normal after suffering (!) a temporary chemical disturbance. When youngsters drink heavily and frequently, however, the organs of the body may be damaged. The central nervous system, including the brain, is affected.

People typically pass through four stages in their response to increasing amounts of alcohol. The numbers on the following chart refer to the level of alcohol in the blood.

Stage 1. (0.05%) Some inhibitions are removed, the person is sociable and confident, but skill and judgment are impaired.
Stage 2. (0.10%) The person tends to overdo things, is talkative, careless and funny. Skill is further diminished, and the will is weakened.

Stage 3. (0.15%) The person sees double, totters, fumbles, is incoherent and boisterous. Feeling and pain are lessened.
Stage 4. (above 0.15%) Action is slow, breathing is difficult. Person staggers, mutters, is indifferent and semiconscious.[2]

Why do people drink?

Adolescents often begin drinking because alcohol makes them feel grown up. It helps them break their ties within the parent-child relationship, and they feel more in charge of their own lives. "I am an individual", they seem to say as they take a drink.

The individuality of the young adolescent, the sense of self, is very fragile. It is barely there. Most of the time, the true self is hidden deeply within the soul or far outside the soul, masked by emotions masquerading as the true self. When too much alcohol is taken or when it is taken too often, what occurs is quite different from what the youngster thinks is happening. Instead of strengthening the individuality, alcohol weakens it, leaving the youngster witless in the face of all his confusing emotions and desires.

In Arabic, alcohol means The Spirit, and alcohol is sometimes referred to as a False God. So, the false God or Spirit doesn't allow the true Spirit to work. Youngsters are not in control of their own conscience. Instead, under the influence of alcohol, they do things they would not do if they had clear heads.

Alcoholism

Awareness is growing that alcoholism is a disease and that certain people do not need to take in a great amount of alcohol to create the need for more. In the words of an old saying, "For an alcoholic, one drink is too many – and a thousand are not enough!" Once a person becomes an alcoholic, he or she deals with the condition for the rest of his or her life. Alcoholism has become a serious problem in Western society.

Alcoholics Anonymous puts out the following twelve-question quiz to help teenagers decide whether their drinking is becoming a problem:

1. Do you drink because you have problems? To face up to stressful situations?
2. Do you drink when you get mad at other people, your friends or parents?
3. Do you often prefer to drink alone, rather than with others?
4. Are your grades starting to slip? Are you goofing off on the job?
5. Do you ever try to stop drinking or to drink less – and fail?
6. Have you begun to drink in the morning, before school or work?
7. Do you gulp your drinks as if to satisfy a great thirst?
8. Do you ever have loss of memory due to your drinking?
9. Do you avoid leveling with others about your drinking?
10. Do you ever get into trouble when you are drinking?
11. Do you often get drunk when you drink, even when you do not mean to?
12. Do you think it is cool to be able to hold your liquor?

If the teenager can answer yes to any one of these questions, it is a sign that the young person's drinking is following a dangerous pattern and that help is needed.

Drinking and danger

I live across the street from a favorite teen hangout. Youngsters drive into the gravel parking lot and put away a couple of six packs of beer or a bottle of hard liquor. They break bottles, yell and spin around on the gravel with their cars, kicking up dust, shouting and arguing. Thoroughly crocked, they speed down the dark street, lights often out, weaving from side to side, challenging friends in another car to race them to the corner. In this condition, they turn onto one of the busiest thoroughfares in Sacramento County. It is not surprising that automobile deaths due to drunkenness have become a national concern.

Drinking is often related to unplanned pregnancy among teenagers. I have talked to girls who had sexual intercourse while drunk and they are not even sure who their partner was. This is not surprising since alcohol lessens inhibitions and weakens self-control.

Despite all the awareness of the problems stemming from teenagers and drinking, many adults do not take responsibility where they can. I had strong words with a parent about a party for teenagers where alcohol was served. The parent felt that I was being unreasonable by suggesting that thirteen, fourteen, and fifteen-year-olds were not able to handle themselves (including those who would be driving home).

Problem drinkers tend to be those teenagers who are impulsive, who over-emphasize their masculinity or femininity, who deny anxiety and dependency, who are compulsive, and who lack self-esteem. How can we prevent them from developing drinking problems? One way is to help them strengthen their personalities. Another is to take away the status given by alcohol. Another is to be alert to our teenager's behavior.

Teenagers with serious drinking problems often describe how their parents did not notice, even when their drinking became extreme. Some parents did notice that something was wrong, but then allowed their youngsters to avoid the questions or to give vague answers. Few parents like confrontations, and those over alcohol or drugs are among the most feared. If parents fail to induce their teenagers to talk about what is going on, they can insist that counseling begin and see if a neutral person will help the youngster explore the problem.

Denial does not help. The first step in helping the youngsters is admitting that they have a drinking problem, and the second step is getting them to admit it. Protecting the teenagers will only help them make excuses for their behavior. Most teenagers with drinking problems are crying for help. Even though they resist help at first, the seed of recovery occurs at the point where the teenagers know that they need help and appreciate it.

Guidelines

For youngsters who are concerned about the effects of drinking or whose parents are concerned about the effects of alcohol on them, there are guidelines with which teenagers can monitor themselves.

They can learn to refuse a drink when it is offered. No apology is needed, no argument or excuse has to be made. They simply must feel clear enough about the issue to say, "No, thanks". They can have a ginger ale or mineral water, so that they, too, are drinking and enjoying the social scene without standing out. If they do take a drink, they can nurse it, so that it lasts the evening, and they can eat while drinking.

They can have an arrangement with their parents to pick them up at a party if they or their date has been drinking and is unfit to drive.

Friends can help each other by being sure that the driver doesn't drink.

They can cultivate the image that it is OK not to drink. Only through awareness and a change in attitude will teenagers take control of their lives rather than handing over the power to the False God.

Chapter Twenty Four

Teenagers and drugs

Turn on, tune in, drop out.
Timothy Leary

This chapter on teenagers and drugs should be read with caution, as the drugs scene is constantly changing, with new drugs coming along all the time – for example skunk cannabis, which is much more powerful then marijuana. If you have questions and need more information, do not hesitate to get professional drugs advice.

As a teenager, I was familiar with drinking, but marijuana, cocaine and LSD did not exist in the high school scene, and certainly not in elementary school. I went to high school in the slums of the Bronx and in a small Florida town. In neither setting were drugs present. Violence, yes. Racism, yes. An occasional pregnancy, yes. But drinking was the main expression of teenage exploration and rebellion.

Today's teenagers are confronted almost daily with the drug culture. It expresses itself in album covers, rock music lyrics, in overdoses among friends or relatives, in deaths of rock stars, movie stars, or athletes, in burnout-damaged friends or siblings, in burglaries and muggings committed by dopers needing money for drugs, in students selling drugs on campus, in social interaction, in experimentation. Hardly a family is untouched by drug experience and damage. Too many young people have been diverted from meaningful and responsible adult lives, spending instead the golden years of adolescence and young adulthood in drug rehabilitation therapy, committed to institutions with brain damage and apathy. Too many young people have lost their teen years in fuzzy clouds of smoke and frightening flashbacks of LSD trips.

Those of us who have been teaching, counseling and parenting for twenty or more years, have experienced the waste of a generation. The drug scene no longer is tied to political and social revolution.

The idealism has gone – but the hard reality of drug use remains with us. The fun is gone, but the pain remains.

Today's teenagers are snorting cocaine and mixing marijuana with alcohol. Drugs have moved from the high schools down into the elementary grades, so that children of ten, eleven, and twelve now are drug-conscious. The good news is that their drug consciousness includes awareness of its dangers as well as a sense of its allure. Teenagers have seen their heroes die because of misuse, and they are more aware of the dangers than were their predecessors of a decade ago. They also are more cautious about confronting the law and less likely to openly defy it.

On the streets, the picture is mixed, too. Marijuana cultivation and use are widespread and tolerated, if not condoned, in American society. At the same time, however, the accumulated experiences with a generation of users plus insights from scientific studies which steadily trickle in, enable us gradually to understand the dangers more clearly. Even as we learn, however, the devastation continues.

Millions of teenagers have experimented with drugs. They have experienced changes in their minds and in their moods. Many try drugs a few times and quit, but many continue and become hooked. Once they become dependent, they move from one drug to another.

What are the common drugs?

The main categories of drugs include stimulants (mainly amphetamines), sedatives (mainly barbiturates), psychedelics (consciousness-expanding drugs such as LSD), hallucinogens (such as marijuana), opiates (such as heroin), although some teenagers sniff glue and inhale fumes, trying anything that will get them high.

Dr L.F.C. Mees, a doctor and teacher in a Waldorf school in the Netherlands, describes the effect of the plants used in LSD, marijuana and heroin in his book, *Drugs: A Danger for Human Evolution?*[1]

Mees looks at drugs from a standpoint of human evolution and asks the question, "How does the drug change consciousness?"

Opium is the traditional drug of the Orient. (Heroin is an alkaloid derivative of opium but has different effects.) According to Mees, opium produces dreams at the expense of the vitality. Opium users prematurely age, they experience picture consciousness, retiring into a world of chaotic imagery.

LSD, mescaline (from the cactus), and psilocybine (from the mush-room) produce ecstasy by affecting the nervous system. The user experiences split consciousness – dreamy pictures during a wakeful state. The person feels very clear and is able to relate sensory images in a new way. Yet, a sense of timelessness is induced, so that he or she experiences the illusion of eternity, infinity, joy and inner peace. This ecstasy gives the person an experience of salvation, instant grace and a mystical world beyond space and time where colors have sounds, and music is experienced visually. Mees points to LSD, mescaline and psilocybine as drugs of the West. LSD is a kind of a fungus, about an inch long, which lives in the ear of the rye. It contains ergotine – one of the most potent herbal poisons. It contracts the finer blood vessels, squeezing out the blood, and causing madness.

Marijuana and alcohol produce a high. Marijuana's main effect is euphoria, but it is not as picture-producing as opium. The substance responsible for the effects of hashish and marijuana is the same resin which forms amber, and tincture of amber has been used as a mild sedative. Marijuana, however, obliterates the feelings. It produces an illusory feeling of merging with other people or beings. Users expe-rience a sharing and a feeling of community. However, the sharing has no real basis. The smiles and camaraderie are products of chem-ical, not of conscious, relationships.

Effects

Drugs drain vitality. LSD produces euphoria. Marijuana produces a high. Opium produces dreams. It is common to experience a mixture of three sensations:

- the boundaries disappear
- a sense of rapture
- two kinds of consciousness at once.

These are considered by some to be worthwhile experiences. For others, however, the experience is one of anxiety and discomfort, while others have intensely frightening experiences. They enter a state of consciousness for which they are not prepared and over which they have no control.

How are they used?

Marijuana is the most common. Although Federal law treats marijuana the same as it treats heroin – as a hard narcotic – it is available everywhere, on campus, on the streets, in school yards. It is used variously, to relax, to generate euphoria, or to induce a pleasant distortion of time and space. In small doses, this is what it does. However, the research on habitual use shows such serious results as memory loss, weakening of the will, and heart damage. In addition, when it is smoked, it causes very similar health effects to those from smoking tobacco. Skunk cannabis, however, is powerful.

Heroin is used in a variety of ways and produces drastic effects. The first stage is smoking, the second is inhaling smoke, and the third is injecting it into veins. During the third stage, the person's need for heroin increases daily. Even a few hours without it bring cramps, sweating and vomiting, which can be relieved only by more heroin or other drugs which mimic its effects. Heroin users become slaves to the drug and will do anything to relieve the craving. At the same time, in the backs of their minds, sits constant fear of infection, AIDS and overdose. To support their habit, they often resort to burglary or prostitution.

The addict's fixation on obtaining heroin eventually alienates him or her from non-addict friends, leaving only a circle of pimps, pushers, and prostitutes as people on whom to rely.

It is ironic that LSD, developed specifically for experimental use under supervision, became a street drug, produced in home chemistry laboratories. It intensifies perceptions and transports the person into another state of consciousness. It can cause terror and either temporary or permanent insanity, also chromosome damage and birth defects.

PCP, also called "Angel Dust" and "supergrass", is included here because of its wide usage and its dangers. Unlike the other drugs which are herbal, PCP or phencyclidine was synthesized for use as a surgical anesthesia, but its use in experiments with human beings was discontinued because of side effects. Its effects on consciousness lie between those of marijuana and LSD. Even in small quantities, it is potent. Users feel numbness and unreality.

A pamphlet from the US Department of Health, Education and Welfare says that PCP users often have trouble describing how they feel when they smoke PCP. Most users agree that it's different from other drugs. They say it feel like they're in another world – a fantasy world which is sometimes pleasant, sometimes not. When the high wears off, users often feel mildly depressed, irritable and alienated from their surroundings.

Symptoms of PCP use include confusion, agitation, a blank stare, difficulty walking, confused speech, distorted vision, difficulty remembering, violent behavior, aggression, or withdrawal. With higher doses, stupor or coma may occur and possibly death.

PCP so disorients people that they can't tell where they are walking or which direction is up. They fall from roofs, out of windows and step in front of cars. Some users have died in fires because they were insensitive to the pain of burning and didn't realize that they were in trouble. They can also become suddenly violent, killing others, or themselves.

PCP is not only one of the most potent drugs but also one of the most widely used. It is readily available, being produced in home laboratories in various forms – powder, tablets, or capsules. It can be smoked, snorted, swallowed, or injected. It is often mixed with marijuana, mescaline, or cocaine.

There is a new group of drugs known as club drugs or party drugs. These are used by teenagers at all-night dance parties known as "raves" or "trances". Because some of these drugs are colorless, tasteless and odorless, they can be added to drinks as a way to intoxicate others, often related to sexual assaults.

Why do teenagers take drugs?

Teenagers take drugs for the same reasons they drink alcohol – for the excitement, the sense of danger, peer pressure and the need to escape from family problems, abuse, emotional stress and despair.

Is your child using drugs?

Some signs of drug use are physical, some behavioral, and some are unusual occurrences that should alert parents to possible drug use.

Physical signs. These signs may point to drug use or some other physical problems. It is recommended that the youngster see a doctor if any of the following persists:
1. Inability to concentrate.
2. Loss of weight and appetite, increased craving for sweets.
3. Blackouts.
4. Red eyes.
5. Persistent colds or coughs.
6. Chest pains, vomiting.

Behavioral signs. As with the physical signs, the following may indicate drug use or other disturbances and should be taken seriously:
1. Inability to organize anything.
2. Paranoia.
3. Restlessness, irritability, nervousness.
4. Sudden hostility, vagueness, apathy, secretiveness.
5. Lying.
6. Strange phone calls, late hours, change of friends.

Unusual occurrences. These signs should alert parents.
1. Prescription drugs missing from the closet.
2. Smell of incense in teen's room to mask marijuana.
3. Drug paraphernalia around house or in teenager's room.
4. Money or things of value disappearing from the house.

What can parents do?

Don't wait until your teenager has a problem. Make it a point to find out about the different kinds of drugs and learn to spot the symptoms. Share what you learn with your teenagers and pre-teenagers. Leave published material lying around. You would be surprised how many teenagers read educational material on drugs, sex and alcohol if their parents don't force them to. Examine what kind of an example you are to your children. Do you take pills as soon as you have a problem? Do you use sleeping pills, stimulants, or sedatives? Are you aware of what programs on drug education are offered by your child's school or by the community? See what you can do to support the program.

If you think your teenager is involved with drugs, be awake and aware. Keep a close watch. Go to your child and express your suspicions. Try to talk about it. Ask questions that may help the teenager think about it. Speak in a concerned manner rather than lecturing.

When we find our youngsters in trouble, our first impulse is often to accuse and vent our own frustration and embarrassment. What is our real goal? Do we want to punish the teenager for causing us stress, or do we want to get help? Be aware that teenagers often lie when they are questioned about drugs. Their loyalty goes to the drug. If your suspicions are strong, persist.

If you are unable to have a fruitful discussion, set firm rules. Distinguish between rules which are negotiable and those which are not. The rules may cover the presence of drugs in the house, curfews, use of the car, parties in the house, and restriction on money.

You have to make it very clear that you will not tolerate drug use in the house and at the same time offer help to the youngster.

This is your moment of truth. Don't give in to self-pity. Face the fact that there is a problem and seek help. You are not alone. Meet with other parents with similar problems. Obtain professional help. Speak to whoever will provide support for the family. Find out about counseling and treatment centers in your community.

There is a group called Families Anonymous, similar to Alcoholics Anonymous, whose first of twelve precepts reads, "We admitted that we were powerless over drugs and other people's lives – that our lives had become unmanageable."

Don't give up. Substance abuse is a very difficult problem to overcome, but it can be done.

What kinds of changes have to happen?

While a youngster is involved in drugs, steps necessary for his or her development are not happening. As we know, adolescence is a painful time. The youngster has to learn to deal with stress, with feelings, with disappointment and frustration. During adolescence, people develop patterns of coping with success and failure. Running away is not the answer. How does one help a youngster develop these life skills after having used drugs as a crutch?

The individuality has to be strengthened. Security has to develop within the self, to replace dependence on a substance. The teenager has to learn to put off gratification, resist temptation and develop inner strength. Learning to trust adults, developing self-confidence, and understanding the need for rules and limitations are major steps in the youngster's release from drug dependence. We cannot pretend that this is easy. Getting off drugs and staying off is one of the most difficult tasks the youngster may ever face.

Most drug programs are step-by-step programs. As the youngster learns to handle small responsibilities, larger privileges are granted.

The long road to recovery involves honesty and will-training. The teenager has learned to lie to parents, teachers and self. The will has been crippled and needs to be strengthened. That is only part of the treatment. The problems that led to drugs in the first place need to be explored and examined.

Strengthening the individuality

If we use drugs to enter another kind of consciousness, or if we use drugs to have spiritual experiences, we have not earned these experiences. We also have no control over them. Instead of moving us forward in our development as human beings, opium, LSD and marijuana push us backward.

The human being is fighting for freedom in the midst of many forces in society that want to enslave, such as advertising, movies, the distorted image of the human being, and the denial of anything spiritual. The teenager feels trapped in the physical body. In a drug experience, the youngster is freed, and it feels good.

Teenagers today have a thirst for imaginative pictures. The dry thinking that goes on in so many schools, the bizarre posters and images on t-shirts, the sick humor that fills so many comic books – all create an inner longing for something higher, something that affirms the human spirit.

It is not surprising that some teenagers turn to drugs for pictures. In the LSD consciousness, another world reveals itself. Earlier, I described the three impressions common to many drug experiences – disappearance of boundaries leading to a false connection with the world; heightened rapture; and a split sense of the self and the world. In these ways, the person is lifted out of the body into an artificial universal experience.

Rudolf Steiner gave exercises to strengthen the soul. For example, one exercise is to observe a plant, its budding, its growing, its blossoming. Then observe its fading, decaying, and withering. If this is done repeatedly, the person develops a strong experience of life forces. To heighten the experience, bring strong feelings into the perception. This helps the person relate to the growing and dying forces in nature and in the self, thus strengthening the self. A person sees how the world of nature and the world of self share similar processes. In this inter-relationship, man and nature are one. Such a strong feeling helps a person retain a centered-ness in life.[2]

Another exercise is to observe one's thinking. Become aware of how thoughts randomly flow in and out of our minds. Try concentrating on one thought for one minute, then two, and so on. See if you can keep peripheral thoughts from wandering in. Don't permit free associations to take over this concentration exercise. Work on concentration every day for a few minutes until you can discipline your thinking.

Still another exercise has to do with feelings. Deepen your gratitude or appreciation for what others do for you. Learn to notice the small gestures, the smiles, the hands reaching to help. Observe your own feelings from outside. What gave rise to sudden anger? Why do you feel sorry for yourself? What caused the hysterical laughing? As you begin to observe your feelings, you master them.

Many of the exercises Steiner gave had to do with developing moral life. He said that a person should take three steps forward in moral development for every step forward in spiritual development.[3]

Conscious self-development is a much slower path than the unconscious path of drugs. Conscious development, however, develops concentration and will power. The person is active in the process rather than passively being at the mercy of whatever appears in a chemically induced brain-storm. Doing the exercises develops a new soul-being created by the person's own activity. In this way, the person unites Eastern and Western consciousness. However, the dreams and the rapture are in balance and do not threaten the soul with annihilation as drugs do.

Our youngsters are hungering for imaginative pictures. When they receive stones instead of bread, when they find dry fact after fact instead of living images, their longing builds to bursting. Using drugs to feed this longing is understandable, but it is dangerous for the individual and for society.

Chapter Twenty Five

Teenagers and food

I'm not hungry. Stop trying to make me fat.
16-year-old girl

"I'm too fat" must be three of the most spoken or thought words of teenage girls and women. Boys are becoming increasingly weight conscious too.

For many years I taught art history to ninth and tenth graders. They are barely comfortable with the proportions of the ancient Greek sculptures of women and the Renaissance madonnas, but they react strongly when the fleshy and curvaceous women painted by Renoir and Degas are shown. Some laugh, some become nervous, some indignant, others mocking. They find it hard to imagine such women as beautiful.

Every culture has its ideal of beauty. Ours is "Skinny is beautiful". The glut of advertising, magazine pictures, television and movie heroines presents the girl and boy with the "ideal woman". Before her body starts to change, the girl knows what she wants to look like. The nine and ten-year-old teeny boppers already have their vision internalized. As their body changes they are determined to force it into a shape most acceptable by their society. The easiest way to make this happen is by not eating. Teenage girls are diet conscious, even diet obsessive. Yet in spite of that many of them gorge themselves on fast food, cookies, potato chips and soda.

It is hard to resist wanting to have the ideal body. How can teenagers know how magazine advertisements are made? How can they know what models go through to stay skinny? Certain body types are naturally thin and others never will be. You don't usually see short models being photographed – clothes photograph best on tall flat-chested girls. The message is "tall and skinny are good, short and rounded are not."

In addition to the trauma of growing up and away from the family, there are other pressures placed on the teenager – the pressure to be popular, to be liked, to be accepted, to dress nicely, and to do well in school. Most teenagers are affected by pressure, but some are more vulnerable to one or another way of escaping it. We have already talked about alcohol usage as one way of dealing with the pain of growing up. Some of the other dangerous means to alleviate pain are eating disorders, drugs, promiscuity and suicide.

Eating disorders

Some teenagers focus their problems onto food – either eating too much or too little food. Food is a symbol of love, and some youngsters turn to food as a comfort, a pacifier to soothe the hurt they feel; others use food as a way of gaining control over those they want to hurt.

Food is one area that is almost completely within the teenager's power to regulate. When it is carried to an extreme it becomes an illness. Diet fads are a mild form of illness, whereas the binge-and-purge cycles of bulimia and self-starvation, or anorexia, are serious health hazards.

Anorexia nervosa

The anorexic starves herself to death. She is compulsive about becoming extremely thin. Ninety-six percent of the victims are female of whom ten percent actually die of starvation.[1] Many others develop health problems which they live with the rest of their lives. There is a growing number of male anorexics.

The anorexic has a fixation on food. She collects recipes, likes to prepare gourmet meals for others, but she doesn't eat. She is very particular about food and when she does eat she has no sense of what her body needs. She exercises frantically because no matter how skinny she is, she is still convinced she is fat. She occasionally goes on a binge, but then vomits to keep from gaining weight. She drives herself unmercifully and wants to be a good person.

The anorexic may drop twenty to forty percent of total body weight, becoming skeleton-like. Her hair will drop out. She will stop menstruating, have low body temperature and low blood pressure. No matter how gaunt or skeletal she becomes she sees herself as fat. Her image of herself is so distorted she will do anything to keep losing weight. We are used to connecting this kind of thinness with concentration camp victims or victims of famine, but it is a shock to see young people in our society look like this. What is even stranger about anorexia is that it is not a disorder that comes from inability to buy or know about good food.

The pattern of the typical anorexic is surprisingly clear. From a middle to upper middle class family, most are super-achievers who have high expectations from their parents and from themselves. They have usually been easy children to raise, not getting into trouble, doing whatever they needed to do to please their parents and be approved of. Some have been doted on, especially by their fathers. They have been "daddy's little girl". Others are ignored most of the time, receiving attention only when they receive good grades or recognition of some kind. In both cases, approval is coming from outside, while the girl secretly feels insecure. She takes life seriously and often internalizes problems between her parents or siblings.

As she enters the teen years, she needs to break away from her family. She develops negative feelings, but is afraid to express them. People are counting on her, especially her mother. She doesn't want to hurt anyone. Her father is usually busy and preoccupied, but he pays attention to her when she achieves something. She adores him. He may have commented that she was starting to put on a little weight. He may only have been teasing her, but she wants to please him. She feels empty inside. She feels insignificant and unable to control her own life. She may stop eating as her way of showing this control, or she may stop eating because of her father's comment. She may connect putting on weight with failure. She may fear not being popular or not getting a man. For whatever reason, she starves herself. Early signs are loss-of-appetite and loss-of-weight. If the subject is raised, the anorexic usually denies that there is a problem and tries to change the subject.

Bulimarexia

Instead of starving herself, this young woman eats plenty – but then vomits up the food. She is not as easy to notice as the anorexic, because she is not skeletal in appearance. She tends to be of normal weight, even slightly overweight. She enjoys food, appreciates a good meal, enjoys socializing in restaurants. After she eats, however, she takes a laxative or induces vomiting. She is fixed on food as much as the anorexic, but her fixation leads her to gorge. In one sitting, often at night and in secret, she may eat as much as five or six meals, but then she takes a laxative or induces vomiting. She maintains her weight by bingeing and purging. A New York Times article called bulimia "the secret addiction" which leads epidemic numbers of young women from the middle and upper classes to consume up to 55,000 calories in an hour or two, induce vomiting, and repeat the behavior up to four times a day. Others use large quantities of laxatives to prevent the retention of such enormous amounts of food.

What kind of teenagers develop bulimarexia? Again, they are mostly female. About 50 to 75 percent are former anorexics, and this is their way of maintaining their weight, because they have not worked out of their food-fixation. Many young women under great pressure to be thin use this method to maintain their weight, especially those who want to be models, dancers and gymnasts.

They are similar to the anorexics in that they want to be perfect in everything they do. They tend to be compulsive about their work, their clothes, their bodies. Their food intake is an area where they can exert control and be in charge without having to worry about someone else's standards.

In anorexia, the danger is death through starvation as well as damage to the gastro-intestinal system. In bulimarexia, the danger is to the gastro-intestinal system. Other problems are severe tooth decay (from destruction of the tooth enamel by acidic vomitus), constant sore throat, oesophageal inflammation, swollen glands, liver damage, nutrient deficiencies and rectal bleeding (from extensive use of laxatives). In both cases, the emotional damage is considerable.

Signs

One young woman at college sneaks into the bathroom at night to eat. Her roommate can hear her crinkling the foil around the brownies her mother sent her. She throws up constantly. Her hair is falling out. In the dining room, she eats nothing. Occasionally, she takes a blueberry muffin and slowly picks out the blueberries, eating them, and throwing away the rest. For four years, she has acted like this, growing thinner each year.

Another girl can hear her roommate gagging in the bathroom every night. The girl seems to be normal during the day, but she has a secret life at night. Secrecy and obsession distort the young woman's personality.

Because so many teenaged girls are obsessed with being thin, it is easy to accuse them of being anorexic or of having bulimarexia. Teens who are struggling to stay thin have much in common with those who are in the first stage of anorexia or bulimia. What is different is the degree of emotional stability that keeps one young woman in balance and allows another to get out of control. Accusations only worsen the situation. If parents suspect that their daughter may be struggling with an eating disorder, they should speak about it, but not push. Youngsters want control over their own lives, and parental pushing is part of what they are trying to escape.

If caught in early stages, anorexia may be cured. The youngster should see a doctor who specializes in treating adolescents with eating disorders. Those in advanced stages urgently require help. Even if treated, they may have anorexia for life and need help in dealing with their feelings and problems. There is no quick cure, and health will return very slowly even after the youngster has dealt with her attitudes and changed her habits.

For many parents, food is a loaded issue. Arguing, nagging, or lecturing about food backfires as the youngster becomes stubborn and unyielding. This stubbornness cuts off communication on important issues and insures that the teenager will not listen.

Compulsive overeating/obesity

Some teenagers react to the emphasis on the ideal body by finding a safe unjudgmental place in their lives, namely the realm of food.

When they were little and hurt themselves, mommy gave them cookies and everything felt better. Now they are hurt too, and food still makes them feel better. It is better to go to the refrigerator and eat a ham and cheese sandwich or to pig out on a bag of potato chips than talk to someone who intimidates them. They become obsessed with food, even to the point of dreaming about it.

When they feel afraid, they eat; when they feel anxious, they eat; when they feel relieved of stress, they eat; or if they want to celebrate something, they eat. When their parents fight, they eat; if they are worried about an exam, they eat; when they feel disappointed, they eat; when they are successful, they eat.

One of the great fears of adolescence is the relationship with the opposite sex. If they get fat, they don't have to deal with it. Most heavy teens, boys and girls, are looked down on. If they are funny, if they play the clown, they will be appreciated as entertainment, but not as dates. Through their heaviness, they can postpone having to face intimacy, relationships and sexuality. Especially where youngsters have had a traumatic experience in early childhood, they seek safety in food, because reaching out may result in another trauma. Feelings are frightening to them, love is frightening, any kind of relationship built on vulnerability is scary. Food is a safe, dependable source of pleasure.

Another reason that teenagers overeat is depression. When they feel bored and empty about their lives, when they lack interest in what is happening around them, they fill their emptiness with food.

Others overeat to rebel. They use it to punish those around them and themselves. If a parent has overstressed thinness and good looks, the youngster may try to get even by eating more.

Whatever the reasons teenagers overeat, one common factor is that they feel worthless. Their self-image is so low that they sabotage themselves and make the situation worse. They feel low to begin with, achieve a temporary high after eating, but then feel worthless again.

It is difficult for those with no weight problem to understand the frustration of the obese person. Occasional attempts to diet do not bear results, and the person gives up. When all the advertisements show skinny people having fun, skinny people finding dates, skinny people modeling clothes, the heavy teenager feels shut out. This intensifies the need for comfort and food fits the bill.

Medical researchers say that fat children and teenagers often become fat adults because fat cells formed during childhood can be reduced in size but not in number. Just as anorexia is a life problem that needs attention even in adulthood, so is obesity. A change in eating habits and exercise is necessary to maintain any weight loss.

What can parents do if their teenagers are overeating?

Remember that the teenager already feels uncomfortable about weight. If the parent communicates judgment, the youngster will usually rebel. Weight has to do with control and self-image. It is much more helpful to ask youngsters how they feel about the weight. Do they want to do something about it? Are they comfortable with it? Are there things they want to do which the weight prohibits? Get a sense of how much the teenagers want to talk about it. Respect them as people. If they indicate that they would like help, contact a group such as Weight Watchers, TOPS, or the Diet Center. Give strong support and encouragement. Do things with the teenager that encourage exercise. Examine the family's eating habits and see what can be done to support the youngster's needs.

Other eating problems

Although teenagers may not be affected by eating disorders as serious as anorexia or compulsive eating, they may be developing poor eating habits.

Many teenagers exist on junk food: snacks made up of sugar and empty calories, and fast-food items. Girls usually combine junk food with diet fads, whereas boys eat constantly and whatever is around.

A steady diet of empty, junk food calories causes a thiamine deficiency and a beriberi-like disease as well as personality problems. Drinking coffee, cola and cocoa – the three Cs – leads to nervousness, anxiety, sleeping problems and irritability. I am always surprised at the amount of candy and soft drinks teenagers consume. When I take high school students on trips, I find their junk food consumption to be a sensitive issue. Yet, they need to be made conscious about it. So much of the teen social scene takes place over hamburgers, sharing a pizza, or having a can of soda. Advertisements romanticize these events, and teens feel that they are in the swing of things when they participate in the junk food ritual, especially soft drinks.

It is difficult to eliminate junk food completely from a teenager's diet. If one succeeds in raising teenagers' consciousness about good nutrition, one then has to be careful they don't go overboard in that direction. Some teenagers become fanatical about good nutrition, and they avoid socializing because they don't want to be contaminated. They can develop a sensible attitude toward food and nutrition, mostly by example. Their meals at home should be nutritious, and healthy food should be available for them to take for lunches and snacks. Having salad items, milk, fruit juice, vegetables, raisins, and nuts available sets a good example and fills the need of the growing teenager who constantly asks, "What's there to eat? I'm hungry."

Chapter Twenty Six

Extreme behavioral problems

We have been on a long journey in this book. We have stepped into the worlds before birth when the human individuality was first awakened to incarnate into earthly human experience, and we have followed the child through the early years into the dawning of self-conscious activity and through the challenges of selfhood.

Some beings have more difficulty incarnating than others and try to avoid becoming part of everyday earthly life; and some incarnate too quickly and become hard and tough. In his excellent book, Man On The Threshold, Bernard Lievegoed, the distinguished Dutch physician, educator and industrial psychologist, develops Rudolf Steiner's thoughts about adolescent development. He describes three "escape routes" that the ego may follow, trying to escape from growing up:[1]

1. Anorexia

Withdrawal back through the gate of birth. The youngster does not want to become an adult but holds back and maintains a child-like appearance. The adolescent has to learn how to become an adult and to accept difficulties and responsibilities of growing up. Therapy to help this youngster aims at strengthening the will to incarnate through reawakening interest in human life and nature, practicing social encounters in conversations, going for walks, doing things with other people so there is a strengthening of communication. This helps the youngster to form warm friendships and to develop enthusiasm for something that is outside himself or herself. The next hurdle is to develop strength, concentration and skill so that he or she can take hold of the random activities that block self-control. She can do this by learning to play an instrument, by learning to draw and paint. Once she has achieved a degree of self-mastery, she needs to bring soul into her gestures. Often the anorexic has a vacant, aloof bearing, and this must be transformed by doing movement with others, especially eurythmy. The final step is the transformation of the death wish into a will-to-live through making sacrifices for others. When this occurs, the anorexic adolescent has accepted life and the illness can be transformed. To do this, at least one person around the anorexic must feel compassion and love and must make a tremendous commitment of time and attention. When the young person sees the commitment and love of the other person, this evokes a similar commitment and awakens purpose in living.

2. Aggressive behavior

The second route is escape into pseudo-adulthood, into extreme aggressive behavior, or into extreme educational difficulties. Whereas anorexia is the typical illness of girls, psychopathic behavior is the typical illness in boys. The boys dive into adulthood too early, skipping the step of adolescence, and they do not experience the transformation of early negation into affirmation as described in Chapter Two. Part of this diving into the earth is their early sexuality. They look for an opportunity to experience something that makes them feel powerful and impressive. They make lots of noise, look for fights, act tough, look for ways to express their anger, and show their skill with machines. They are unable to accept blame or problems when they come up. Instead, they lash out at others as the cause; they often are hyperactive and unable to take control of themselves. They can find no meaning and fanatically push other people around. They often talk big, have contradictory moods of apathy and constant movement, cannot make real connections with people but find strength in a group. They have great amounts of energy for protest, but are unable to connect spiritually with what is going on around them. They lack subtlety in their feelings and perceptions, and act in extremes. Their physical bodies are well developed, but they often become over-developed to the point of caricature. In spite of all their power and strength, their behavior drives them into self-destruction and risking death through daring ventures.

Inwardly, this psychopathic personality feels vulnerable and weak. Many boys do not become psychopathic but are off-balance in one or two of the elements such as being obsessed with power and needing to justify their existence by joining strongly authoritarian groups or by being surrounded by constant chaos, resisting form or order in their lives.

There is no clear direction on how to heal the psychopathic personality once it is far advanced. Adults need to observe the early signs of the problem and help the youngster move into true adulthood rather than jumping over this stage and adopting a false adulthood. Puberty is most important to help him accept responsibility for his actions and to be concerned about other people. What goes on in school and at home between seventh grade and tenth grades is important in helping the boy who has these tendencies to find a healthy relationship to the social life.

3. Escape into euphoria.

"Being high" or excarnation by means of alcohol and drugs, leads to addiction and eventual loss of awareness that one is indeed on the earth at all. Lievegoed describes how this group of young people usually pass through puberty in a normal way, but they do not take hold of themselves. They pass through the third-fourth year change and the ninth-tenth year change without experiencing a strong sense of self. They dream through these experiences. Because they are weak and have not made much of an impact on life, they need support from outside and usually use alcohol, marijuana, stimulants, and possibly heroin. If the youngsters have a neglected childhood that may intensify the unwillingness to take hold of their lives. They find life dull and can do nothing about it but rely on substances to relieve them of the pain for a while. We have spoken of this in detail in earlier chapters. Their inner life has to be strengthened so they are not as dependent.

Help for parents and teachers

Lievegoed describes how all three forms of emotional imbalance lead to self-destruction. The young person facing these difficulties is a picture of the courageous soul facing evil and striving to overcome it. Lievegoed's attitude is very important for us as parents and teachers. It is devoid of judgment but full of clarity. It is not for us to judge young people who are suffering as being good or bad, but rather as needing help. The relationship between their higher selves and the earth is out of order and needs to be set right. This can only be done through the love, determination and devotion of other human beings. Because of the difficulties our society is undergoing, such extremes of behavior are becoming more common and need special attention.

When we step back and look at the three escape routes described by Lievegoed, we have a picture of the subtle process each human being goes through. We could say that each person has a gesture in life – to withdraw from life, to plunge too deeply into life, or to need crutches in order to meet life. When imbalance occurs, the person over-reacts and the gesture becomes exaggerated, leading to illness.

What is our work then? As adults concerned with our children or working professionally with children and teenagers, we can learn to read these gestures. As we gain experience with youngsters with emotional problems, it becomes possible in some cases to spot problems in their early stages. This can begin as soon as the first seven years. Kindergarten teachers can identify those children for whom the gesture of holding back from life, of plunging too fast and too hard into life, and too weak to meet life is becoming exaggerated. Teachers of fourth and fifth graders are able to identify and help those youngsters who still have exaggerated tendencies because they have not been able to work them through in the normal childhood experiences. By the time the high school teacher works with these attitudes, some cases may be quite advanced and special help needed. For many, however, these tendencies are not pathological and they respond positively to warmth and support in their environment. If we learn to recognize these pathologies, we will be better able to offer appropriate help for those in whom they are mere tendencies.

Chapter 27

Teenagers and media

Media such as newspapers, telephones, telegraph, television, and movies have been around for a long time. As media has become much more sophisticated and more affordable, it has moved from the adult population to the teenager population, and even down to children under three.

As soon as one form of media is introduced, another comes along and creates a new fad. The forms of media include: television with cable, DVDs, cell phones, digital cameras either on cell phones or self-contained, video games, internet computers, iPods, and blackberries.

These new forms have increased the possibility of connecting people in different parts of the world, simplified research, allowed businesses to reach huge numbers of customers, allowed soldiers to communicate from the battle field, and inspired endless advances in medicine, manufacturing, and distribution. Today teenagers and pre-teens are the biggest population base for media use. This is **Generation M**.

We can ask why this is. From a developmental viewpoint it makes a lot of sense. Pre-teens and teens are trying to figure out their identity. They like to find out what's new, try on different identities, meet new people, and communicate what they like and don't like. They like the instant response that comes with text-messaging, and they like the creativity of blogs and profiles. They like the chat rooms in which they can express themselves and say whatever comes to mind. The social-networking craze with such programs as MySpace began with young adults, spread to college students, and is very popular with the 12–13 year olds and teenagers. It is not surprising.

A key developmental need of pre-teens and teenagers is to figure out relationships, both in their immediate environment and those far from home. Rather than develop pen-pals across the globe, the on-line community is more instant and satisfying than waiting for letters to be sent by train or plane.

Another key developmental yearning is to have more freedom. In my teen years, the bicycle was the vehicle for that kind of exploration, but today parents have concerns about physical safety, and also harm from strangers. Teens look for ways to secretly communicate outside of their parents' earshot. They look to make friends who do not have to be scrutinised by their parents' eyes. On-line contact has become a place for freedom.

Since teenagers devote more than a quarter of their day to media, it is worth looking at each kind specifically.

Television – For many decades television has been the main form of media in children's and teen's lives. Concerns about violence and sexuality, images of women, explicit scenes about drugs, alcohol use, abuse, and consumerism have been the common issues. Concerns with TV have to do with how much exposure, the content, and what other activities are being neglected. Children in heavy TV viewing homes read less and learn to read later than those in other homes, although many parents still believe TV helps more than it hinders learning. The greatest harm seems to be for young children who confuse fantasy with reality, who are fixated on the images instead of creating their own mental images. Girls tend to watch sitcoms; boys tend to watch sports. With pre-teens the biggest impact on homework and especially on reading is based on three things – they have a TV in their room, the TV is left on all the times, or there are no rules about TV watching. Parental guidance is needed to keep TV use in balance. Use of cable and DVDs has expanded the offerings, challenging parents to be more watchful. In addition, the repetitive showing of a video intensifies the content of the images.

Movies pose similar challenges as TV, either in the theater or shown at home. Here violence and sexual imagery are the strongest issues. One only has to go to the movies and watch the previews to sense what the industry is putting out. The sensory overload desensitises youngsters to the images and the foul language, the objectification of women, and the feeling of the world being a dangerous place. The conscious manipulation of viewers through subliminal imagery and increased volume exploits the pre-teens and teens who are vulnerable to this kind of stimulus.

Video Games have become part of the landscape for children. Since the 1970s when they were first introduced, they have become a popular pastime for children and teens, as well as for adults. The biggest game players are 8–10 year old boys, while girls listen more to music.

Media and computer games have been pointed to as a stimulus for violent acts committed by children. These have to do with children's acting out what they see, not understanding the difference between reality and fantasy, and having poor impulse control. It is especially important that parents understand their children's level of development and their sensitivities. The question is often not whether there is some violence or aggression which has always been in fairy tales or other literature, but the intensity and graphic quality of violence and the context. Parents need to be alert to this and differentiate between entertainment and fun and harmful influences. How to do this? Spend time playing the games with your children, discuss the values in the games, and educate yourselves on the ratings of video games (see the website of Entertainment Software Rating Board in which every computer game is discussed and rated).

Most parents are not familiar with the particular games and seldom have rules about which games should and should not be played. Parents can play a role in discussing video games with their pre-teens and teenagers to develop discernment. Although the use of computer games is more prevalent with youngsters before their teen years, the habits formed often carry over into adolescence. Healthy teenagers tend to leave their obsession with video games behind them as they become interested in other activities.

Cell Phones – Telephones have been a pre-teen and teen obsession for years. However, the cell phone makes contact immediate wherever they are. It has also offered parents a way to keep in touch with their children and brought a sense of security. As with all media, the problems come with overuse so that they aren't getting other things done, and with using the cell phone while driving. While this is an issue for teens of driving age, it is not for pre-teens. The cell phone extends the time youngsters can be in contact with friends. Cell phones with cameras can increase cheating on tests, or taking pictures of a test answer and sending it to a buddy. It can also be used to take embarrassing pictures of a classmate and putting it on line. The allure of the cell phone is that the teenager can be reached at any time and any place, and that creates immediate communication. Rather than leaving a message on the phone or asking a parent to speak with a friend, the teenager creates an anonymous community that does not include parents.

Internet – Computers are becoming a universal presence in our lives. They outpace the use of TV. As with TV, however, one of the main issues is parental guidance, how much time youngsters spend on it, the games, the email contact with strangers, the way that short-cut language can affect spelling, and more importantly, the way that a youngster can e-mail opinions about a classmate that can be very harmful. "Flaming" of other people is the term now used for saying things online you'd never say to someone's face.

Teenagers, especially those under seventeen or eighteen, have trouble understanding consequences of their actions. Because email is instant, there is no time to reflect on what one is going to say. Ruining someone's reputation, using foul language, being inappropriately gross or mean are ways that teenagers have caused harm to others. The harm is intensified because they can download the email onto a website or email it to hundreds of people, many of whom have not requested the material being sent to them.

iPods – Music is very important among older students, many of them using MP3 players and iPods. The most popular genres are rap and hip hop, then alternative rock, then gospel, country, technic, and heavy metal. Young teens also like having their iPods. The parental responsibility is to have an idea of what is being downloaded, as well as the isolation factor because the youngsters are wired. This is true across all generations. It is hard to make eye contact or exchange small talk with anyone who is wired into music. The problem is intensified because adults download music as much as teenagers do, although they may have less time to listen.

On–line social networks such as MySpace is a recent craze. Teenagers love the creativity of creating a profile, placing photographs, their favorite stars and bands, and sharing their inmost thoughts. Unfortunately, they do not realise that these are public documents. Even with passwords, they can be entered. In their innocence, they may give their addresses or phone numbers, and make contact with viewers who may share a common interest.

Visitors to the site can make comments or contact the person directly. This interaction expands the teen's community of friends. Just as teenagers have always looked for a place to hang out, meet friends, put on a persona, flirt, and test their limits, MySpace offers this. "It's just like a big community where people can talk and hang out." Why does MySpace have special allure for pre-teens and young teens? Developmentally they are becoming aware of their own identity. Who am I? What do I like? What do my friends like? What do they think about me? They can try on different identities and change them from day to day. Instead of going to the local drive-in of my youth or the mall, it's a place to hang out and meet friends and strangers. Even though programs set up an age limit, pre-teens lie about their age in order to develop their profile.

The major concerns with MySpace have to do with how much information and what kind of information is put on the site. Young teens have little sense of their effect on other people, on how public the site is. One teacher got on MySpace and within a few minutes he knew who was drinking and what was going on at parties with his students. This lack of realisation can cause problems when older visitors visit the site and arrange to meet the youngster, exchange sexual imagery and connotations, and where the teenager gives too much information of his or her residence. It is important for them to realise that the information they put on MySpace can be accessed by others. This is important for high school students who are applying to colleges or for jobs. Increasingly, college admissions offices, prospective employers, and others they want to impress are searching MySpace and other such sites. Another aspect is that what is put on the site can be found by people who are not their close friends and can be printed out and passed along in e-mails and instant messages or copied and shared on networks totally removed from the knowledge of the original creator of the site.

There is no doubt that media can be addictive for children, teens, and adults. The biggest antidote to this is parental awareness and awareness. Parental attitudes and increased communication with their children are the strongest means of bringing balance to the youngsters' involvement with media.

On the broader front, there are important questions to ask. The MacArthur Foundation is committing $50 million over five years to "fund research and innovative projects focused on understanding the impact of digital media on our youth and how they learn." According to MacArthur President Jonathan Fanton:

> This is the first generation to grow up digital – coming of age in a world where computers, the internet, videotapes, and cell phones are common, and where expressing themselves through these tools is the norm. Given how present these technologies are in their lives, do young people act, think and learn differently today? And what are the implications for education and for society?"

Does on-line use of social networks mean that people are less social? Pew research shows that users are communicating more often than recent generations, particularly with emails, and possibly more often than any previous generation. "While bowling alone, they are networking together."

One issue has to do with multi-tasking. Between the ages of 8 and 14 youngsters learn how to focus their attention among a variety of inputs, including the cell phones, TV, internet and music. They become efficient at this, but the question remains, the more they multitask, the less attention they can devote to any one activity. Another issue is that they tend to respond very quickly, rather than thinking about a question or re-reading a letter before sending it.

Most students multi-task while they are doing their homework, i.e. talk on phone, instant message, watch TV, listen to music, surf the Web. There is very little single-minded attention given. Most students are happy, well-adjusted, have lots of friends, get good grades, aren't unhappy or in trouble. They get along well with parents. Those who are least happy or get poorest grades tend to spend more time with video games and less time reading with peers.

What is needed for healthy development for tweens (children between 8 and 13) and teens?

1. Strengthen relationships. Youngsters need meaningful and long-lasting attachments, especially as anxiety has become one of the most common problems, and mental health problems, in general, have increased.
2. Develop authoritative communities in which people are committed and connected to one another over time, and who are role models of moral behavior and who nurture children, and who set clear boundaries and limits. It is especially meaningful when they are multi-generational, have a long-term focus, and encourage spiritual development, emphasising the dignity of all human beings and the love of one's neighbor.
3. Set limits on time and content of media. Explain the dangers of putting personal information on MySpace profiles or on blogs. Emphasize respect toward their classmates and friends in their use of media. Let your children know that if there is something unsafe or harmful they encounter, that you are there to support them.
4. Schools should set limits on cell phone usage and text messaging in class.
5. Parents and teachers should help students self-regulate, find a balance in media usage, and keep the lines of communication open.

Conclusion

Another race hath been, and other palms are won.
Thanks to the human heart by which we live,
Thanks to its tenderness, its joys and fears,
To me the meanest flower that blows can give
Thoughts that do often lie too deep for tears.
                                        William Wordsworth

It is not easy to grow up in these times. Adolescents struggling to realize themselves as individuals are vulnerable to influences they cannot deal with and which cause many of the problems we see today. Helping children develop into adulthood is a long arduous process, and just when we think we are over one hurdle, another presents itself. Although there are things we cannot have control over, there is much we can do that nourishes and strengthens the higher self. The attitudes of the young mother and father in the care of the baby creates a foundation for the development of the higher self during adolescence. The activities which the three- or four-year-old imitates during the early experiences of selfhood are the basis for healthy development. Nourishment of the child's feelings during the middle years of childhood opens the child's heart to beauty and goodness. Being exposed to attitudes of respect, concern and integrity during puberty helps adolescents discover truth in the world and purpose in themselves.

I have tried to describe the process of incarnation and the development of the self in childhood and to provide directions for parents to take in the journey of parenting. Of course, I have been mindful during this process of my own mistakes, and so the book itself has been an experience of awakening. As so often happens when one sets out on a journey, there are many surprises along the way. Although many experiences are painful, we gain perspective and humor as well. We are not prepared for the journey until it is over. Then we exclaim, "If only I knew at the beginning what I know now!" I feel that way too. This book has been part of my journey. It has been difficult to consider it finished since every new experience has caused me to rethink what I have written.

So too, being a parent is never finished. Relationships between parent and child change, but they continue into adult life. The difficulties and the joys of adolescence are seen in a different light after our formal parenting years are over.

Among other things, being a parent confronts us with our own parents. We may be symbols of authority to our own children, but we are still sons and daughters to our mothers and fathers. Often into old age, we continue trying to fathom our connections with the parents who gave us life and guided us into adulthood.

While I do not expect the reader to accept without question what I have brought of Rudolf Steiner's ideas, I wanted to share them for those who might be interested. I expressed them freely in the way that I understand them, and I hope that I have not been untrue to them.

I have experienced the awe and thrill of discovering that being a parent is, in the final analysis, to participate in a grand drama on both a spiritual and an earthly level. It excites me to contemplate the creative powers of those spiritual beings involved in forming the physical structure of the child. I am awed equally by the complexity of cosmic patterns and by the daily wonders of human existence, even at so elementary a level as the healing of a bruise.

The natural development of the child is mirrored in the unfolding of adult life cycles. Both are rooted in patterns; yet each has its uniqueness. The parent has the advantage of having experienced the childhood stages of development, whereas children live in the moment, trusting those around them.

An often-asked question at parent meetings is, "In addition to all the descriptions of childhood and adolescence that are usually given, is there anything else that can help us?"

We parents are also growing, and being a parent gives us a wonderful opportunity to work on ourselves, to work with our own tendencies, to develop patience and understanding, to learn to read our children, to become more forgiving of ourselves and our children.

In his book, *Knowledge of Higher Worlds and Its Attainment*, Steiner describes some exercises by which adults can strengthen their own egos. These include cultivating an attitude of reverence, wonder and devotion.[1] They include gaining discipline over one's thoughts and actions. They include nightly looking back and reviewing the day, as a way of becoming objective about our own behavior. This helps us see ourselves from outside without getting tangled in our emotions. (Steiner says this exercise is most effective if one starts one's review at the end of the day and recalls the day's events in reverse sequence.)

We, along with our adolescents, are struggling to live in a world between form and freedom. We cannot do it alone. We need to help each other, and we are also helped when we develop trust in the working of the spiritual world. Something we all need today is courage – courage to develop meaningful relationships within our own lives, to respect our children's individuality, to stand by decisions when we feel alone and weak and to do so without knowing all the answers or even being able to ask all the questions. We need the courage to participate in the evolution of tomorrow from today even when we know that what we hold most firmly cannot escape change. We need courage to be thankful for adversity, to make statements that are neither popular nor generally supported, to explore the unseen world of human evolution, to form a vision of a better world, and to live our lives in gratitude for freedom.

> In the free being of Man
> The Universe is gathered up,
> Then – in the free resolve of your heart
> Take your own life in hand –
> And you will find the World,
> The Spirit of the World will find itself in you.
>
> Rudolf Steiner.[2]

Appendix I

Bibliography

Bell, Ruth, and Wildflower, Leni Zeiger, *Talking With Your Teenager*, Random House, N.Y. 1983

Easton, Stewart C., *Man and World in the Light of Anthroposophy*, Anthroposophic Press, Spring Valley, New York, 1975

Elkind, David *All Grown Up and No Place to Go*, Addison-Wesley Publishing Co., 1984, Reading, Mass.

Elkind, David, The *Hurried Child*, Addison-Wesley Publishing Co., 1981, Reading, Mass.

Ginott, Dr Chaim G., *Between Parent & Teenager*, Avon Books, a division of The Hearst Corporation, published by arrangement with The Macmillan Company, 1969, New York

Glas, Norbert, *Adolescence and Diseases of Puberty*, Education and Science Publications, East Gannicox, Cainscross Rd., Stroud, Glos. U.K., 1945

Harwood, A.C., *The Recovery of Man in Childhood*, A Study in the Educational Work of Rudolf Steiner; Hodder & Stoughton, London, 1958

Hinds, Katherine, *Bulimia*, Brown Alumni Monthly, Sept. 1982, Vol. 83, No. 1 Brown University, Providence, Rhode Island.

James, Charity, *Beyond Customs: An Educator's Journey*, Agathon, New York, 1974

Jocelyn, Beredene, *Citizens of the Cosmos*, Continuum Publishing Co., N.Y., 1981

Kozol, Jonathan, *The Night is Dark and I Am Far from Home*, Continuum Publishing Co., 1975, New York

Lievegoed, Bernard, *Man on the Threshold, The challenge of inner development*,

Hawthorn Press, Stroud, England, 1985 (1983 Uitgeverij Vrij Geestesleven, Zeist, Holland.)

Lievegoed, Bernard, *Phases, Crisis and development in the individual*, Rudolf Steiner Press, London, 1979

McCoy, Kathleen, *Coping With Teenage Depressions*, Signet Book, New American Library, N.Y., 1982

Mees, L.F.C., *Drugs, A Danger for Human Evolution?* Regency Press, London, N.Y., 1973

Pearce, Joseph Chilton, *Magical Child, Rediscovering Nature's Plan For Our Children*, E.P. Dutton, N.Y., 1977

Richards, M.C., *Toward Wholeness: Rudolf Steiner Education in America.* Wesleyan University Press, Middletown, Conn., 1980

Steiner, Rudolf, *Human Values in Education.* Rudolf Steiner Press, 35 Park Road, London, 1971

Steiner, Rudolf, *A Modern Art of Education.* Rudolf Steiner Press, 35 Park Road, London, 1928

Steiner, Rudolf, *Soul Economy and Waldorf Education*, Anthroposophic Press, Spring Valley, New York, 1986

Steiner, Rudolf, *Waldorf Education*, Rudolf Steiner Press, London.

Steiner, Rudlof, *Study of Man*, General Education Course; Rudolf Steiner Press, 35 Park Road, London, 1966

Steiner, Rudolf, *Waldorf Education For Adolescence*, Kolisko Archive Publications for Steiner Schools Fellowship Publications. Michael Hall, Forest Row, E. Sussex, U.K., 1980. Distributed by St George Book Service, P.O. Box 225, Spring Valley, N.Y. 10977

Winn, Marie, *Children Without Childhood*, Penguin Books, 1981, 83

Appendix II

Study questions

The questions following can be used for you as self-examination or for the purposes of discussion. You can use many of the questions as a way of evaluating yourself with the children who are in your care. The questions can be taken in a general way or very specifically related to your own children.

Part One: The Nature of Adolescence

Chapter One: How do you get to be an adolescent?
1. What are the characteristics of each seven year period between birth and twenty-one?
2. In each phase, what is the nature of the child's thinking?
3. In each phase, how does the child best learn?
4. What are the signs of the seven to fourteen year-old- phase beginning and ending?
5. Why is it important to differentiate between the phases?
6. What are some of the ways the parent would relate to the child in each of these phases?

Chapter Two: Stages of adolescence
1. What are the characteristics of the period of negation?
2. How do young adolescents relate to adults during the period of negation?
3. What is the basis of these actions?
4. How does the crush help the adolescent overcome his or her negativity?
5. What kinds of pressures are on the teenager during the period of transition?
6. What role does self-esteem have in the transition from negation to affirmation?
7. Give examples of the kinds of changes we might see in a teenager's behavior from early adolescence to later adolescence.
8. What are some of the beneficial ways young people can spend the time from eighteen to twenty-one?

9. What are the results of not having close friends or intense interests during the period of transition?

10. What kinds of activities will balance eroticism and the will to power?

11. How do drama and world events help teenagers gain perspective?

Chapter Three: The search for the self

1. Characterize the major crisis within each seven year period.

2. How does self-awareness change during each seven year period?

3. How does the ninth-tenth year change affect adolescence?

4. How does the child's relationship to adults change during the ninth-tenth year change?

5. What are the losses and compensations that occur around the ninth-tenth year change?

6. What aspects of the child's life help him or her to work through the ninth-tenth year change in a positive manner?

7. What kinds of questions are being asked during the sixteenth/seventeenth year change?

8. What are some ways teenagers confront their mortality? Why is this important?

9. What is the role of loneliness in becoming self-conscious? Is it necessary?

10. In what way is the captain a useful image of the ego that comes into focus at twenty-one? Can you think of other images?

Chapter Four: The birth of intellect

1. How does a young teenager build his or her worldview?

2. In what ways is thinking related to power?

3. Discuss the similarities and differences between the thinking of sixteen-seventeen year olds and adults.

4. How is thinking related to eroticism? Can you think of any examples.

5. Examine Plato's image of the charioteer. How is this helpful in understanding teenagers?

6. What is meant to awaken the intellect gradually?

7. How does intellectual consciousness relate to imaginative consciousness?

8. In what way does materialism enter into the thinking of adolescents?
9. What are some of the ways youngsters can awaken lively thinking? Why is this important?
10. Why is it important not to rush youngsters into intellectual thought?
11. What are the dangers of keeping a youngster in imaginative thinking too long?

Chapter Five: Release of feelings
1. How does the feeling life differ before and after puberty?
2. How does the development of emotional maturity relate to the development of thinking?
3. What role is played by self-indulgence?
4. What is the importance of separation during adolescence?
5. How does family life affect the child's emotional health?
6. What are some of the ways unsuspecting adults prematurely end childhood and bring on adult consciousness?
7. What are the ways a child establishes a healthy sense of self?

Chapter Six: Understanding our sons and daughters
1. How does the girl's sense of self differ from the way the boy's sense of self develops?
2. How might this affect a girl's relationship with her father? mother?
3. How can an early marriage bring special challenges to the young woman?
4. In what way does the boy's emotional life develop?
5. Are the characterizations given in this chapter true to your experience? What major exceptions are you aware of?
6. Because boys may experience their feelings in a different way from girls they are often accused of lacking feelings. How can parents help boys come to feel more comfortable about their feelings? Are the parents doing or saying things that tell the boys they should not show their feelings?
7. What are the dangers to girls and to boys of immature emotional development?
8. Give some examples of how the boy identifies with what he does with his physical body. Give some examples of how the girl identifies with her feelings.

9. Do you notice changes in the way children carry themselves or speak as they come into adolescence. What are they?

10. What special capacities does the teacher, parent, social worker have to develop to work with teenagers?

11. Give examples of ways teachers can meet the arrogant girl, the brash boy.

12. Discuss different kinds of discipline that would meet specific situations. Discuss what the teacher would do and how the teacher would do it. How does the teacher carry out discipline that meets the needs of the young person without losing objectivity?

13. The teacher, parent, social worker has to examine his or her own emotional strivings because the teenager will consciously or unconsciously attack areas of weakness. What areas of emotional maturity are you still working on that makes you especially vulnerable?

14. Think of examples out of your own life when you were rude or callous and how you felt afterwards.

15. What is meant by the statement, It doesn't hurt for the teacher to let the boy know that the action was not very serious but that it could not be ignored? Is this being too soft on the boy? Give an example and examine how this approach would be effective.

16. What is meant by the statement, ignore most of it (the girl's behavior) and approach the girls with 'delicacy and grace'?

17. What happens with head-on confrontations? Why are they not effective?

18. Why is it important to respect the privacy of teenagers? Is it appropriate for parents regularly to read letters, diaries, etc. behind the backs of their children? Is it appropriate in some situations? If so, which?

19. What is the relationship between images and morality?

20. How do the images of beauty and power affect teenagers? Can you give examples out of your own experience or that of the young people you know?

21. How do the qualities of boys and girls complement each other? Give examples out of your own experience.

22. How do the teenagers you know express their individuality, their sexuality? Do they overdo it? underplay it?

23. Has the issue of homosexuality come up in your family? How have you dealt with it? What guidelines are you working with to understand homosexuality? Are you sensing a bias for or against homosexuality with your teenagers?

Chapter Seven: Introduction to the temperaments
1. How is the temperament formed?
2. What are the four temperaments?
3. Are there good and bad temperaments?
4. What is the relationship between the temperament and the physical constitution?
5. Which temperaments are more inward? more outward?
6. When does the childhood temperament begin to show?
7. How can parents nurture the positive aspects of a child's temperament? Give examples.
8. What happens to the temperament at puberty?
9. What temperaments do you have most strongly? Which one do you have least of?
10. What challenges does your temperament present to you? How are you working with it?
11. What temperaments do you find most easy to be around? Why?
12. What temperaments irritate you, why?
13. What is the basic rule in working with temperaments?

Chapter Eight: The melancholic temperament
1. How would you characterize the melancholic temperament?
2. What can you do to help a melancholic child deal with change?
3. What comments have you heard children make that tells you they have a melancholic tendency?
4. What are the great strengths of the melancholic child? Can you give examples out of your own experience?
5. What can you do to assure the melancholic child in social situations?
6. How can you deal with the melancholic child who wants everything to be perfect?

7. How does the melancholic child relate to food? Is this a problem for you?

8. In what situations in your family life does the melancholic child bring special blessings? In what situations does he or she require special sensitivity?

9. Who are the melancholic child's friends? What do they do together?

10. What are the physical ailments the melancholic child complains about most?

11. How can the parent support the melancholic child without indulging him or her?

12. Why is it important for the melancholic child to know of other people's or animals' suffering?

13. Examine the routine of the melancholic child. Is it too rigid, too loose? Why is routine important for this kind of child?

14. Can you tell when a melancholic child is happy? humorous? upset?

15. What kinds of jokes does the melancholic child especially enjoy?

16. How does the melancholic child deal with family stress?

17. What kinds of changes are occurring in the melancholic child during adolescence? Do you find any merit to the comment that the melancholic child often becomes the choleric adult? Do you have examples?

Chapter Nine: The sanguine temperament

1. What are the characteristics of the sanguine temperament?

2. What are the strengths of the sanguine child?

3. What are the struggles of the sanguine child?

4. How can a parent help the sanguine child strengthen his or her will?

5. What is the chief motivation of the sanguine child?

6. How can the environment of the sanguine child bring calm?

7. How can a parent help focus a sanguine child?

8. What changes does the sanguine child undergo as he or she enters adolescence?

9. What stresses and blessings does a sanguine child bring into the family?

Chapter Ten: The phlegmatic temperament

1. What are the characteristics of the phlegmatic temperament?
2. What are the strengths and weaknesses of the phlegmatic child?
3. How does the parent motivate the phlegmatic child?
4. What is the phlegmatic child's relationship to food?
5. How is the phlegmatic child in school?
6. What is the greatest challenge for the teacher of the phlegmatic child?
7. How does the phlegmatic child change in adolescence?
8. How does the adolescent emphasis on appearance affect the phlegmatic child?
9. How does a parent avoid over-indulgence or over-protection of the phlegmatic child?
10. What are the challenges of the phlegmatic child to the family?

Chapter Eleven: The choleric temperament

1. What are the characteristics of the choleric child?
2. How does the choleric child exercise leadership in the family?
3. What is the relationship between the choleric child and the adults around him or her?
4. How does the choleric child relate to his or her siblings?
5. How can the choleric child learn to relax and not take the burden of the world on his or her shoulders?
6. Does the choleric child fly into rages? What sets them off?
7. Does the choleric child assume too much responsibility?
8. How does the parent communicate love to the choleric child?
9. How does the choleric child change during adolescence?
10. How can the teacher reach the choleric child?
11. What is the challenge of the choleric child in the family?
12. What are the blessings of the choleric child?

Chapter Twelve: The development of character in adolescence.

1. When does character development take place?
2. How can parents aid in character development in the seven to fourteen stage? in the fourteen to twenty-one stage?
3. What are character traits? Can you describe these traits in people you admire?
4. How does character differ from temperament?

5. What are the ways adults can influence character development?
6. Give some examples of teenagers who are making decisions in their lives that will build character.
7. What is the role of standards provided by teachers or parents?
8. What opportunities can we offer in our communities to enhance the development of character?

Part Two: The Challenge of Adolescence

Chapter Thirteen: The needs of teenagers
1. Why is the soul-life in flux?
2. What are the basic needs of adolescence?
3. Why is there tension between the needs of the adolescent?
4. How can parents help teenagers balance the need for physical activity and the need for stillness?
5. How can the family balance the need for intensity and the need for routine?
6. How can the teenager be involved in working out this balance?
7. How can the parent decide whether boredom expressed is appropriate boredom or true ennui?
8. How can adults help teenagers to feel needed? Give examples from your experience.
9. How can teenagers bring about change?
10. How can we nourish the inner life of the teenager?
11. What is the group my youngster belongs to? What needs is it fulfilling?
12. Does the teenager get to spend time alone or away from the group?
13. Does the teenager depend on the group for self-esteem?
14. Will the teenager stand up against the group? What happens then?
15. Will the teenager ask for help? why? why not? What can I do to help the youngster feel it's fine to ask?
16. What is the teenager's role in the family? What does the teenager contribute to the family's well being?
17. Are there opportunities for the teenager to feel needed and to bring someone cheer?

18. How can the teenagers help the family in holiday celebrations?
19. What is the relationship between the teenager and younger children in the family?
20. How is the teenager's need for facts being satisfied?
21. Is the teenager's need for imagination being nurtured? How?

Chapter Fourteen: Teenagers and the family

1. How does the image of the volcano and the mask relate to teenagers?
2. What are some of the ways the teenager views the parent?
3. What are some of the stresses placed on teenagers in the family depending on where they are in the line-up?
4. What special burden is on the oldest child?
5. How do children usually handle being caught in the middle of parents who are divorcing or divorced? What can the adults do to help the youngsters?
6. What are some of the stresses on the child after divorce?
7. What fantasies may develop for a teenager regarding a divorced parent who doesn't appear very often? How can the youngster be helped to work this through?
8. How can divorcing parents help teenagers avoid feeling guilty for the divorce?
9. The teenager of a divorced family often lacks the guidance he or she needs. How can parents be aware of not vying for the teenager's approval?
10. How can divorce affect the teenager's view of long-term relationships?
11. Is the teenager carrying too much responsibility in the family?
12. How can single parents and teenagers support one another emotionally? Give examples.
13. How does a divorced parent's remarriage destroy a teenager's fantasy?
14. How can remarriage help a teenager? Can you give examples?
15. What are some of the patterns of teenagers and their step-parents that you are aware of?

Chapter Fifteen: Teenagers and friends

1. What is the special role friends play in a teenager's life?

2. What stresses do teenagers experience in friendships?

3. What role does conformity have in a teenager's life? Give examples.

4. What kinds of cliques are in your child's school? How does he or she relate to the cliques?

5. What is the special blessing of a platonic relationship?

6. What stresses are placed on teenagers in dating?

7. How can parents handle a situation involving their child which they consider negative?

8. How can parent restrictions actually help a teenager feel cared for?

9. What can be done when a teenager feels lonely and without friends?

Chapter Sixteen: Teenagers and the schools

1. Why is there such a lack of trust in schools?

2. What is the role of the school in our teenager's life? Do we approve of its role? What could change?

3. How has television affected the teenager's involvement in school?

4. How have jobs affected the teenager's relationship to school?

5. What choices of schools are available in your community? Are you satisfied with this?

6. What is the role of the public school in American culture today?

7. What happens when big schools replace small schools?

8. What is the relationship between my youngster and his or her teachers? Are there opportunities for conversations?

9. How does the school my youngster attends function as a community?

10. What kinds of changes have occurred in the curriculum of the public high schools over the past twenty years?

11. What is a smorgasbord curriculum? What are the implications?

12. How have changes in society affected the schools?

13. How have teachers dealt with the changes in society?

14. What is the special value of teachers working closely with students?

Chapter Seventeen: An introduction to Waldorf education

1. When did Waldorf schools originate? Where? in what situation?
2. What children first attended the Waldorf school?
3. What happened to the Waldorf schools under the Nazi regime?
4. What are the basic principles of Waldorf education?
5. What is the stage of consciousness of the nine-ten year old? What image describes this?
6. Why is history so important in fifth grade?
7. How does the history of Rome parallel the life of the child?
8. What is the basic approach of the Waldorf kindergarten?
9. What are the main aspects of the lower school?
10. How is the artistic approach carried into the Waldorf high school?
11. How would you characterize the ninth, tenth, eleventh, and twelfth grades?

Chapter Eighteen: The teenager and the arts

1. What is the special gift of the arts to teenagers?
2. Why is art so important in nourishing the inner life of the teenager?
3. How does art relate to thinking and feeling?
4. How does imagination change during the adolescent years?
5. What is the special role of music in the teenager's life?
6. Give examples of the most popular musicians today. What do they stand for? What kinds of models are they?
7. How has music changed in the last thirty years?
8. What is the appeal of heavy metal music?
9. What effect might the powerful beat have on teenagers?
10. In what ways can music be a healing force on young people?
11. Have you listened to contemporary music lately? What have you especially liked, not liked?

Chapter Nineteen: Power and loyalty

1. What is the teenager trying to prove through power? Can you relate to this?
2. Why is power such an issue between teenagers and their parents?

3. How do teenagers have power over adults?
4. How do we feel when we think we are powerless?
5. What areas are negotiable with your teenagers? Are there areas which you will not allow the teenager to make the final decision? What are they? Why?
6. How is loyalty expressed in your family? Why?
7. The youngster is caught between loyalty to friends and loyalty to parents. Describe situations of this kind and what can be done about them.
8. How is the I-thou relationship relevant to teenagers?

Chapter Twenty: The role of love
1. What kinds of love will the teenager experience in life?
2. What does going steady mean in your community?
3. Why is it helpful for a teenager to have a view of the many kinds of love?

Part Three: The Problems of Adolescence

Chapter Twenty-one: Problems of self-esteem
1. What is self-esteem? How does it affect the teenager?
2. How does advertising affect self-esteem? Give examples.
3. What makes teenagers vulnerable?
4. What were your concerns when you were a teenager?
5. How do teenagers cope with parental expectations? Give examples.
6. Can expectations be positive? negative? both? explain.
7. Why is it normal for teenagers to have periods of depression?
8. What are the signs of depression?
9. What changes have occurred in your youngster's life that might lead or have led to depression? Was it resolved?
10. How do teenagers relate to the loss of innocence?
11. What are some of the ways teenagers relate to separation and loss?

Chapter Twenty-two: Pregnancy and the teenager
1. Why is pregnancy so common in teenage life today?
2. Do you know any teens who have been pregnant?

3. How did they handle their pregnancy? What have you learned from this experience?

4. What kinds of considerations should a pregnant teenager think about before making any decision?

5. In what ways can a teenage mother experience success? How can I help?

6. What are the ways the parents and other adults can be supportive to a pregnant teenager?

7. What is the responsibility of the father of the child? Is it being handled maturely?

8. What agencies are available in the community to help a teenager who is pregnant?

9. How can the young woman be prepared to accept the spiritual responsibility of her child?

10. Is the pregnant teen being given nutritional counseling?

11. What are the advantages and disadvantages of the pregnant teen marrying?

12. What is the father's responsibility?

13. What is being done to help the young couple understand the responsibilities of marriage?

14. What kind of support system is around the young couple to help them make the adjustment?

15. What adults in the community does the young couple trust and have confidence in to help them?

16. Are there religious conflicts influencing the decisions? Be clear what they are. How can they be acknowledged?

17. Is there advice from the young woman's religious community?

18. Who makes the final decisions on the question of birth, adoption, abortion, marriage?

19. What are your experiences with adoption? Examine the advantages and disadvantages of adoption.

20. What is your attitude toward abortion? Is it relevant to the situation?

21. Why are so many teenagers getting pregnant?

22. Does the teenager know about birth control?

23. What are some of the dangers of abortion?

24. What is the spiritual aspect of abortion?

25. What are some of the dangers of teen pregnancy?

26. How can these be avoided?
27. What can be done to awaken boys to an understanding of their sexual activity and to their responsibility?

Chapter Twenty-three: Teenagers and alcohol
1. Why is alcohol the drug of choice among teenagers?
2. How does alcohol affect judgment?
3. What are the two types of alcoholic beverages?
4. What determines the rate of absorption of alcohol?
5. How does alcohol affect the brain?
6. What are the four stages of response to alcohol?
7. What are some of the reasons teenagers drink?
8. How does alcohol affect the sense of self?
9. What are the twelve questions Alcoholics Anonymous gives for a teenager to decide whether or not drinking is a problem?
10. What are some of the characteristics of the problem drinker?
11. What are the first two steps in helping teenagers admit they have a drinking problem?
12. What are some of the guidelines that can help a teenager monitor himself or herself?

Chapter Twenty-four: Teenagers and drugs
1. How have publicized deaths of popular heroes affected the use of drugs?
2. What are the patterns of drug use in your community?
3. What are the common drugs?
4. How available are drugs in your community?
5. Why do teenagers take drugs?
6. What are the physical signs that your teenager may be using drugs?
7. What drug education programs and drug treatment programs are available in your community?
8. Why do teenagers lie about drugs?
9. How do drugs affect a teenager's development?
10. How can you support a teenager who is struggling with drug use?
11. Discuss the thirst for imaginative pictures. How is it being met?

12. What are some of the soul-strengthening exercises given by Rudolf Steiner?

Chapter Twenty-five: Teenagers and food
1. What is our culture's idea of beauty?
2. What is the ideal body presented to our teenagers?
3. What are some of the ways teenagers turn to food to solve their problems?
4. What is the condition of anorexia nervosa?
5. What is the typical pattern of the anorexic?
6. What is the condition of bulemarexia (or bulimia)?
7. What are the similarities in the two conditions, the differences?
8. What are the dangers of each condition?
9. What are the signs of food abuse?
10. What kind of knowledge does the teenager have about the dangers of anorexia and bulimia?
11. How does the compulsive personality present itself?
12. What is the relationship between compulsiveness and food disorders?
13. What is the relationship between emotional needs and food? Give examples.
14. What is a common factor in people who overeat?
15. What are some of the frustrations of the obese person?
16. What signals are being given to the obese teenager that he or she is unworthy?
17. How can teenagers gain support in changing their eating and exercise habits?
18. What are the nutritional dangers of a junk food diet?
19. How can parents encourage healthy nutrition in their teenager's diet?

Chapter Twenty-six: Extreme behavioral problems
1. What are the three escape routes described by Lievegoed?
2. Discuss anorexia in relationship to an escape route.
3. How can we help youngsters accept difficulties and responsibilities of growing up so they will not look for an escape route?
4. What is the escape into pseudo-adulthood? Give examples.
5. What in our society encourages this escape?

6. What can we do to help such a youngster?
7. Can we spot the early signs?
8. What are the signs of escape into fantasy?
9. How can the sense of self be strengthened?

Conclusion

1. How can the parent strengthen himself or herself?
2. How can parents build a strong support group to help each other and to help their youngsters?

Appendix III

The ages of children

School grades, classes and years in Britain and the USA

Between Form and Freedom uses the grading system for grouping children by age which is common in schools in the United States. Whereas in Britain, children normally go to a secondary school when they are eleven – in the USA, children remain in 'grade school' until fourteen, when they go to high school.

Waldorf (Steiner) schools use a similar classification to that of the American system, except that outside the USA grades are called 'classes' e.g. Class 2.

The ages groups begin on September 1st and finish on August 31st of each year. Developmental psychologists and teachers are in a continued debate about 'school'/class readiness for infants – and the dates may be shifted backwards from September 1st to April or May 1st in certain schools. The American and British classes are given below:

	4–5 years		Reception
	5–6 years		Year 1
1st grade	6–7 years	Top infant	Year 2
2nd grade	7–8 years	1st year junior	Year 3
3rd grade	8–9 years	2nd year junior	Year 4
4th grade	9–10 years	3rd year junior	Year 5
5th grade	10–11 years	4th year junior	Year 6
6th grade	11–12 years	1st year	Year 7
7th grade	12–13 years	2nd year	Year 8
8th grade	13–14 years	3rd year	Year 9
9th grade	14–15 years	4th year	Year 10
10th grade	15–16 years	5th year	Year 11
11th grade	16–17 years	Lower 6th	Year 12
12th grade	17–18 years	Upper 6th	Year 13

References

Foreword
1. Sister Grace Pilon, *Workshop Way*. She teachers at Xavier University, New Orleans, Lousiana. Her publications are available through Xavier University.

Chapter 3
1. J. Chilton Pearce, *The Magical Child, Rediscovering Nature's Plan for our Child*, E. P. Dutton, New York, 1977, pp27, 28.
2. Luxford, Michael, *Loving the Stranger, Studies in Adolescence, Empathy and the Human Heart*. Great Britain: TWT Publications, Camphill Books.
3. Staley, Betty, *Adolescence, The Sacred Passage, Inspired by the Legend of Parzival*, Fair Oaks, Ca:, Rudolf Steiner College Press, 2006.

Chapter 6
Biddulph, Steve and Sharon, *Raising Boys, Why Boys Are Different and How to Help Them Become Happy and Well-balanced Men*, Berkeley, CA: Celestial Arts, 1999.
Elium, Don and Jeanne, *Raising a Son, Parents and the Making of a Healthy Man*. Beyond Words Pub. Co., Oregon, 1992.
Elium, Don and Jeanne, *Raising a Daughter, Parents and the Awakening of a Healthy Woman*, Berkeley, CA: Celestial Arts, 1994.
Garbarino, J. *Lost Boys: Why Our Sons Turn Violent and How We Can Save Them*. New York: Anchor Books, 2000.
Gurian, M. *Boys and Girls Learn Differently*, San Francisco: Jossey-Bass, 2001.
Kindlon, Dan, and Thompson, Michael, *Raising Cain: Protecting the Emotional Life of Boys*. New York: Ballantine, 2000.

Chapter 7
1. R. Steiner, *The Four Temperaments*, Anthroposophic Press, Inc. New York, 1944, p.39.

Chapter 11
1. A. Morgan, *Today: The Best Loved Poems of the American People*, selected by Hazel Felleman, Garden City Books, Garden City, New York, 1936, pp.67–69.

Chapter 12
1. R.W. Emerson, *The Heart of Emerson's Journals*, edited by Bliss Perry, Dover Publications Inc., New York, 1939, p39 Cambridge, undated 1928.

Chapter 13
1. From album, *Breakfast in America*, by Supertramp. Words by Rick Davies and Roger Hodgson, 1979 Almo Music, Corp, and Delicate Music (ASCAP) Supertramp Umbrella Chat International, P.O. Box 1703, Burbank CA, 91507.

2. Charity James, *Beyond Customs: An Educator's Journey*, Agathon, New York, 1974, see p.265, Ch.13,2.

Chapter 14
1. K. Konig, *Brothers & Sisters*, Floris Books, Edinburgh.

Chapter 15
1. A. de Saint Exupery, *The Little Prince*, Harcourt, Brace, Jovanovich, N.Y., London, 1943, 1971.

Chapter 16
1. D. Elkind, *All Grown Up and No Place To Go*, Addison-Wesley, Reading, Mass. 1984 p.137.
2. E. Greenberger & L. Steinberg, *The Debit Side of Adolescent Employment*, Education Week, 10.12.1986 p24. Excerpt from their book *When Teenagers Work: The Psychological and Social Costs of Adolescent Employment*, Basic Books, 1976.
3. Ibid p.24.

Chapter 17
1. R. Steiner, *Education of the Child in the Light of Anthroposophy*, Rudolf Steiner Press, London, 1979.
2. R. Steiner, *The Supplementary Course, Education for Adolescence.* – now published as – *Waldorf Education for Adolescence*, Kolisko Archive Publication for Steiner Schools Fellowship, Forest Row, E. Sussex, U.K. Distributed by St George Book Service, P.O. Box 225, Spring Valley, New York, 10977.

Chapter 18
1. R. Steiner. Originally in R. Steiner, *Wahrsprachworte*, Dornach, Switzerland, as quoted in Gerbert, Hildegard, *Education Through Art*, Verlag Freies Geistesleben, Stuttgart p.24.
2. A. Bloom, *The Closing of the American Mind*, Simon and Schuster, N.Y. 1987 p.72.
3. Steven C. Martino, Rebecca L. Collins, Marc N. Elliot, Amy Strachman, David E. Kanouse, and Sandra H. Berry, *Exposure to Degrading Versus Nondegrading Music Lyrics and Sexual Behavior Among Youth*, published in Pediatrics on-line, 2006.
4. David Fricke, *Rolling Stone, String*, as carried in the Sacramento Bee, March 20th, 1988, pp.3,4.

Chapter 19
1. Robert Frost, *The Poetry of Robert Frost*, editon Edward Connery Lathem, Holt, Rinehart and Winston, N.Y. 1969, p.34.

Chapter 21
1. D. Elkind, *All Grown Up and No Place To Go*, Addison Wesley, Reading, Mass. p33.

Chapter 22
1. From the report, *Teen Pregnancy: What is Being Done? A State by State Look*; issued by the House Select Committee on Children, Youth and Families, March, 1986. Quoted in, *House Panel Finds Efforts to Prevent Teenage Pregnancy Failing*, by Mina Tugend, Education Week, March 5th, 1986.
2. *Ten Tips for Parents to Help Their Children Avoid Teen Pregnancy*, Campaign to Prevent Teen Pregnancy, 1998.

Chapter 23
1. Chaim Ginott, *Between Parent and Teenager*, Avon Books, N.Y. 1969, p.192.
2. Shirley Schwartzrock, *Facts & Fantasies About Alcohol*, American Guidance Service, Circle Pines, Minnesota 55014–1796, 1984.

Chapter 24
1. L.F.C. Mees, *Drugs: A Danger for Human Evolution*, Regency Press, London & New York, 1973.
2. Rudolf Steiner, *Knowledge of the Higher Worlds and its Attainment*, Rudolf Steiner Press, London.

Chapter 25
1. K. McCoy, *Coping with Teenage Depression – A Parent's Guide*, Signet Books, New American Library, N.Y. 1982, p.182.

Chapter 26
1. B.C.J. Lievegoed, *Man on the Threshold*, Hawthorn Press, Stroud, UK, 1984.

Chapter 27
1. Rideout, V., D. Roberts, and U. Foehr, eds, *Generation M: Media in the Lives of 8–18 Year-olds*. A Kaiser Family Foundation Study, March 2005.

Conclusion
1. Rudolf Steiner, *Knowledge of the Higher Worlds*, Ibid.
2. Rudolf Steiner, *Verses and Meditations*, Anthroposophical Publishing Co. London, 1961, p.47.

Author's Acknowledgements

I have been an educator as long as I can remember. As a nine year old I had my own class on the steps of our Bronx apartment house. Yet, after a few college education courses and some months teaching in New York City public schools, I vowed I would not become a teacher. However, it was due to the efforts of my history professor at City University of New York, Dr Stewart C. Easton, with whom I have a wonderful thirty-year friendship, that I became acquainted with Rudolf Steiner and Waldorf education, and renewed my commitment to education.

Since 1978 this book has been a constant presence in the life of my family. It has accompanied us on vacations and has often determined the schedules of our weekends. I thank my children Andrea, George, and Sonya for their patience during those times when I had to finish a few more paragraphs before we could go swimming or exploring. Many of the examples in the book are drawn from their childhood and adolescence.

Meredith Kurtz, and Virgilia and Henry Dakin were the godparents of the book, providing vision and encouragement at different stages of its conception.

I thank Franklin Kane for the two decades of shared parenting which provided the experiences of family life which I cherish.

Thanks to Julia Connor for the title, *Between Form and Freedom*. From the moment she suggested it for a workshop, it seemed the perfect description of adolescence. Thanks to Julie Moyer for her artistic interpretation of my words into her drawings and painting. I am grateful to Martin Large at Hawthorn Press for his persistence and encouragement.

A special thanks to my husband Jim Staley for his support and patience. He walked the fine line between being critical editor and supportive husband.

Last, I acknowledge my deep gratitude to Rudolf Steiner's understanding of the human being and to my many colleagues and friends in Waldorf education with whom I have shared a commitment to educating young people.

Waldorf Schools Contacts

Those interested in finding out more about Waldorf (Steiner) education may contact the following addresses:

Association of Waldorf Schools of North America
17 Helmlock Hill
Great Barrington
MA 01230

Steiner Schools Fellowship
Kidbrooke Park
Forest Row
East Sussex
RH18 5JB

Ordering Books

If you have difficulties ordering Hawthorn Press books from a book-shop, you can order direct from:

United Kingdom
Booksource
50 Cambuslang Road
Glasgow
G32 8NB
Tel: 0845 370 0063
Fax: 0845 370 0064
Email: orders@booksource.net

USA/North America
Steiner Books
PO Box 960, Herndon
VA 20172-0960
Tel: 0800 856 8664
Fax: 703 661 1501
Email: service@steinerbooks.org
Website: www.steinerbooks.org

Or you can order online at www.hawthornpress.com

For further information or a book catalogue, please contact:

Hawthorn Press
1 Lansdown Lane
Stroud
Gloucestershire
GL5 1BJ
Tel: 01453 757040
Fax: 01453 751138
Email: info@hawthornpress.com
Website: www.hawthornpress.com